AF864451

THE MASTER ARCHITECT SERIES II

DARYL JACKSON

Selected and Current Works

THE MASTER ARCHITECT SERIES II

DARYL JACKSON

Selected and Current Works

First published in Australia in 1996 by
The Images Publishing Group Pty Ltd
ACN 059 734 431
6 Bastow Place, Mulgrave, Victoria, 3170
Telephone (61 3) 9561 5544 Facsimile (61 3) 9561 4860

Copyright © The Images Publishing Group Pty Ltd 1996

All rights reserved. Apart from any fair dealing for the purposes of private study, research, criticism or review as permitted under the Copyright Act, no part of this publication may be reproduced, stored in a retrieval system or transmitted in any form by any means, electronic, mechanical, photocopying, recording or otherwise, without the written permission of the publisher.

National Library of Australia Cataloguing-in-Publication Data

Jackson, Daryl, 1937–
Daryl Jackson: selected and current works.

Bibliography.
Includes index.
ISBN 1 875498 52 4
Master Architect Series ISSN 1320 7253

1. Jackson, Daryl, 1937–. 2. Architecture, Modern—20th century—Australia. 3. Architecture—Australian.
I. Title. (Series: Master architect series 2).

720.92

Edited by Stephen Dobney
Designed by The Graphic Image Studio Pty Ltd, Mulgrave, Australia
Film separation and printing by Everbest Printing H.K.

Contents

INTRODUCTION

Introduction

Yet another synthesis

By Daryl Jackson

As a practising architect operating in a discourse of increasing complexity, I feel the need to clarify my position—to outline a theory. A theory offers a conceptual framework for practice and a basis on which to generate, comprehend and criticise work; hence the title of this essay, which is posed as a spiritual, even ironic question.

My theory is personal and value-based. It is presented as a series of dynamic themes linked over time by a unified intent. It is prejudiced on at least two counts. Firstly, by the belief that architecture is, above all, a cultural pursuit, reflecting and developing the conditions and aspirations of the society it serves and feeds upon. Secondly, by the belief that the future of Australian architecture is intrinsically bound up with a larger concern: the metropolitan form of the city, from suburban fringe to commercial and institutional centre.

Conditional culture

Australian culture is caught within a series of dialectics: an inherited, implanted form of Western culture, it is constantly being adapted and mediated by Antipodean socio-political conditions which are the product of geographical detachment. Through the heritage of our parent cultures, we address our real (and imagined) habitat of open space: an environment of unique climate, topography, built form, flora and fauna, into which Australia's increasingly divergent cultural milieu continues to forge an existence.

While we are geographically detached, we are simultaneously tied to the rest of the world via a communications system that supports intellectual, economic and material exchanges. But this is nothing new. For the last 150 years or so, our prominent and impressive beachhead capital cities have mediated between incoming international culture and rich Antipodean mythologies based on the power of the land and the epic battles of the people. There need be no contradiction about living in an urban Australia, appreciating a rural Australia, and participating in the modern world.

Evolutionary synthesis

Australian culture, in all its richness, growth and diversity, is one I am pleased to be part of and to which I enthusiastically respond. This response requires me to embrace a complex and dynamic evolutionary approach.

As an architect, I want to be in touch with a continually expanding, universal intelligence, and I want to work upon a wide range of material in the construction of our place. This is the nature of Modernism, or indeed of science, the arts or architecture in general; and it is an attitude which demands that change and experience be constantly embraced, to find yet another synthesis.

Vision and idea

A synthesis that embraces and participates in change must be based on vision, just as architectural theory and criticism are formed around visionary ideas. In the process of design, ideas are transformed to encapsulate in a project the designer's visionary intent; ideas instantly apprehend the general and specific to transform the perceived "ideal" value into an actual experience. The process is both intuitive and rational. The ideas can develop from a myriad of sources: behavioural, technical, internal, external, visible, invisible. They can be derivative or original, but the end result must transcend and transform the purely functional and pragmatic to include the poetic and visionary as well.

Idea-making on behalf of society is a necessary function of architecture. The future can be as we imagine it.

Modernist critique

Modernism has always encouraged propositional, visionary explorations. Yet the revolutionary and visionary fervour that marks the Modernism of this century has had its limitations.

The admirable social hypotheses of the early 20th century about a democratic society have always been confused by ideas of personal freedom and individuality. There is an undue emphasis on self-awareness and the importance of the individual. This has hindered the development of new collective viewpoints about design that could benefit the cultural condition of society as a whole.

Consequently, design issues are too frequently seen as particular and separate. Any connection between designers and society is limited. Rarely is any critique of society expressed through their work, and those Modernists unprepared for complexity have aligned themselves with the simple economic goals of an "industrial" or "commodities" society. This was not the original intention. The homogeneous nature of the original Modernist code has now broken up into a more fertile, wider range of ideas to be applied to architecture.

Modernism still has much to offer: emphasis on the social condition, and the desire to embrace technology and change are tenets of the Brutalist ethos that I continue to support. The spatial revolution, perhaps Modernism's crowning achievement, remains a keystone to my compositional tactics, Cubism in particular. Revealing and celebrating the content; complexity and abstraction; deconstruction and reconstruction; shift and refocus of meaning; and object/subject fluctuations—all are appropriate devices for the expression of today's social dialectics.

However, the point at which Cubist abstraction lost its figurative associations stands as a warning. Architecture's associative function—its power to convey meaning—has been all too easily dismissed. Yet it is the critical umbilical magic that links human purpose to tectonic premise—the very structure of our art.

Complexity and evolution

The heterogeneity and pluralism of contemporary society permits a wider, more wholesome divergence of thought about the substance and expression of architecture, leading to a critical review of precedent and content, social conditions and the urbanity of the city. There is now a broader base for architectural concerns that includes issues of context, meaning, history and, above all, a renewed understanding of ideas about continuity as well as change.

I am reminded of a discussion of Joyce's novel *Ulysses* by Noel Riley Fitch:

> *Ulysses* contains eighteen episodes, each written in a different style to match the contents, as if eighteen authors had written the book. The most innovative technique...was the use of the interior monologue or what Joyce called the uninterrupted unrolling of thought.[1]

For me, each design project represents that kind of process: each is episodic and real; each is different and deals with, and is uniquely affected by, its particular parameters.

Presence and legibility

The essential purpose of architecture is to celebrate human presence. Architecture's role is to affirm where we have come from and to invoke a vision of where we are going. It must also reinforce and enhance our emotional and physical presence in symbolic and functional systems of expression.

The objects in our lives have no meaning other than via associations. Things recall, represent and challenge other familiar things and stimulate enquiry. For architecture, such associations are fundamental; real delight, beyond the time-honoured demands for distinctive presence and functional purpose, comes only from a representative, artistic intention and substance. Legible imagery is crucial to the way architecture works. As Suzanne Langer states:

> The importance of an art symbol cannot be built up like the meaning of a discourse, but must be seen in totality first; that is, "understanding" of a work of art begins with an intuition of the whole presented feeling. Contemplation then gradually reveals the complexities of the piece, and of its import ... in art the complex whole is seen or anticipated first.[2]

This I define as "configuration" or "strategy". We have been taught to analyse, sieve and construe data as a basis for understanding the way things work, but in architecture the essential task is confrontational. To put it *all* together, poetic synthesis and the integrity of the whole are essential.

1. Fitch, Noel Riley. *Sylvia Beach and the Lost Generation: A History of Literary Paris in the Twenties and Thirties.* New York: Norton, 1973, p. 67.

2. Langer, Suzanne Katherine. *Feeling and Form: A Theory of Art Developed from Philosophy in a New Key.* London: Routledge & Kegan Paul, 1953.

Style and configurative ideas

How things appear (their iconography) is of critical importance to architects. Traditional definitions of "style" have to be reviewed. Modernism handed down a model of the "master" architect stamping out a personal "style" which was easily recognised and usually consistent in content and symbol over a life's work. The current intellectual climate supports stylistic divergence. In our free, scientifically advanced state, with its permissive artistic codes, we are presented with relativities, not a world of absolutes.

For me, style expresses a consistent way of thinking, seeing, and doing. I work with a series of configurative models, a broad schema or language of ideas which enables me to "image" or structure the brief as "concept". While there is consistency in the process, each building is unavoidably different. For me, design is the central act, a process that is evaluative, critical and creative. Each design reflects my particular sensibility for highly legible configurations of assemblage and form. A range of compositional tactics are deployed, depending on the commission. This vocabulary is not static, and I am always searching for devices that might better communicate ideas.

There is consistency in the compositional process and in the intelligence attached to authorship. Always there is a strong commitment to imagining, formulating and correlating, sieving and dismissing, refining and testing, and finally implementing each project.

City building

Ever since I began practising architecture (in 1960), one sustaining idea has gathered strength: a renewed belief in the urbanity of the city. Central to this is a conviction that each architectural intervention is not only an object in its own right, but also contributes to a vision of the city as a whole. Similarly, the form of the city is itself crucial as object, and not just as a product or subject of its architecture. Buildings may be mortal but cities and the ideas they embody are immortal.

In Australia there are six prototypical physical contexts: the wilderness, the countryside, the country town, the outer suburbs, the historical inner-city suburbs, and the institutional and commercial city centre. Each possesses a different morphology of built form. Each demands a different understanding, with responsible solutions based upon the particular physical and social conditions.

Because of the social, economic and physical complexity of the city, aesthetic issues have to be addressed in parallel with all the inherent forces: the expression of content—emotional and physical—is as imperative as the expression of object.

Urban form and public space are still largely controlled by economic determinism. There is an absolute need to review the manner in which the architecture of the larger metropolitan frames is achieved. Of particular urgency is the need for new, powerful, formal imagery for the public and commercial zones of the suburbs—imagery which introduces a civic/social dimension from which we may learn to celebrate and value each other, not just the material artefacts we possess. This means rethinking the patterns of habitation, commerce and conviviality, and rendering the built components as figurative objects, so that the city has meaning and memory beyond the simple expression of fiscal values.

Australia's future lies in the consolidation and reconstruction of its beachhead cities. The role of the architect is to formulate another urban *reality* that is understandable, useful, legible, challenging and memorable. City building requires optimism and opportunity, love and care, critique and theory. The idea that we are building worthwhile habitable places must be paramount. It remains the architect's role to drive a personal dream which can, at best, include other people's truths. The key is to be able to interact with the people one builds for: to be able to look, listen, learn, and importantly, to lead.

The best part about being in Australia is the belief that its future is going to be more important than its past, and that the dream continues to be driven by the joy of incompletion.

SELECTED AND CURRENT WORKS

Education

Methodist Ladies College Music School

Design/Completion 1992/1994
Kew, Victoria
Methodist Ladies College
7,500 square metres
Rendered concrete block, painted fibre cement sheet with metal deck roof

Located at the centre of the college, the Music School conveys its importance via an external colonnade at the eastern edge of the building. A multi-purpose auditorium seats 360 people for performance, rehearsals or lectures, while a two-level foyer incorporates a stepped performance area for informal occasions. A rehearsal hall and instrumental suites, studios, classrooms and laboratories accommodate teaching, performance and instrument storage. The building is cubist in its sculptural form, in part acoustically determined; the interior of the auditorium is finished in timber panels to mimic the idea of "instruments".

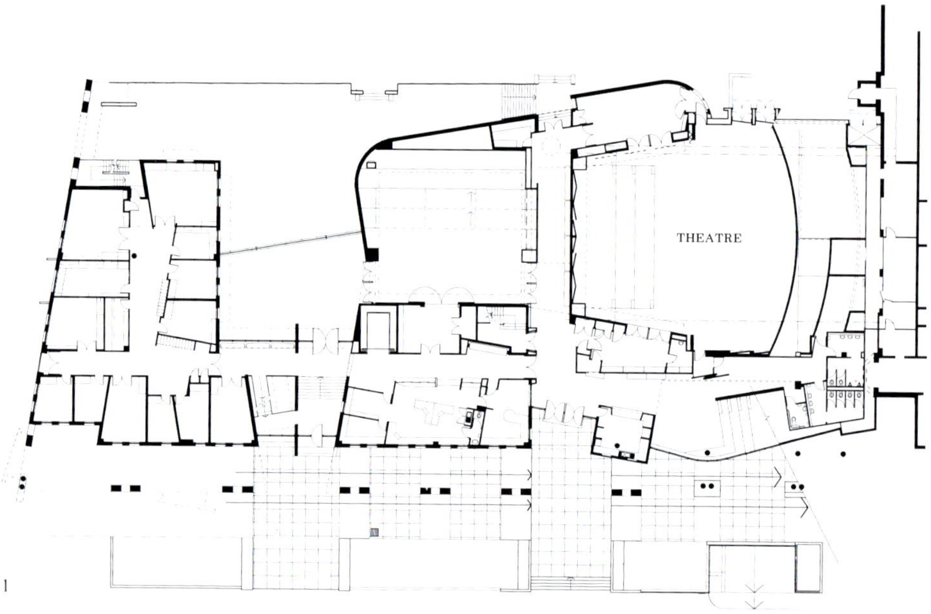

1

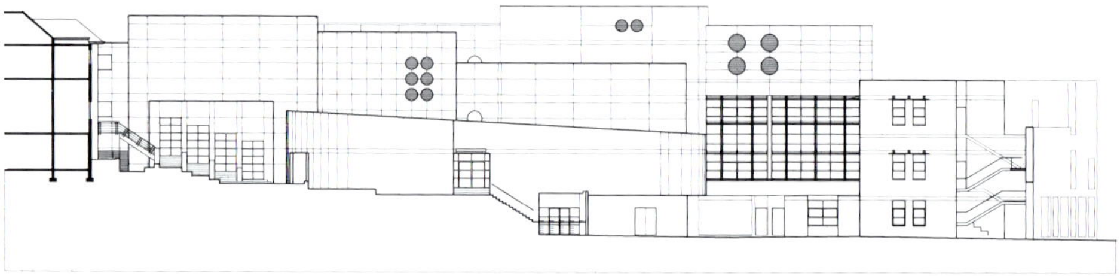
2

3

1 Ground-floor plan
2 Elevation
3 Building entry
4 Window detail

4

5

6

5 West entry to auditorium
6 Ceiling detail
7 Main auditorium
8 Performance foyer
9 Circulation staircase and gallery

7

8

9

Wesley College Senior School

Design/Completion 1988/1992
Glen Waverley, Victoria
Wesley College Melbourne
Associate architects: McGlashan Everist, Melbourne
6,200 square metres
Reinforced concrete frame
Concrete block and fibre cement sheet cladding, metal stud partitions and metal deck roof

An open cloister-like courtyard is the focus for the various educational spaces of the Senior College at Wesley's Waverley Campus.

The two-storey structure comprises four stair towers representing the four student "houses" of the College, each highlighted in the appropriate house colour. Classrooms, offices and study areas are situated on either side of the quadrangle and the centrally located student cafeteria opens directly onto the courtyard.

The new structure serves as the first point of arrival for those visiting the campus and houses offices for the Principal and administrative staff.

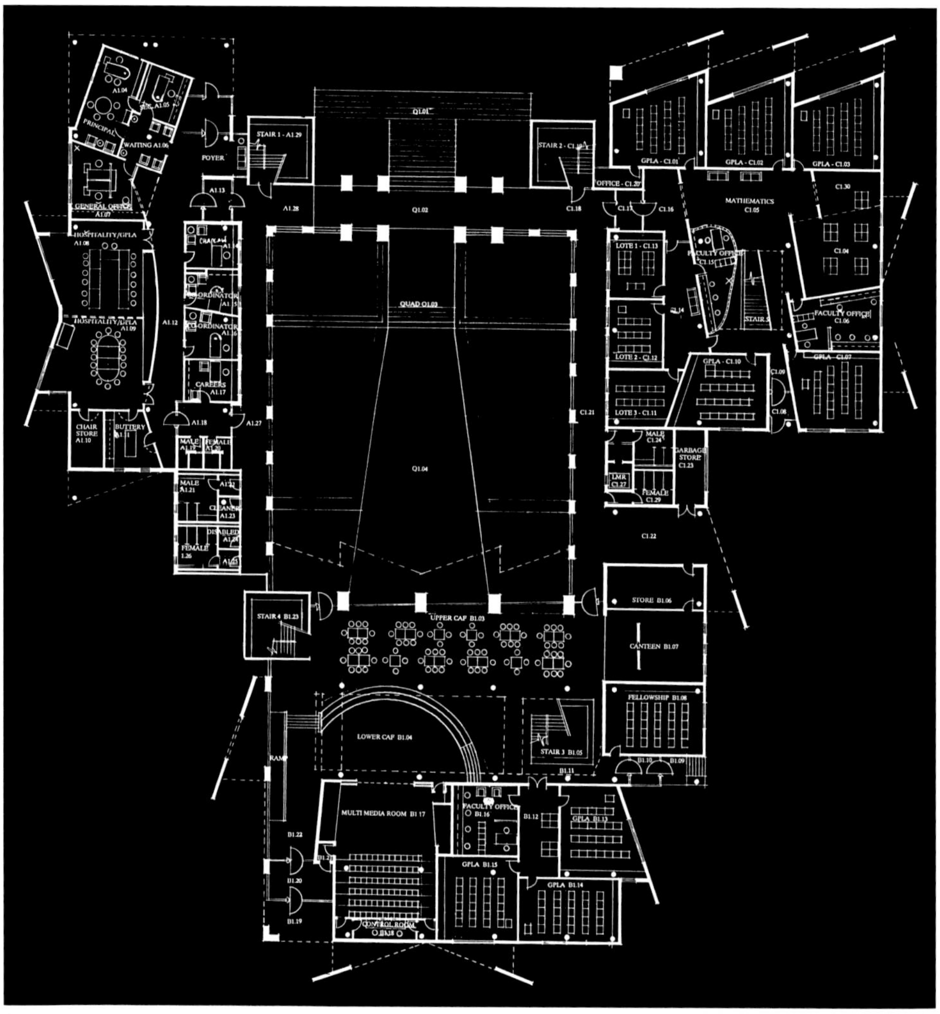

1

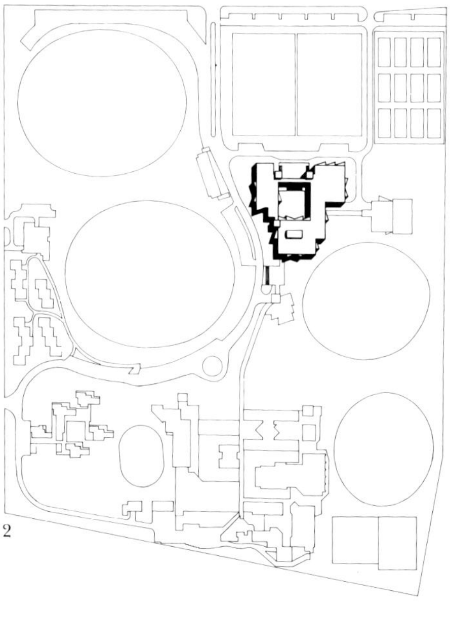

2

1 Ground-floor plan
2 Site plan
3 Ground-floor cafeteria
4 North elevation, main entry

3

4

5

6

7

5 Top-lit interior staircase
6 Main entry
7 Bridge link overlooking courtyard
8 Internal stairwell

8

Australian Film, Television and Radio School

Design/Completion 1985/1989
North Ryde, New South Wales
Australian Film, Television and Radio School
Architects: Daryl Jackson Robin Dyke Pty Ltd
in association with Basil Carter
7,000 square metres
Reinforced concrete frame
Concrete block and fibre cement sheet cladding, metal stud partitions and metal deck roof

Grids and networks are ways of organising things that need to communicate.
The new school links with its educational neighbour, Macquarie University, and with the surrounding street grid, which bisects the university grid at an angle. An interior "street" joins and distinguishes the school's component elements, linking secondary routes, staircases and informal meeting places. Their intersection is celebrated in a proscenium which arches over the street (a conscious symbol of theatre). Architectural incidents mark the street as it progresses from entrance "marquee" (an emblem of cinema) to a canteen at the end. This space overlooks the open valley beyond, through a large sunscreen porch. The skin is taut, banded and layered into its landscape setting. The major interior volumes of studios, support spaces and plant rooms are expressed externally with a solid, cubist feeling for mass.

Continued

1

2

1 Design sketch
2 Main building entry
3 Axonometric study

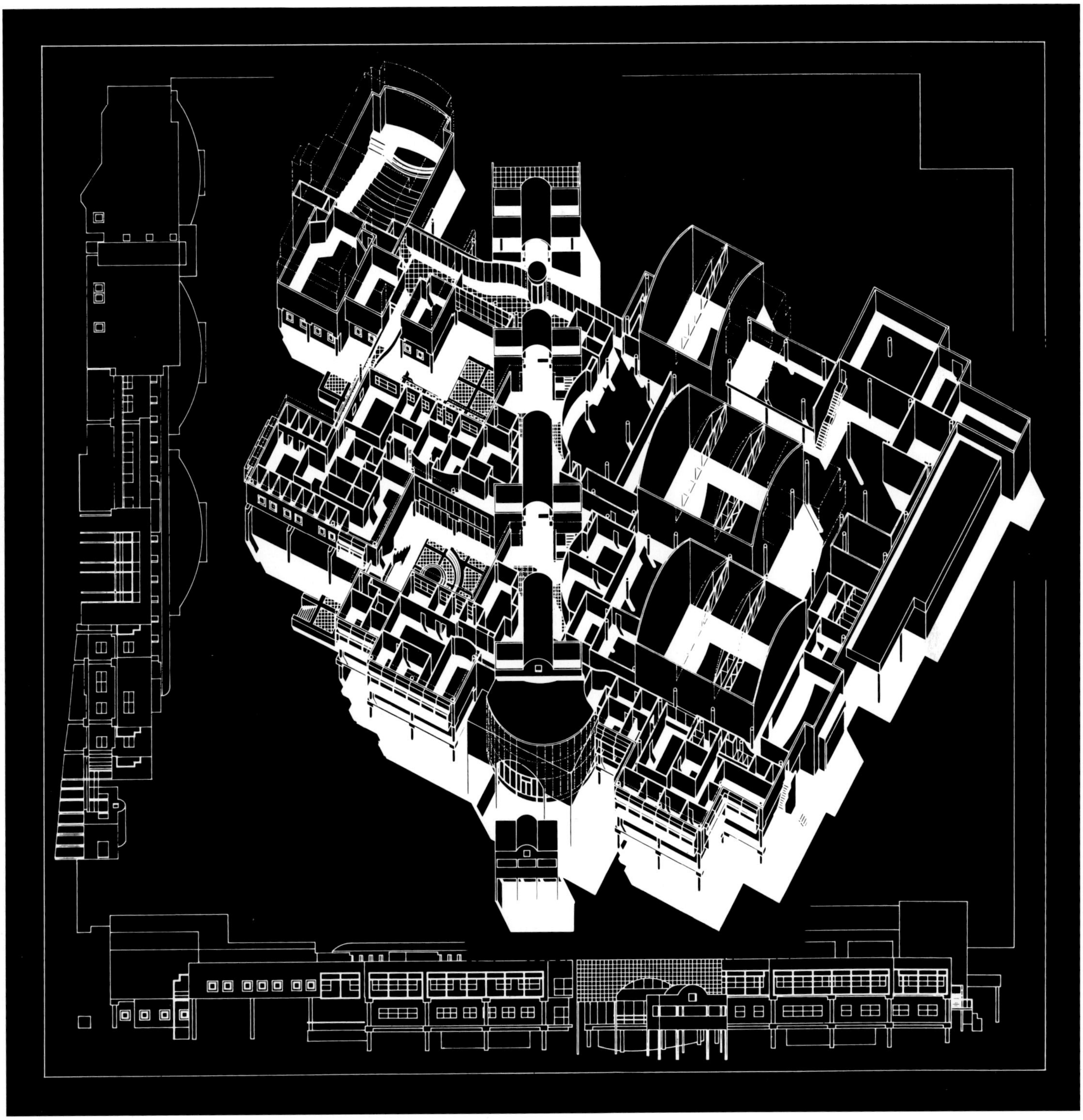

3

4 View out to courtyard
5 Studio
6 Level 2 floor plan
7 Circulation space
8 Exterior view

The enclosure is solid and dense where acoustic isolation is necessary (in studios and control rooms) and open and veranda-like where offices, library, and workplaces demand natural light and ventilation. Alternative access patterns, and connections to courtyards, theatres and workshops create a "labyrinth" designed to stimulate the imaginations and communicative skills of the scholars.

4

5

6

7

8

Canberra School of Art

Design/Completion 1978/1981
Acton, Australian Capital Territory
Department of Education
Architects: Daryl Jackson Evan Walker
11,000 square metres
Solid brick, steel frame, metal deck

The new School of Art buildings reinterpret the 1940s Modern of the old high school. Studios, workshops, apartments and an art gallery are added to this two-storey Art Deco block which symmetrically straddles the street axis. The additions form a series of open and closed work spaces, recalling Canberra's urban garden setting. The plan celebrates the role of the street address axis, while a primary circulatory spine organises and connects old and new. A red brick plinth with white bagged and painted brick walls keys the college to the ground plane; the window designs extrapolate a pattern from the existing proportions; and a recessed frieze at the height of the existing entablature offers juxtaposition.

1

2

3

4

5

6

7

8

1 Foyer
2 South entry
3 Axial journey
4 Courtyard kilns
5 Roof terrace
6 Library portico
7 Craft studio
8 Gallery
9 Main street entry
10 Axonometric study

CANBERRA SCHOOL OF ART

9

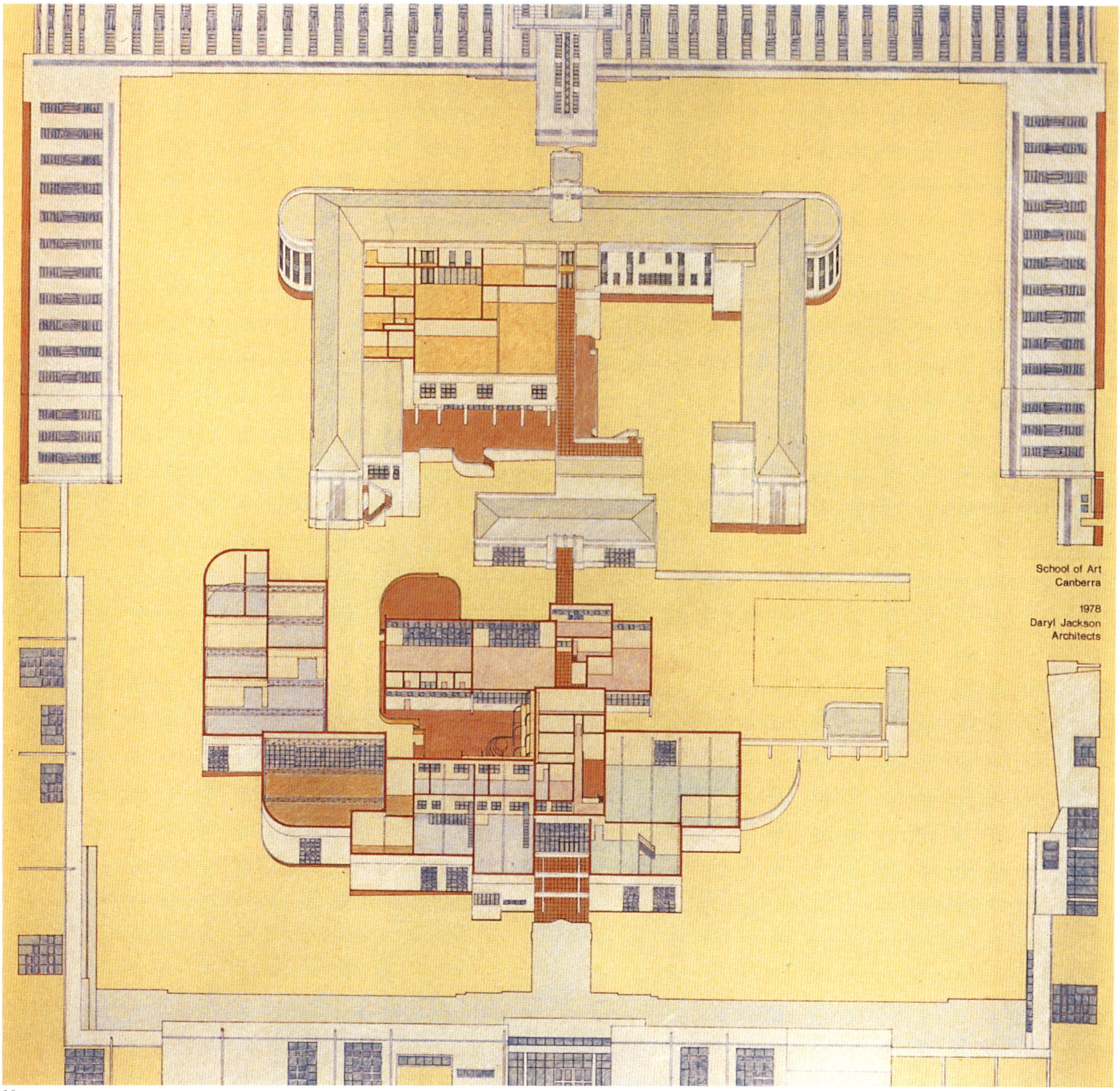
School of Art
Canberra
1978
Daryl Jackson
Architects

10

Canberra School of Music

Design/Completion 1971/1976
Acton, Australian Capital Territory
National Capital Development Commission
Architects: Daryl Jackson Evan Walker
12,000 square metres
Reinforced concrete, steel roof frame, metal deck

At the time this project was designed, highly modelled, monumental architectural expressionism was out of favour among Canberra architects, and bland, faceless offices for the bureaucrats were the rule, supplemented at the civic level by a neo-classical National Library built in the early 1960s. The School of Music was to stand alone in the middle of a ring road, with an adjacent 1940s high school to be demolished to make way for a through road. (A change in thinking later allowed the school to be recycled as the School of Art.) The interior had to be acoustically isolated from the anticipated exterior traffic noise.

The boldness of form results from a desire to produce an assertive cubist arrangement whose parts explore landscape and figurative metaphors to establish an architectural presence. The long horizontals are emblematic of landscape, while vertical stair towers

Continued

1

2

1 Street facade
2 View of corner
3 Sculpture
4 Axonometric study

3

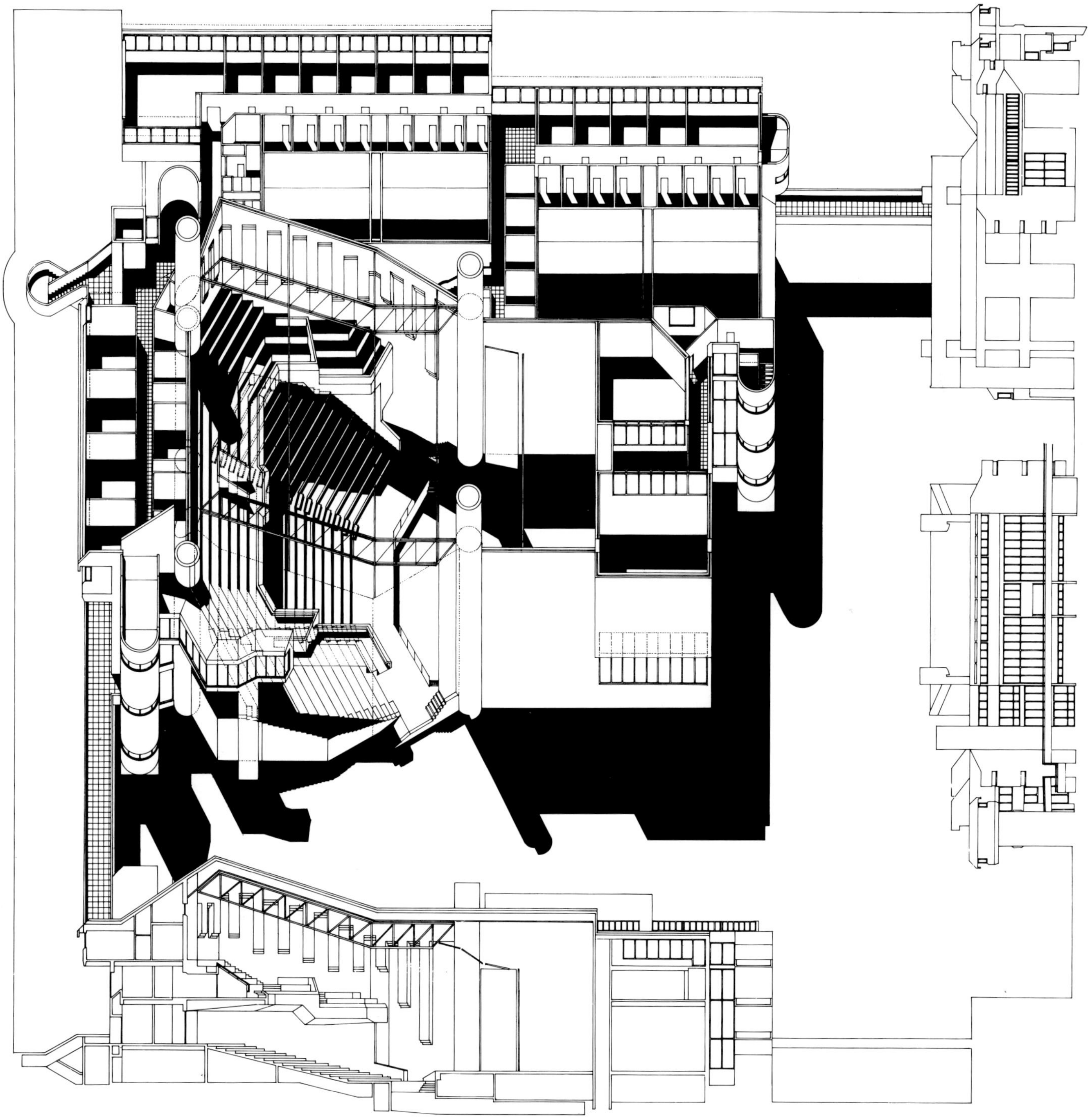

4

suggest life—upright opposing figures in a sculptural theme. Externally modelled circulation routes animate the otherwise static solid walls of the 1,500-seat auditorium. Office, stairs and galleries appear as additional encrustations on the basic enclosure, and impart a plastic sense of particular function and meaning.

The ring road was never built, leaving the school standing as an isolated landmark in a horizontal field, in need of one of the key elements of its sculptural form—a footbridge across the one remaining nearby road. This imbalance remains to be redressed.

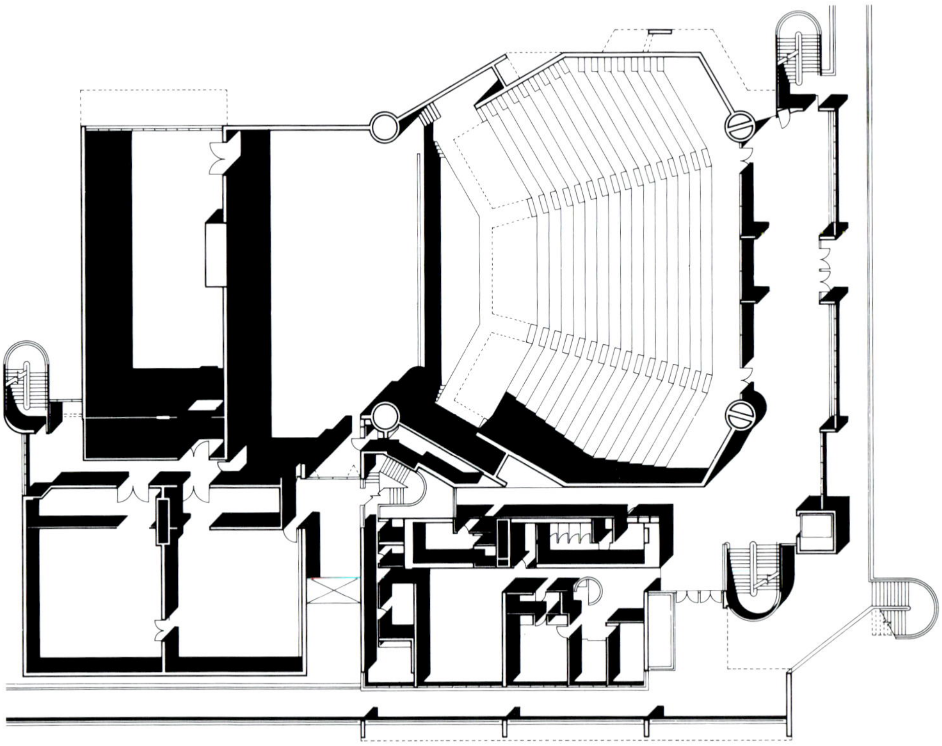

5

6

7

8

5 Ground-floor plan
6 Circulatory staircase
7 Theatre
8 Lecture theatre
9 Section
10 Aerial view of theatre stage

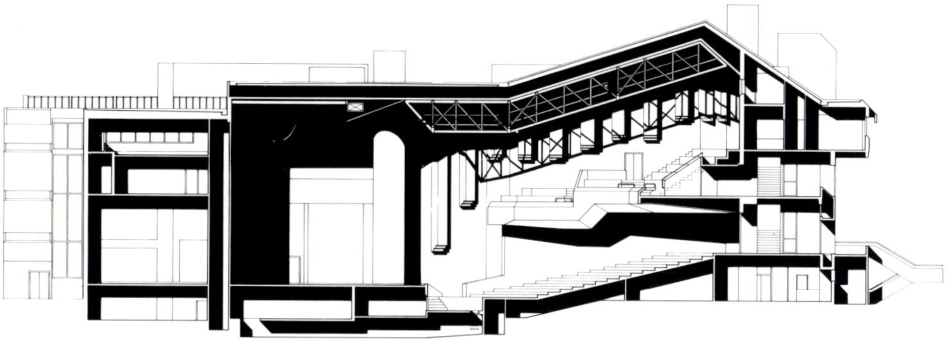

10

Technical and Further Education Complex, Swinburne University

Design/Completion 1985/1992
Hawthorn, Victoria
Swinburne University of Technology
7,223 square metres
Concrete frame
Red brick cladding, Robinson panel, metal sunshades

Hawthorn is a red brick suburb, and the new Swinburne buildings are designed to co-exist. Red brick base walls two storeys high, with an upper floor of blue metal panels matching the sky.

The three buildings are grouped along a brick paved pedestrian street which leads to a series of "front doors" signifying the various departments.

The new street continues uphill to bind the old and new parts of the campus together.

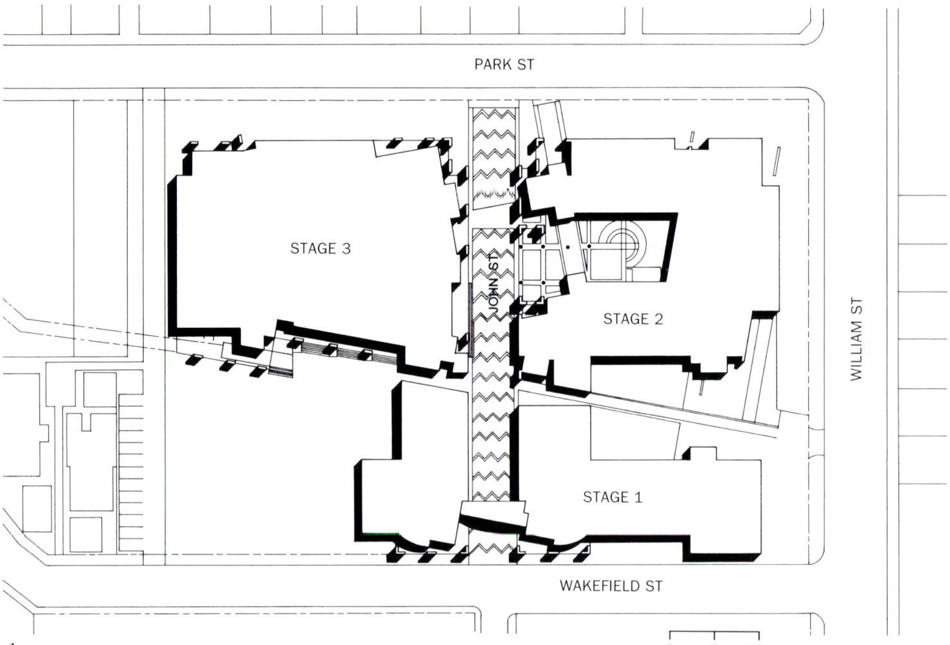

1

2

1 Site and location plan
2 Building detail
3 Stage 2: ground-floor plan
4 Stage 2: first-floor plan

3

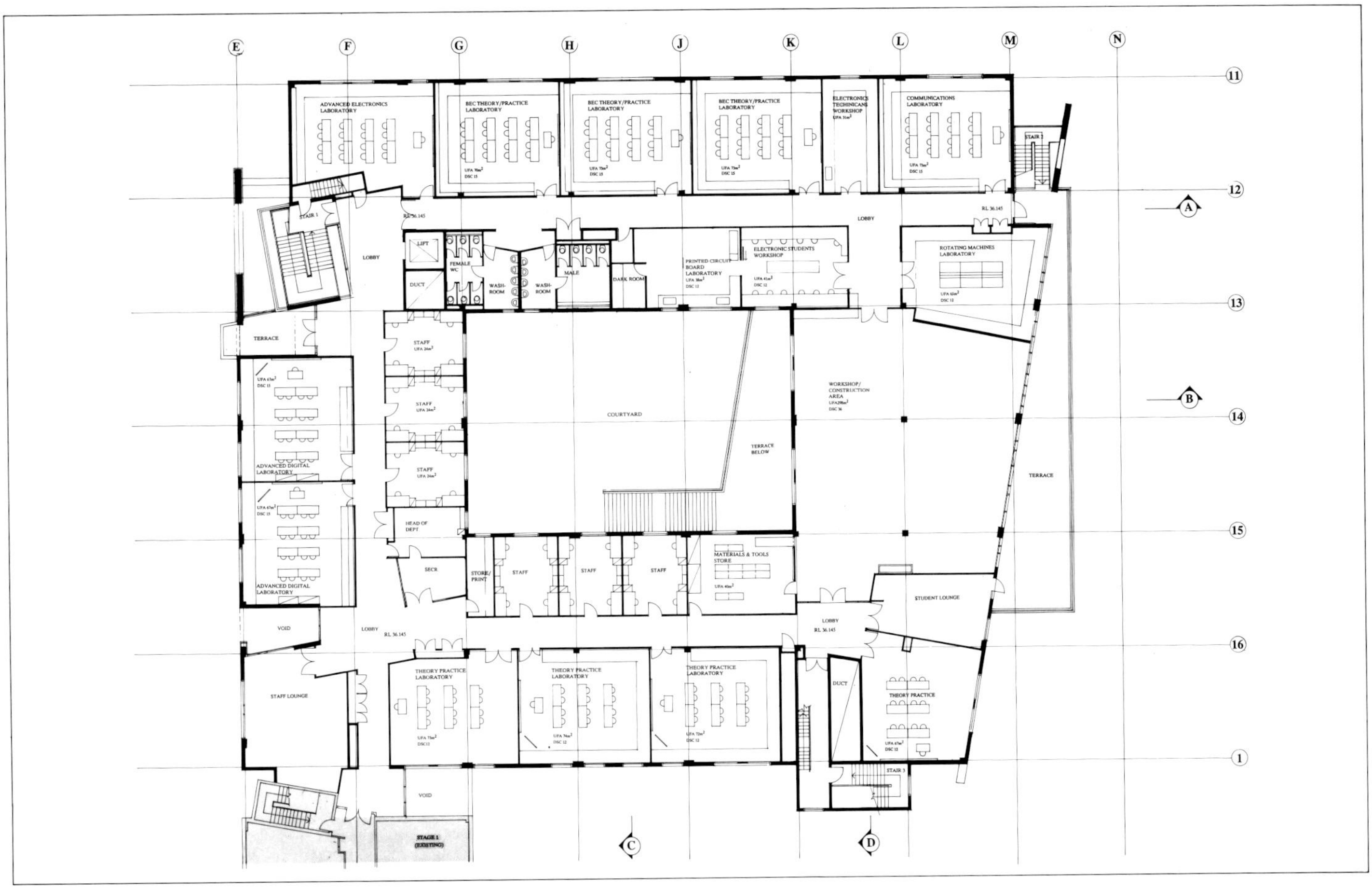

4

5

6

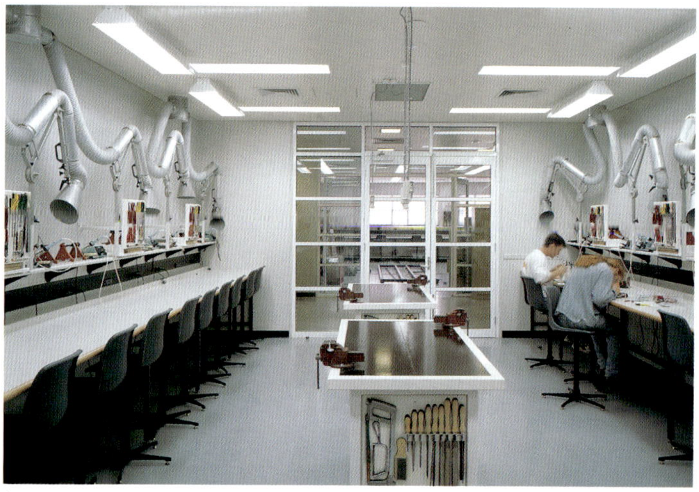

7

8

9

5 Wakefield Street elevation
6-7 Workshop
8 Exterior
9 Internal stairwell
10 John Street exterior

10

Swinburne University Master Plan

Design/Completion 1992/to date
Lilydale, Victoria
Swinburne University of Technology
Site area: 28 hectares
Infrastructure of roads, lighting, landscaping and all site services

Master planning is really the preparation of strategic understanding and tactical expression that anticipates and allows projects to emerge and to match educational objectives in a way that makes best use of the site.

From the Lilydale hill site, views take in the lake below and the Yarra Valley hills beyond. The plan is structured to draw each building into a planned framework which sees faculties stepping down the slope away from the upper level point of arrival.

The only constants to date are the distribution of elements: car parking to the west; buildings oriented to north and east for maximum solar effectiveness; and patterns of vehicular access and low-rise massing to maintain viewlines.

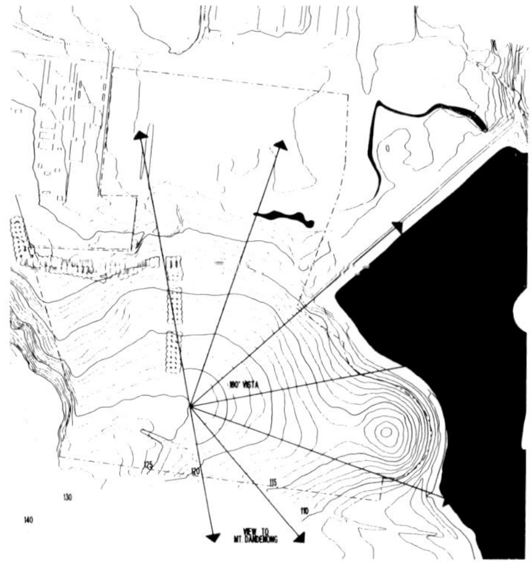

1

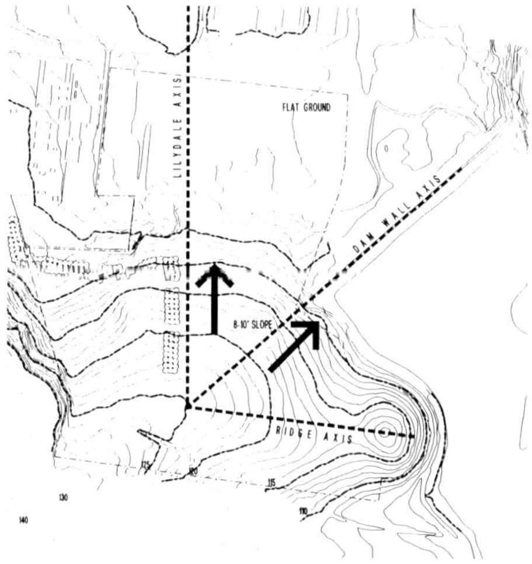

2

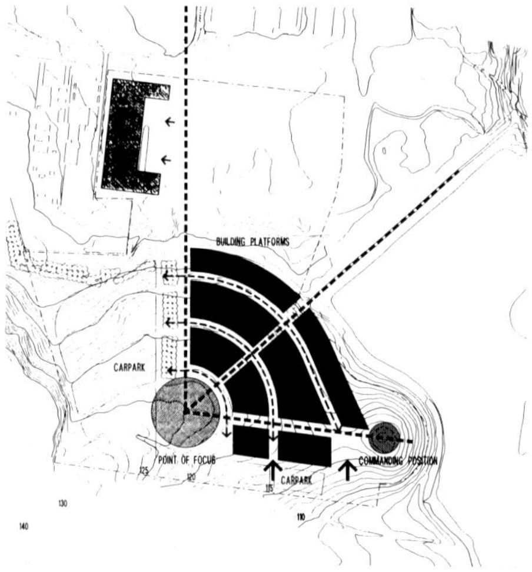

3

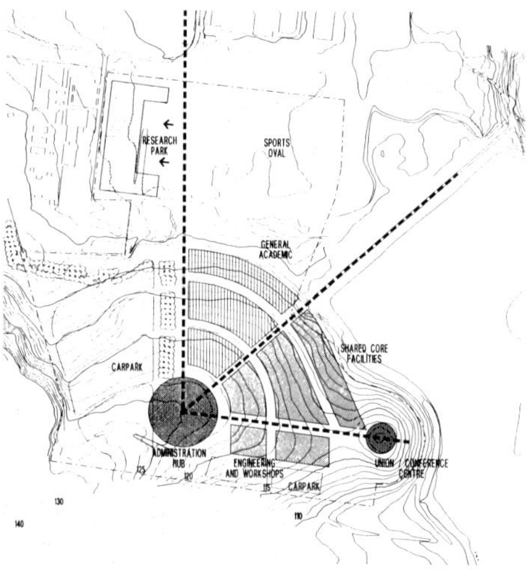

4

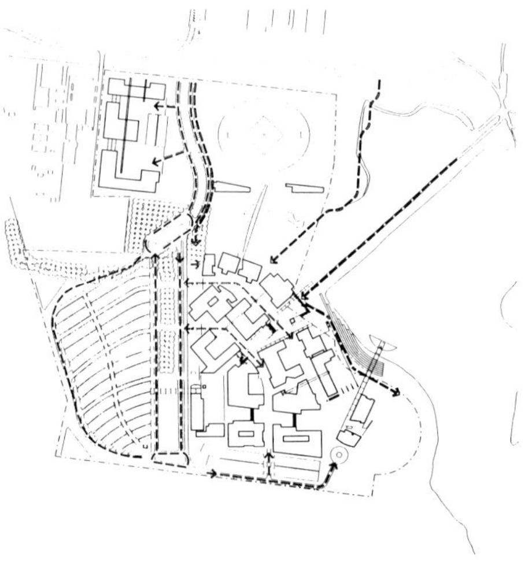

5

1 Views and climate
2 Topographic register
3 Academic zones
4 Building platforms
5 Access
6 Plan framework

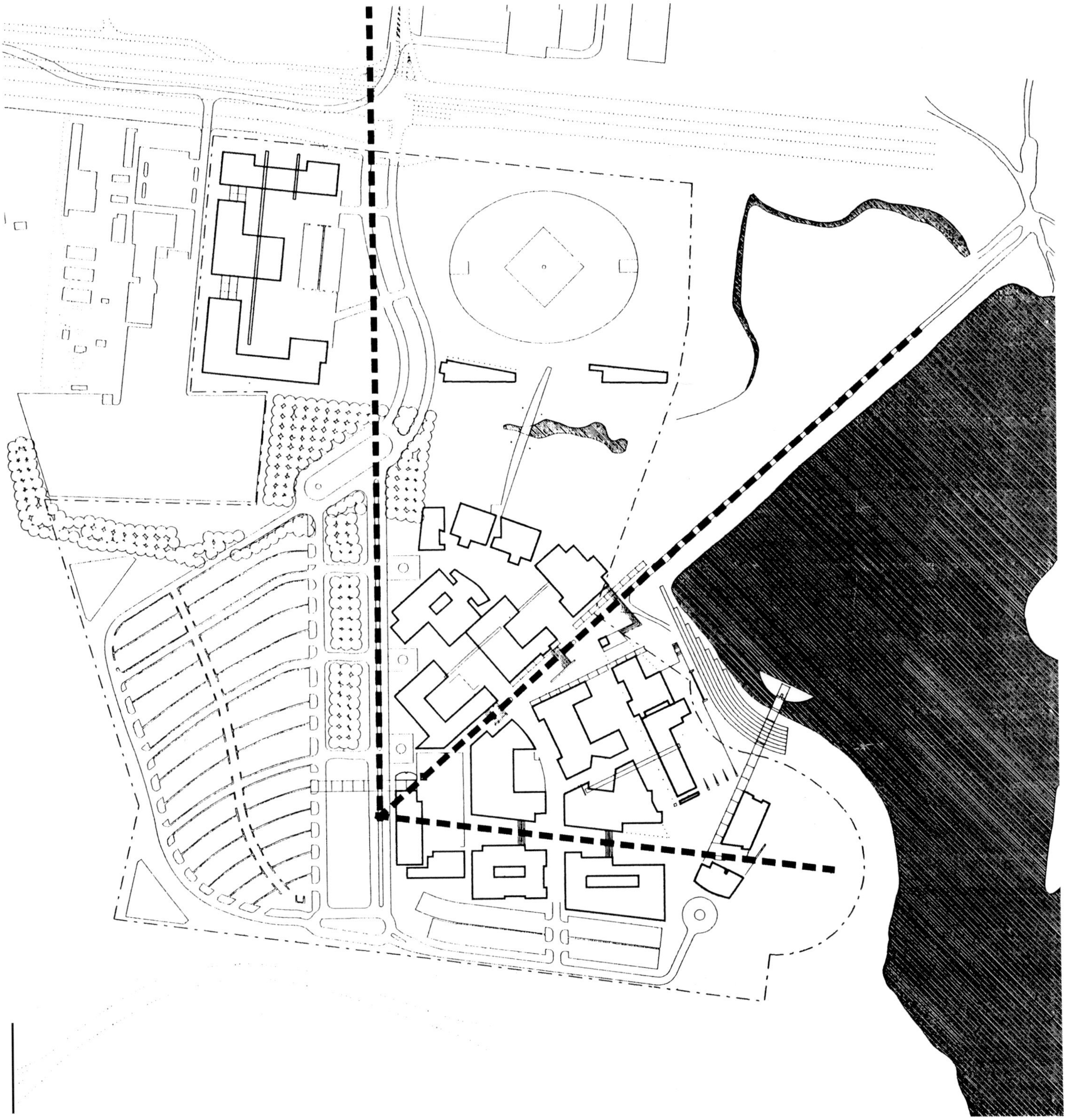

6

Bond University Master Plan

Design/Completion 1986/1989
Burleigh Forest, Queensland
Bond University Management Ltd
Architects: Daryl Jackson Robin Dyke Pty Ltd
Site area: 100 hectares
Service infrastructure, roads, hard and soft landscaping

The design promotes an Arcadian vision of boulevards, tree-lined streets and squares leading down to a water basin and lake beyond. The layout opposes the natural, yet uses landform to establish an urban structure. A formal axial figure is generated from the topography: two pine-covered knolls are joined by a diagonal broadway (academic spine), with cross streets for academic and social buildings. The buildings form urban edges and street facades.

Swampland is transformed. An expansive lake is the centrepiece for a landscape to be planted with flowering exotic species, while a water basin is the formal focus of the boulevard and student activities. The residential perimeter is dominated by an interpretation of landscape, with shafts of space cut into the pine forest. Built form follows the contours rather than the formal geometry of the academic core. Monumentality and enduring values are suggested in a plan structure that appears rational, timeless and solid.

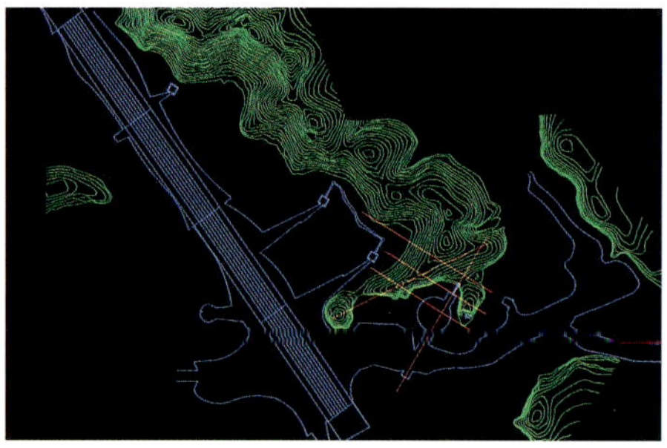

1

2

3

4

1 Topography
2 Master plan
3 Phase 1 plan
4 Entry towers
5 Section at Student Union
6 Plan of Student Union
7 Student Union

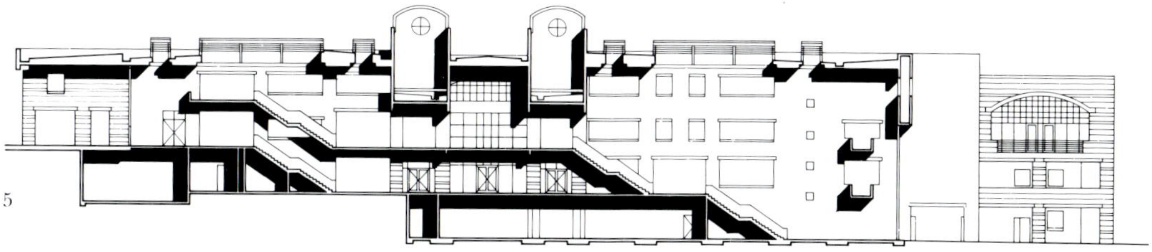

5

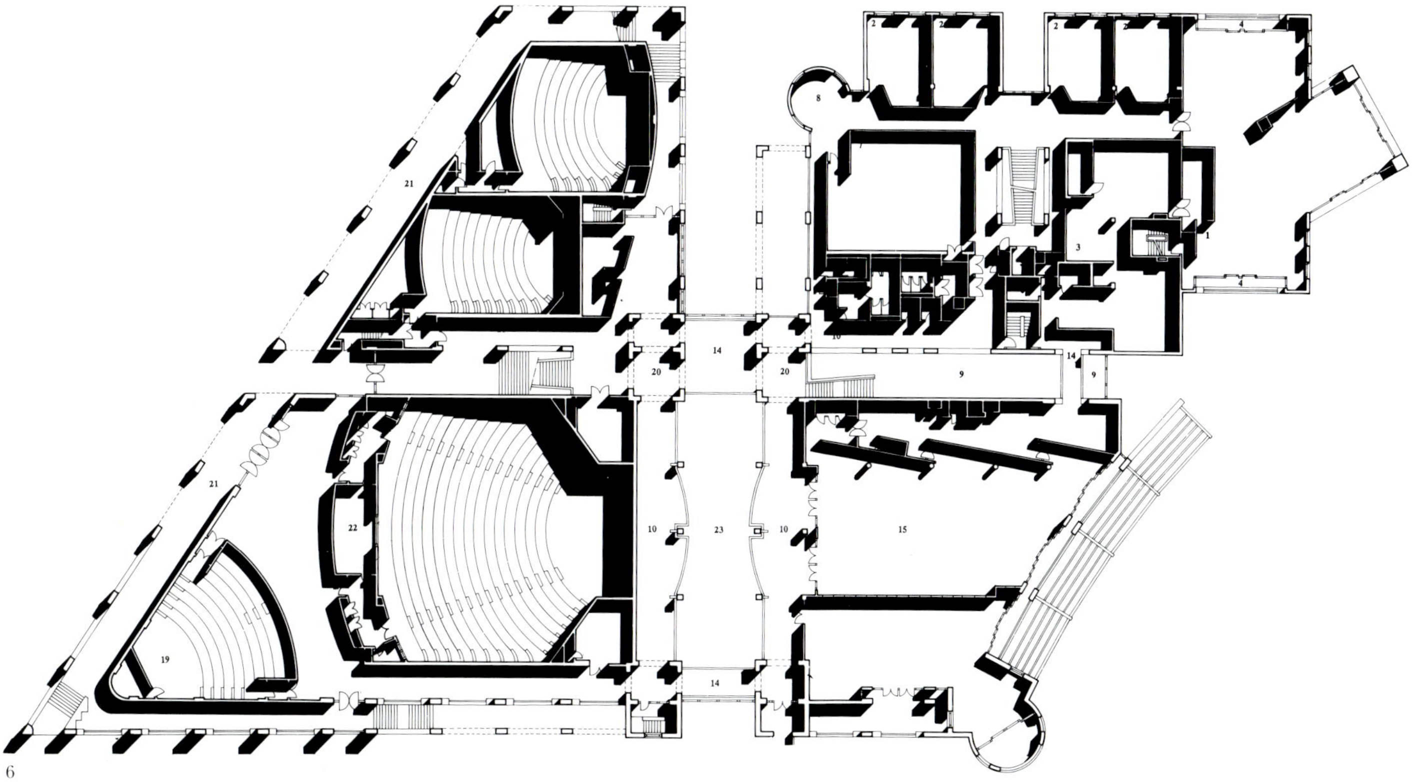

6

7

8 Union stairwell
9 Facade sunshades
10 Belltower stair
11 Aerial view from entry
12 Fabric roof detail
13 Belltower

8

9

10

11

12

13

Graduate School of Management, University of Melbourne

Design/Completion 1982/1987
Carlton, Victoria
Melbourne Business School Ltd
9,600 square metres
Reinforced concrete structure and floor slabs, external walls of load-bearing in situ concrete and load-bearing precast concrete, internal dry walls

The School of Management wraps itself around a courtyard, addresses an inner Melbourne square of large trees, and reflects in its outer face the character of this historic section of Carlton. The building's front deliberately reveals the inside arrangement of two floors of residential rooms placed above the academic tutorial and lecture areas. A two-storey arcade extends through the academic zone, leaving the upper two storeys as a simpler, stepped-back wall plane.

The arcade is at the same scale as the adjacent terraces that line the square. The "negative" openings of the arcade match the scale and rhythm of the "positive" house profiles: contextual fit is symbolic rather than real. A staircase collects the residential and day-scholars and distributes them throughout the complex. Groupings occur at every level, with the greatest number at the public ground level, next to the street and courtyard entrances.

1

2

3

1 North court elevation
2 Shade detail
3 Sunshade silhouette
4 Axonometric study

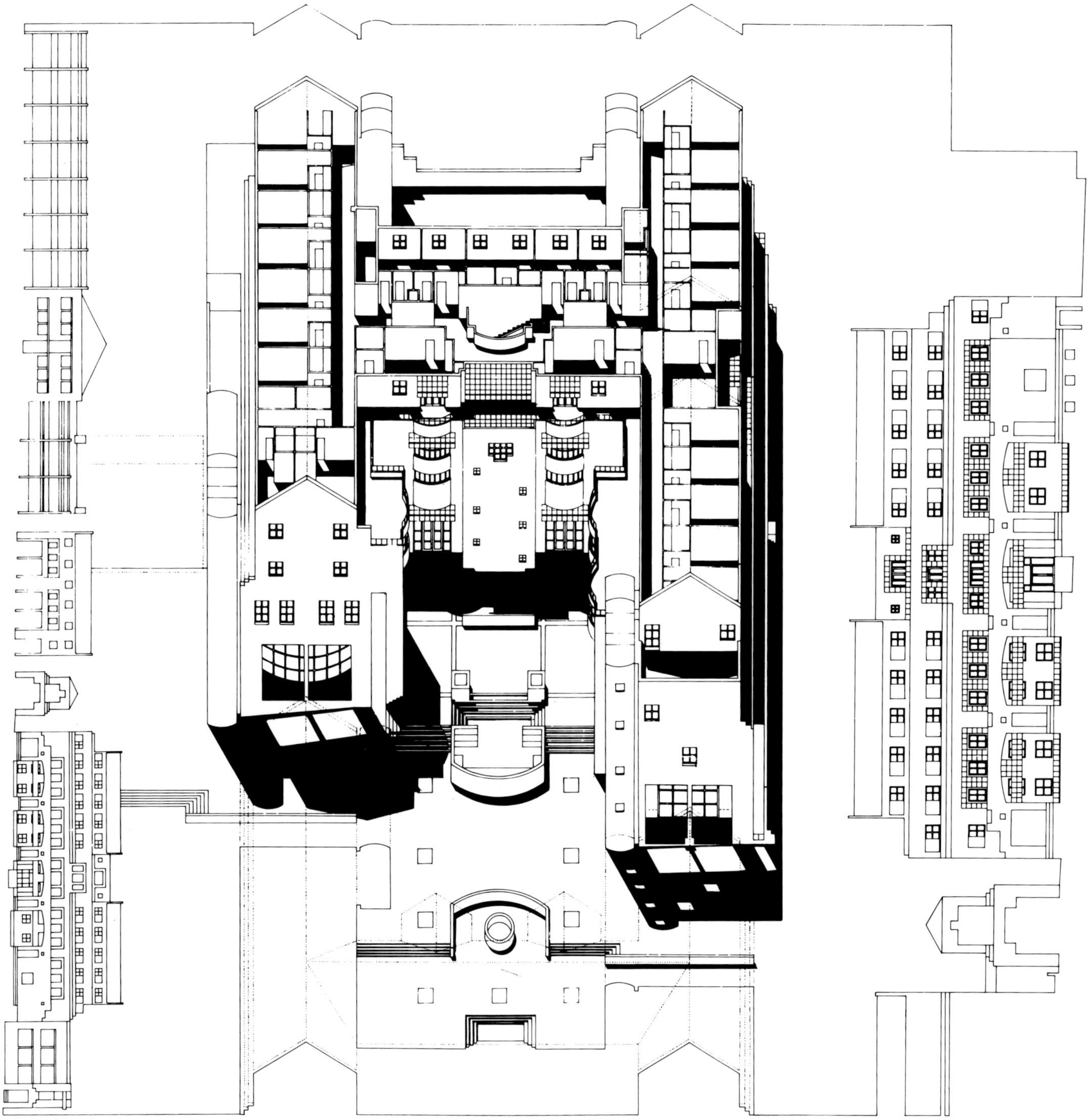

4

5

6

5 View from the park
6 Theatre
7 Lightwell
8 Cafeteria
9 Foyer

7

8

9

IT & EE Building, University of Melbourne

Design/Completion 1992/1993
Carlton, Victoria
University of Melbourne
12,000 square metres
Reinforced concrete frame with in situ band beams and one-way slabs on a grid; precast panels; projecting glass bays; colorbond metal cladding; metal sunshades

The School of Information Technology and Electrical Engineering at the University of Melbourne demanded facilities for the rapidly growing fields of computer science and electrical engineering on the lower levels, with related sectors of commercial research leasing the upper floors.

This dual function meant that the interior spaces had to serve the needs of the students by providing adequate lecture theatres and seminar rooms, while simultaneously being capable of accommodating corporate functions. The high-technology solution provides two front doors to the street: one for tenants and another for students. This registers in the streetscape via the ramp and stair access.

The front elevation splits at the centre to maintain urban scale with the neighbouring buildings yet project a number of upper-level glazed and angled office bays into the street to signify new ingredients. The roof form rotates to diminish the mass and celebrate occupancy.

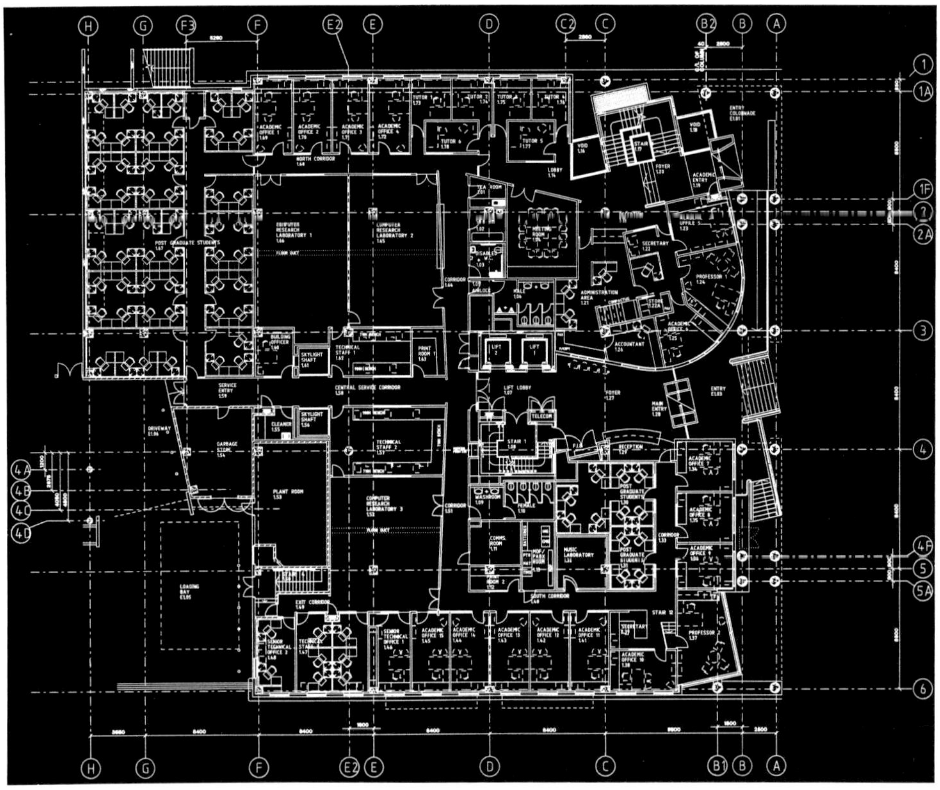

1

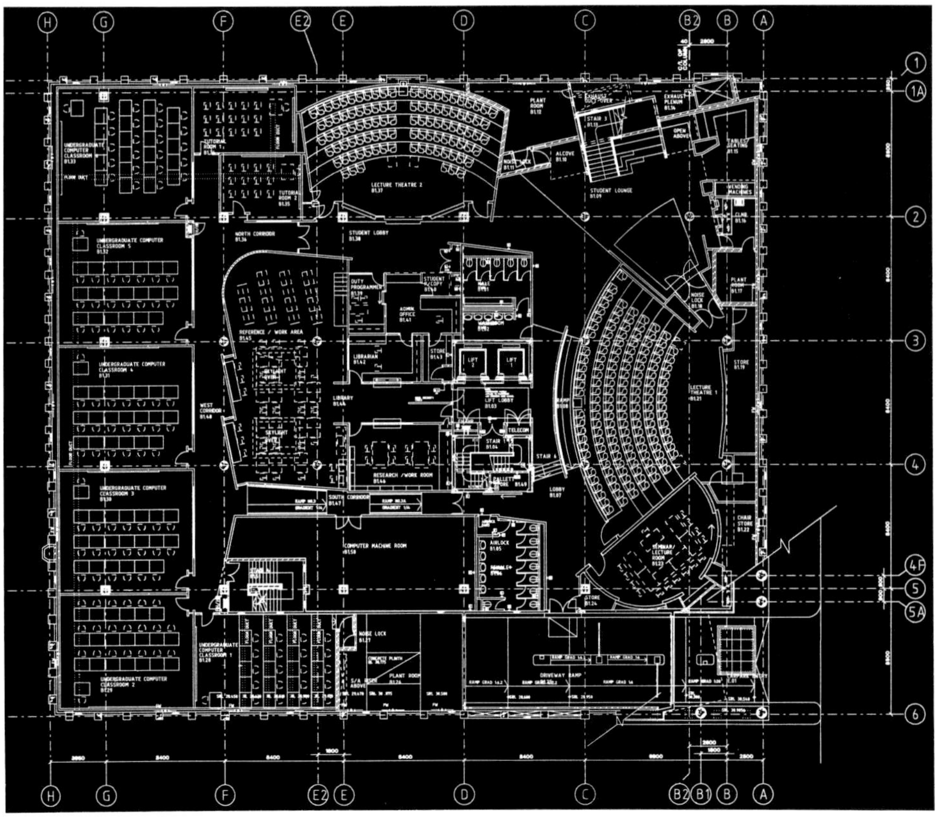

2

1 Ground-floor plan
2 Basement plan
3 View from Lincoln Square
4 Street facade

3

4

5

7

6

8

5 Lecture theatre
6 Foyer
7 Computer room
8 Lecture theatre
9 Bay window detail

9

Griffith University Plan Reviews

Design/Completion 1992/1993
Brisbane, Queensland
Director of Faculties Management, Griffith University

Three existing campuses now comprise Griffith University, and all three are part of this siting review. The salient questions are how to build into and onto each layout, how to maintain vegetation and habitat, and how to generate compatibilities of building massing, car parking and access. Each plan form presents special opportunities, yet the conflicts emerge: existing occupants' attitudes about comfort and fit versus long-term growth and the future.

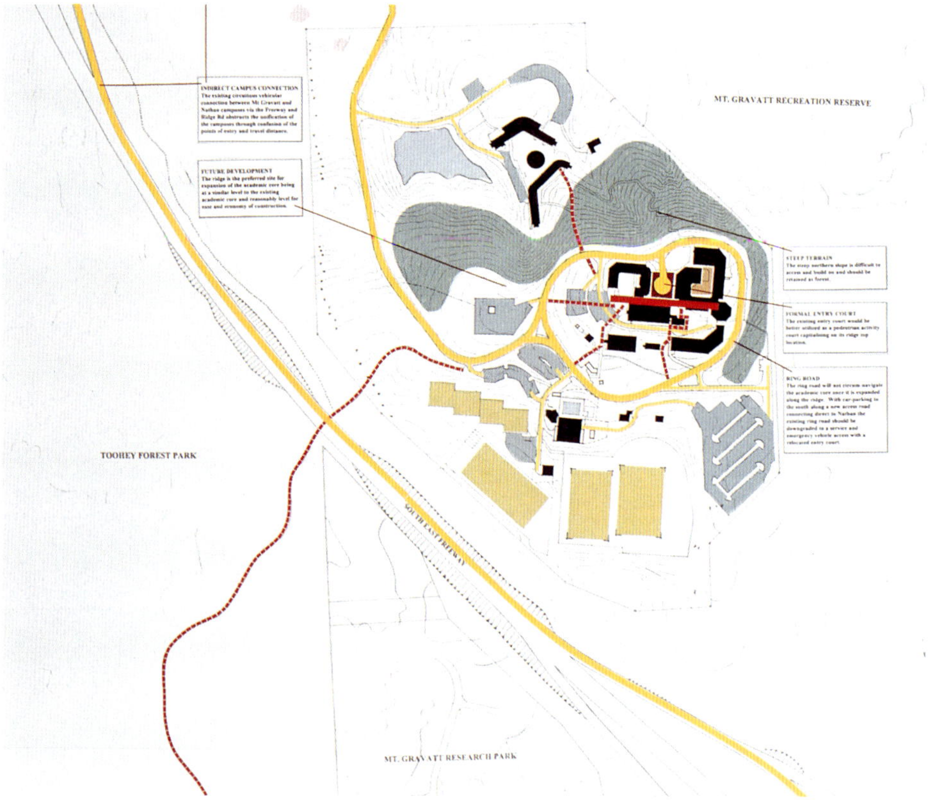

1

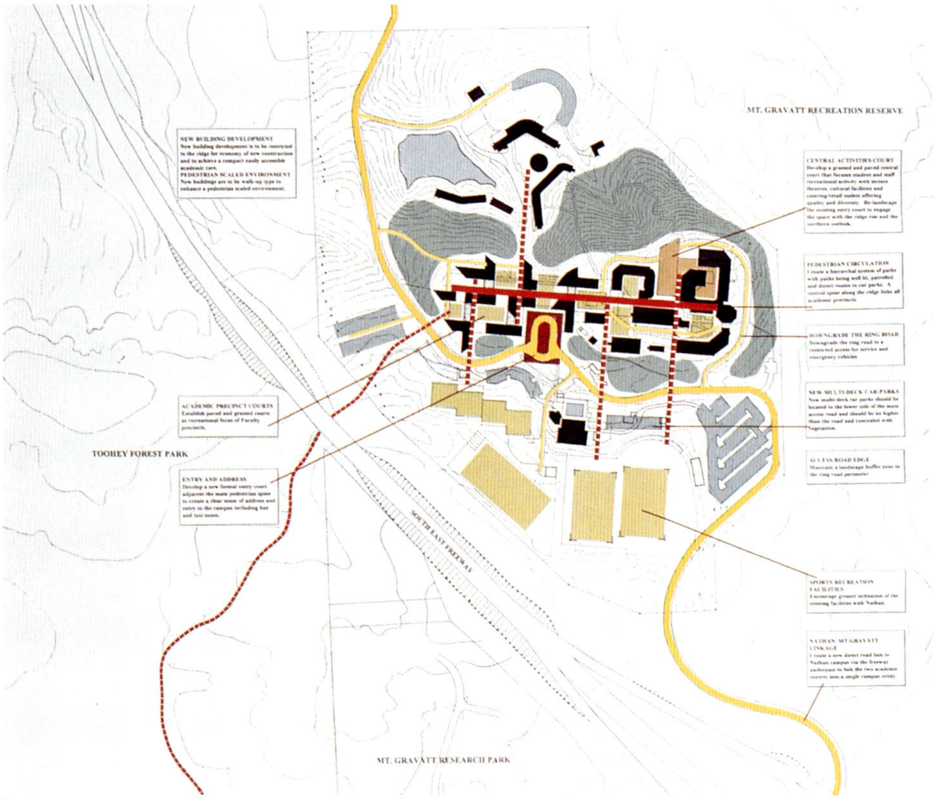

2

1 Nathan Campus: existing
2 Nathan Campus: expanded
3 Mt Gravatt Campus: existing
4 Mt Gravatt Campus: expanded

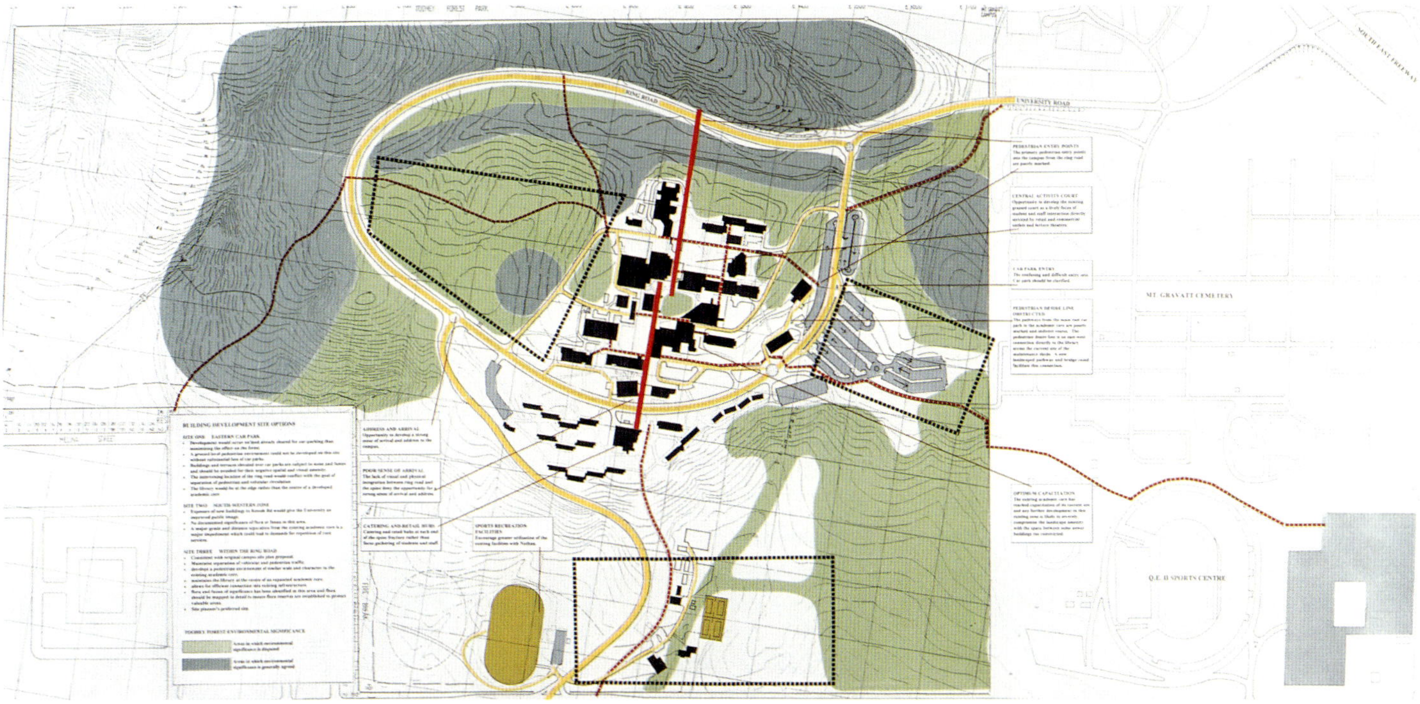

3

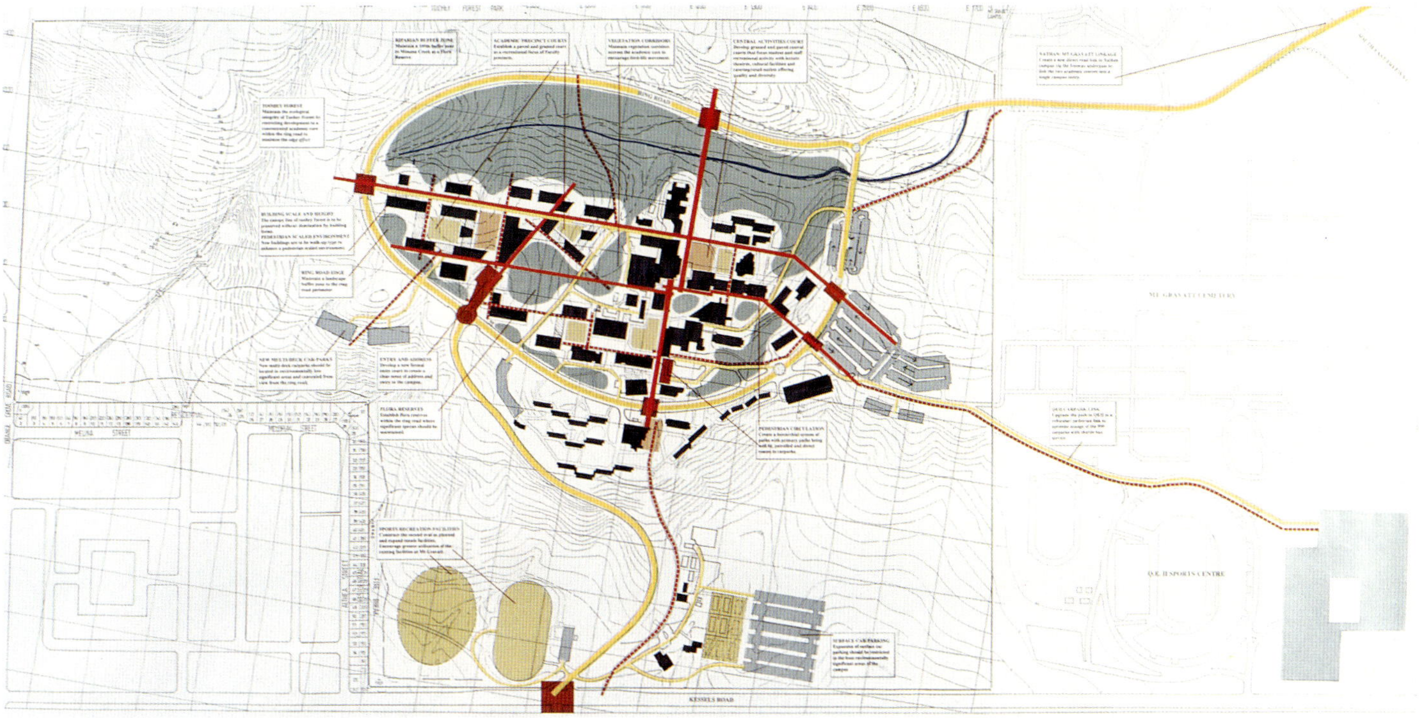

4

Monash University Multi-Disciplinary Centre

Design/Completion 1984/1987
Clayton, Victoria
Monash University
2,378 square metres
Load-bearing brick structure with concrete floor slabs
Brick cladding with bagged and painted bands, aluminium windows and metal deck roof

The Monash Multi-Disciplinary Centre, which houses a number of small facilities and an art gallery, creates an edge and a sense of entry to the Monash University campus. As a small building, it required a strong presence to deal with the surroundings. A curved form responding to the sweep of the ring road is in formal contrast to the Cartesian grid that orders the campus. A grid overlays the curve as a reference to the campus and as a means of generating a complex composition. The orthogonal form of the ground floor art gallery extends from the primary curved form to address the courtyard and the campus.

Internally, the meshing of orthogonal and curve generates a circulation spine of variety—a spatial narrative along a path. Voids over the circulation stair tie together the various disciplines on the upper levels in volume and light. The curved forms at each end are elevated as a gateway to emphasise the dynamism of the composition and allow passage underneath.

1

1 Floor plans
2 North-west corner
3 Toplit staircase
4 South facade
5 Entry

2

3

4

5

Northern Territory University Master Plan

Design/Completion 1990/1992
Brinkin, Northern Territory
Northern Territory University
Associate architects: Woodhead (Aust) NT Pty Ltd
Site area: 57.56 hectares

The Arafura Sea, which separates the north coast of Australia from the Indonesian archipelago, forms an edge to the university site. The master planners' task was to expand the existing university college to a campus model capable of accommodating an expanding student population over a 10-year program. The additions consisted of a new library, student amenities, and faculties for arts, law, sciences and education, as well as the integration of a range of other disciplines from another site.

The plan both apprehends and expands upon the existing layout. A series of open outdoor "rooms" or courtyards, designed to clarify and integrate old and new, is integral to the plan idea. So, too, is the creation of a landscaped pedestrian environment as a core, with perimeter access and car parking around the edges. Two telescoping armatures of new faculty buildings embrace a gradually sloping strand which brings the land–water connection into play.

1

2

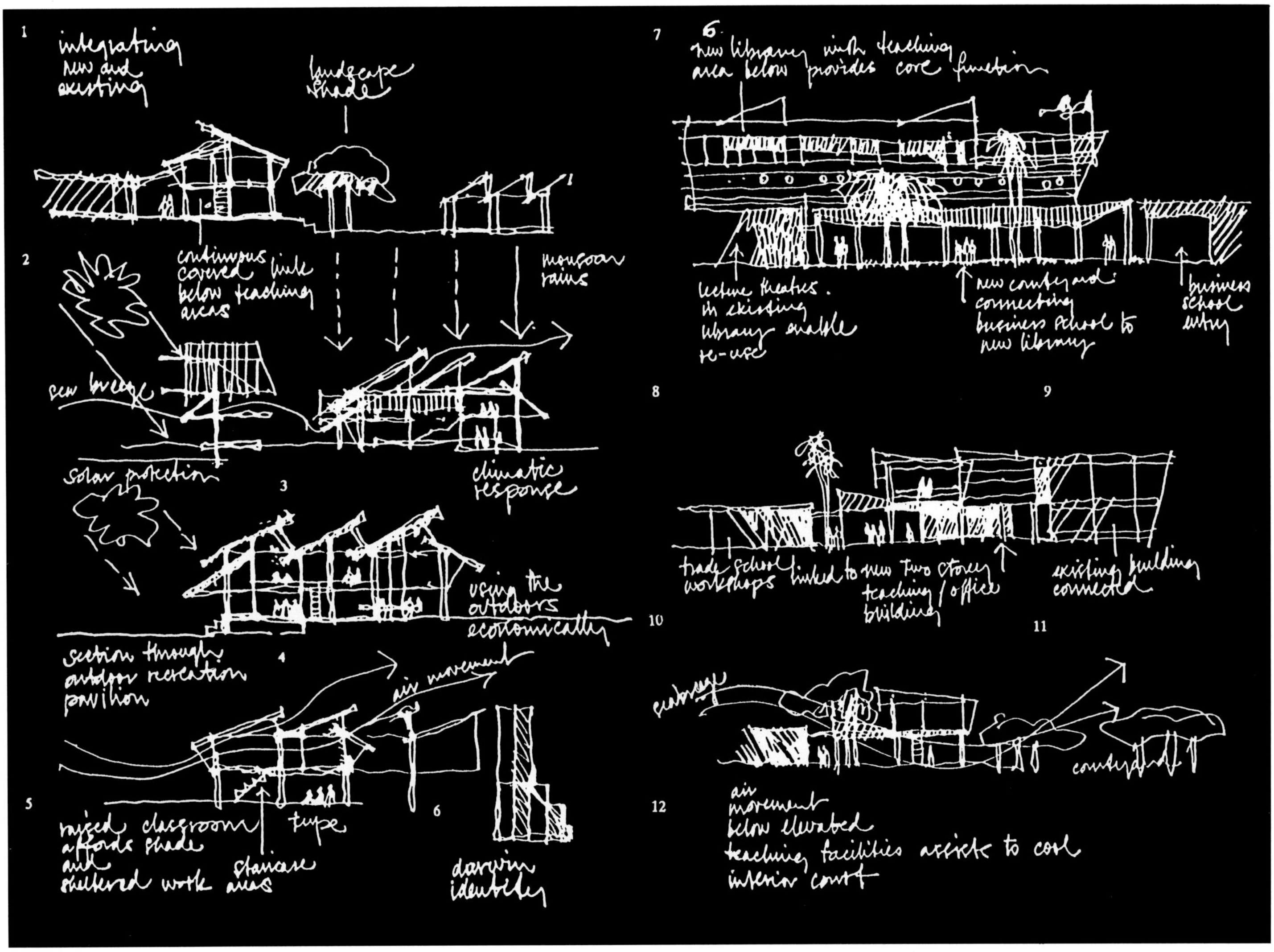

3

1 Overall master plan
2 Perspective sketch of proposal
3 Design sketches for tropical architecture

Arts/Law Building, Northern Territory University

Design/Completion 1992/1994
Brinkin, Northern Territory
Northern Territory University
Associate architects: Woodhead (Aust) NT Pty Ltd
5,500 square metres
Reinforced concrete frame with in situ band beams and concrete floor slabs
External walls of rendered blockwork; corrugated metal panelling on steel frame; metal sunshades

Darwin is tropical, the climate typically wet and hot, or dry and hot. Sun protection, air movement and roof cover are of paramount importance. A long thin academic building with an "open" central loggia or veranda forms a common entry to the separate faculties of arts and law. Long rows of private offices for staff contrast with cubist blocks, wrenched out of the basic block, which offer identity to the library, moot courts and other special uses.

Strong primary colours; shaded, deeply recessed lightweight walls; and skeletal steel stairs complete the assemblage.

1

2

1 Window detail
2 Building in its landscape
3 Staircase detail

3

Boiler House Lecture Theatre, University of Canberra

Design/Completion 1991/1993
Bruce, Australian Capital Territory
University of Canberra
Architects: Daryl Jackson Alastair Swayn Pty Ltd
2,000 square metres
Renovation of existing steel-framed boiler house: steel frame, fibre cement, metal deck roofing

This 600-seat lecture theatre at the University of Canberra is a recycled boiler house. The building's original industrial architecture remains, with a new foyer and stair tower, represented as a series of "reverse" form additions of deliberately contrasting expression. The boiler house is a closed form: the foyer is open. The solid enclosure of the old building is contrasted with the tautness and skin-like feel of the interior additions.

2

1

3

1 Theatre interior
2 Main entry
3 Entry facade
4 Theatre interior

4

South Brisbane College of Technical and Further Education, Food Technology Building

Design/Completion 1990/1993
South Brisbane, Queensland
Bureau of Employment, Vocational and Further Education and Training
7,000 square metres
Reinforced concrete frame
Fibre cement infill wall treatment and aluminium sandwich panel sunshading

This food technology building provides a retail area at street level, with three upper floors offering facilities for training in Butchery, Bread Baking and Pastry Cooking as well as Travel, Floristry and Cellaring. Bread baking and pastry cooking occupy the top storey, reaping the benefits of the high ventilated ceiling.

In tropical Brisbane, the need for sunshading is of primary importance. Natural light is maximised, without allowing direct sunlight into practical rooms. Sunscreening and balconies work towards the same end. A roof terrace over a central service facility between the two building forms a landscaped student gathering area.

1

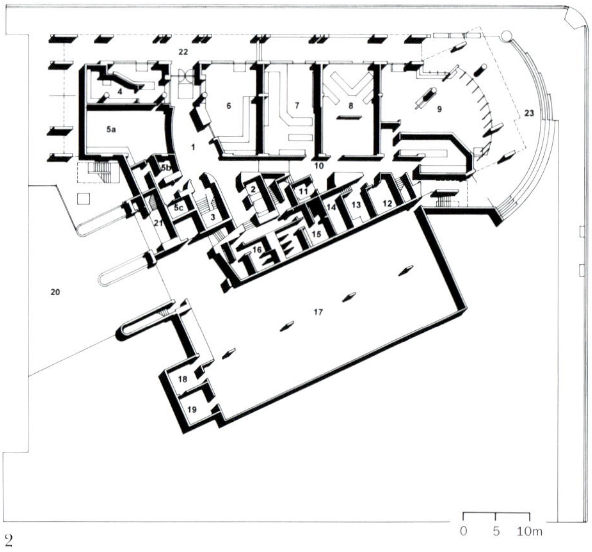

2

LEVEL 1 COLCHESTER ST. LEVEL

1 FOYER
2 PASSENGER LIFTS
3 CIRCULATION STAIR
4 FLORIST SHOP
5a FLORIST PRACTICAL
5b STORE
5c COLD ROOM
6 TRAVEL SHOP
7 BUTCHER SHOP
8 HOT BREAD SHOP
9 COFFEE SHOP/TAKE AWAY
10 SERVICE CORRIDOR
11 GOODS LIFT
12 SCULLERY
13 FOOD PREPARATION
14 DRY STORE
15 FEMALE TOILETS/CHANGE
16 MALE TOILETS/CHANGE
17 CAR PARK
18 COMPRESSOR ROOM
19 TRANSFORMER ROOM
20 SERVICE YARD
21 BUTCHERY SCHOOL DELIVERY
22 COLCHESTER STREET COLONNADE
23 OUTDOOR SEATING AND TABLES

3

1 LEVEL 1 FOYER
2 LEVEL 1 CARPARK
3 LEVEL 2 BULK STORE / DELIVERIES
4 LEVEL 3 BUTCHERY STORE
5 LEVEL 4 LECTURE ROOMS, COMPUTER ROOMS, STAFF ROOMS
6 LEVEL 5 BAKERY SCHOOL

4

5

6

1 Main entry: corner of Colchester Street and Tribune Street
2 Entry level floor plan
3 Section
4 Interior service court
5 View down Colchester Street
6 Interior of coffee shop

Lake Ginninderra College

Design/Completion 1986/1987
Belconnen, Australian Capital Territory
National Capital Development Commission
10,468 square metres
Reinforced concrete, steel columns and beams for upper floors
Brickwork, lightweight panel system on steel frame, white off-form concrete

The college, for students in the final two years of high school, provides a microcosm of the city in both form and experience. The school is organised into four teaching disciplines. Each has an autonomous precinct with an individual expression. The manual arts precinct has an industrial expression, with saw-toothed roofs and castellated beams. The central roof-light of the library is supported by a steel roof truss, expressing the idea of structure and reading as a universal sky across this space.

The quadrangle is the central public space and is defined by a colonnade with paved steps providing informal seating. The corners of the quadrangle are marked by entry towers representing earth, air, fire and water, each colour-coded and top-lit by distinctive roof-lights. The historic and symbolic references of quadrangle, colonnade and tower are mediated by cubist formalism. Overhead is the orator's platform which is reached via one of the classrooms.

Continued

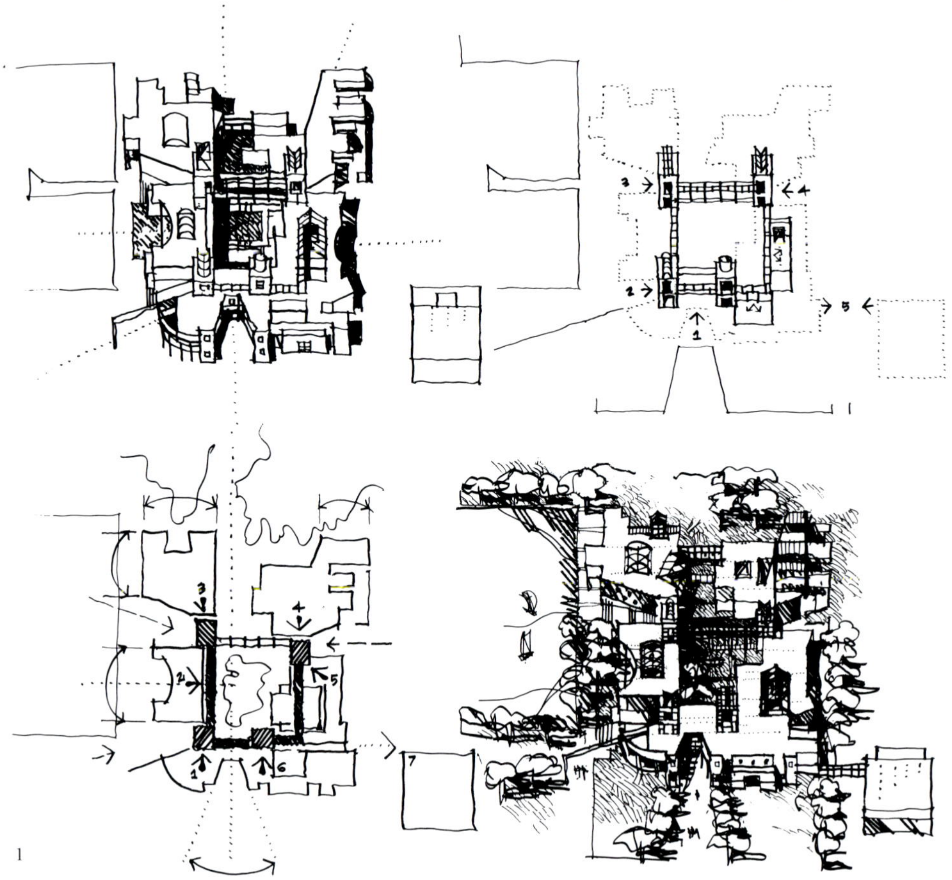

1

2

1 Design sketch based on courtyard
2 North-west quadrangle
3 Elevated walkway
4 Street elevation

3

4

Circulation is the basis of expression: diagonals and curves, in plan and section, modulate the spaces along paths leading users through the building. Activity is revealed and function expressed. Corridors move along facades, and selected rooms are twisted from the orthogonal pattern to project from the facade. From inside, these devices inform the user of activities beyond the compound, and project internal space into the landscape.

The building is an object in the landscape, and also a generator of the future urban condition that will develop here. The brick base suggests the built form of the city, while the upper level green wall panels refer to the surrounding hills and lakeside location.

5

6

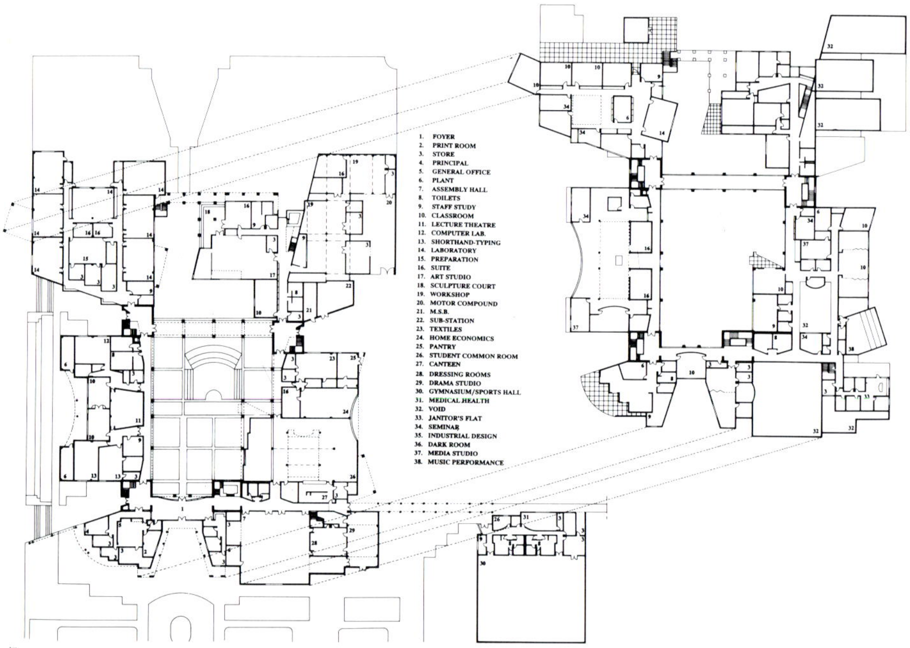

7

8

9

5 Top-lit staircase
6 Skylight detail
7 Ground and first-floor plans
8 Student common room
9 Studio
10 Lake edge elevation
11 Exterior view
12 View through porthole

10

11

12

SELECTED AND CURRENT WORKS

Sports

Australian Institute of Sport Grandstand

Design/Completion 1989/1991
Bruce, Australian Capital Territory
ACT Public Works Department
Architects: Daryl Jackson Alastair Swayn Pty Ltd
1,000 square metres
Concrete block walls, steel frame, metal deck

The aerofoil roof of the grandstand acts like the brim of a hat, shielding the spectators from the sun and the rain. The supports lean forward, giving an aggressive and dynamic expression. At one end of the grandstand, a judges' tower provides an independent but complementary structure. The steel elements are taut, tensioned and tough; the enclosed changing and work areas, by contrast, are solid, independently structured cubic forms of painted concrete masonry. The formal contrast between mass and density and the lightweight roof form establishes the essential values.

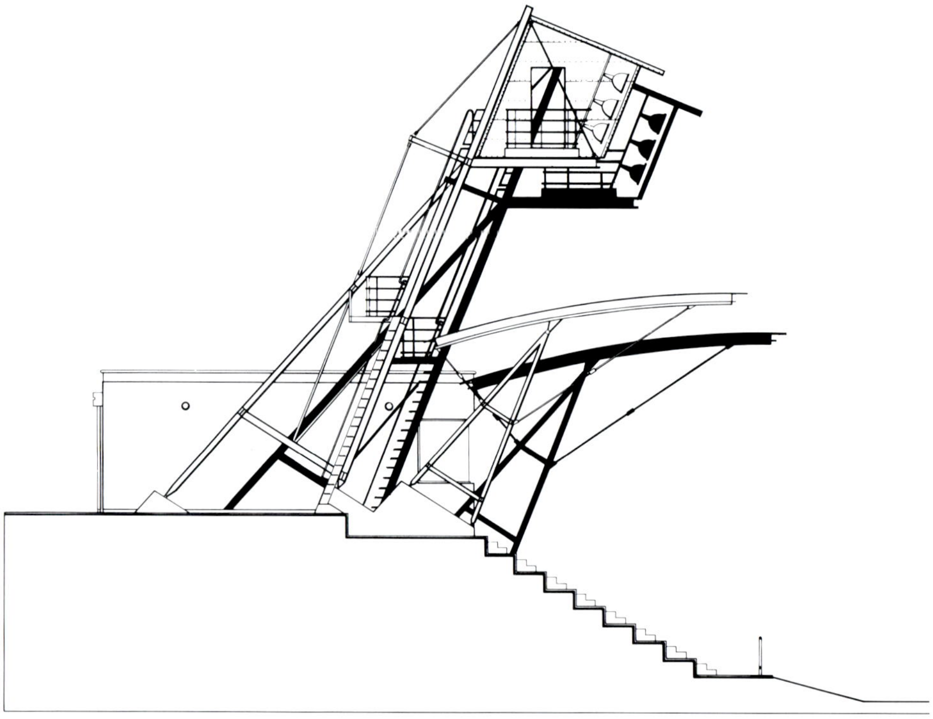

1

2

1 Side elevation
2 View of judges' tower
3 Grandstand elevation
4 View of grandstand from running track

3

4

Cannons Gymnasium

Design/Completion 1989/1994
Cannon Street Station, London, UK
Cannons Sports Club
Architects: Daryl Jackson International Pty Ltd
5,500 square metres
Existing brick arches with inserted steel and concrete floor plates

Below the arches of Cannon Street Station, just south of the financial sector of London, lies Cannons Gymnasium. The original, massively arched brick structure remains untouched: the series of six arches accommodate the varied facilities of the gymnasium, including aerobics, squash, swimming, weights and circuits. Two lightweight mezzanine levels were introduced throughout the structure, with steel staircases at either end allowing for a complete system of access. While the new is new, the old remains intact. The interior has the feel of a stage set, with the workout activities as a form of theatre.

1

2

3

1 Indoor swimming pool
2 Interior workout spaces
3 Within the vaults: entrance foyer
4 Vaulted gymnasium area

4

5-6 Cross sections of arcades
7 Floor plan
8 Lounge/bar area

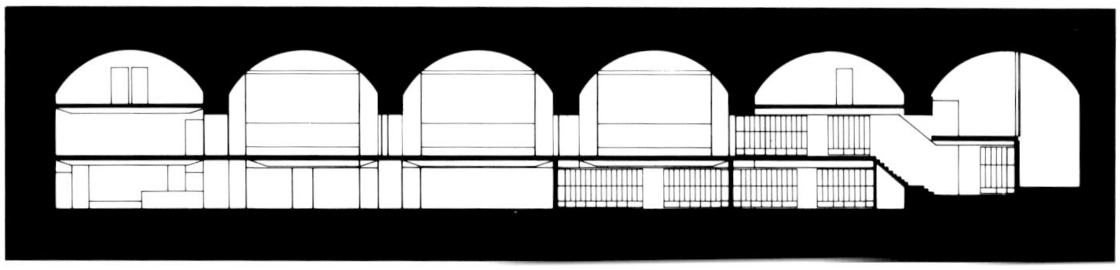
5

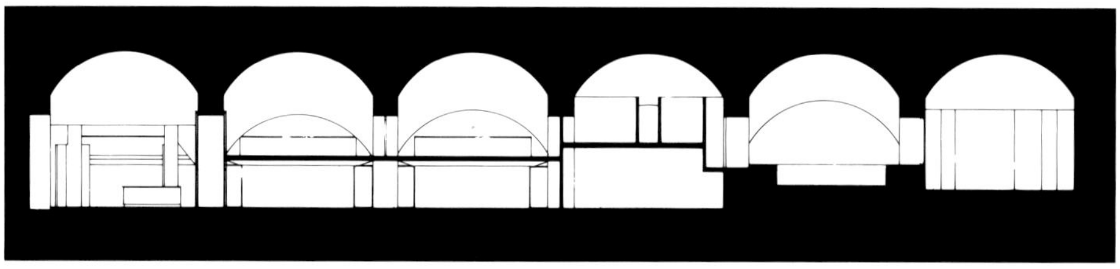
6

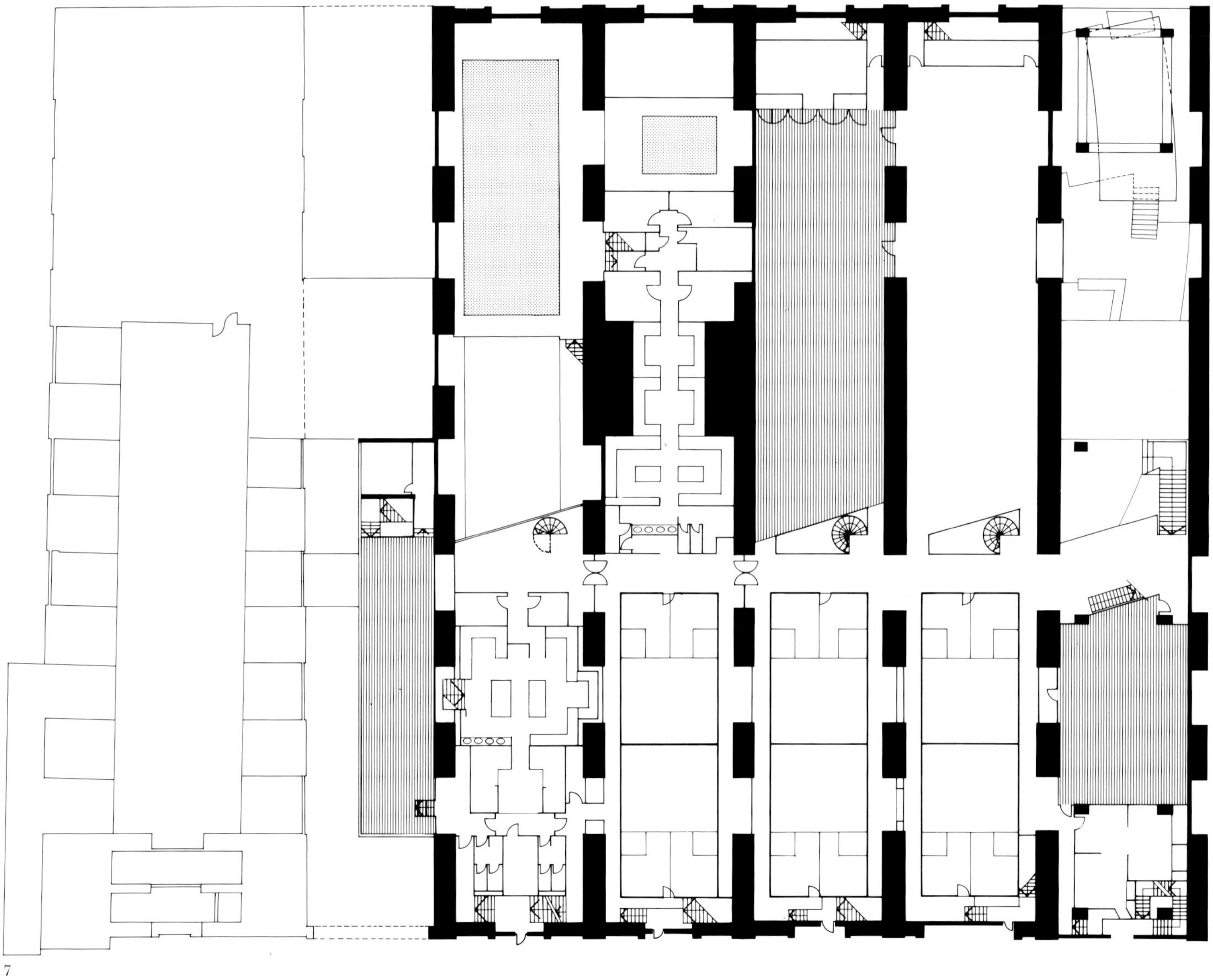
7

8

National Water Sports Centre

Design/Completion 1987/1990
Carrum, Victoria
Dandenong Valley Authority
1,827 square metres
Steel frame with metal cladding and metal deck roof

As an object in open space, the judges' stand for the sculling events required a tiered seating arrangement for each of eight judges. A triangulated plan form carried this stepped armature towards the water with an enclosure immediately adjacent.

The three level structure is self bracing. Judges and commentators occupy the two lowest levels, and the public climb to the top of the stand.

1

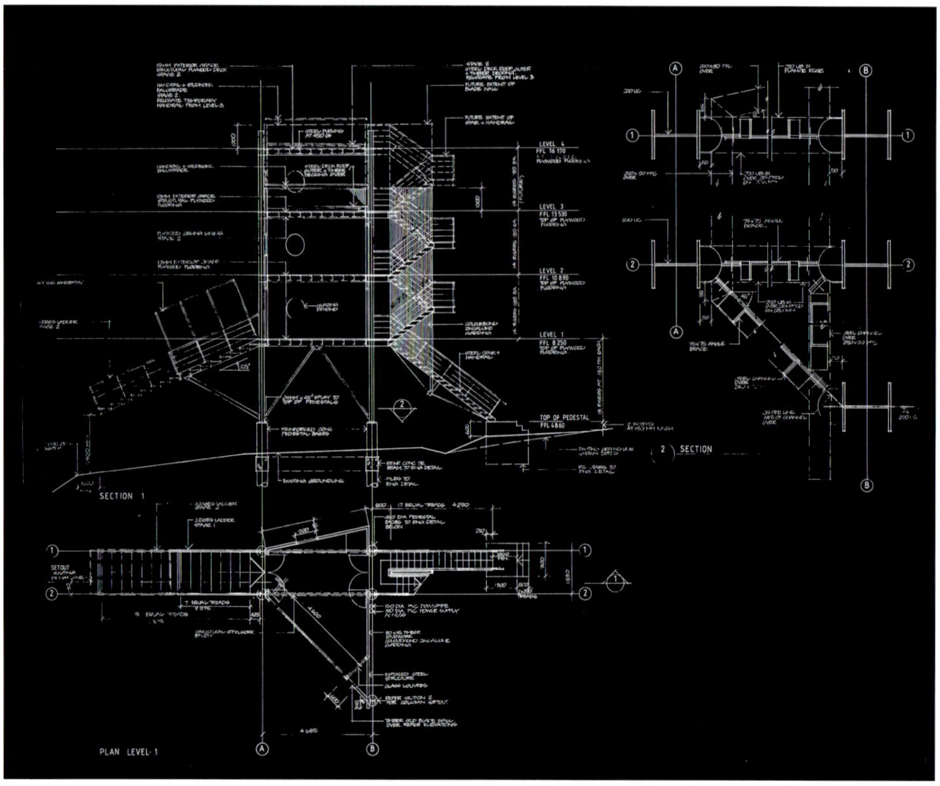

2

1 Judges' stand
2 Floor plan and section
3 Boatshed and stand
4 Public stair
5 Steel structure and skin

3

4

5

Australian Institute of Sport Training Halls

Design/Completion 1982/1984
Bruce, Australian Capital Territory
ACT Capital Works Department
20,000 square metres
Steel frame
Timber sports floor, plasterboard and metal cladding

High-quality training facilities (and programs) are fundamental for supporting the ambitions and talents of young athletes. In Canberra, the Australian Institute of Sport has developed such a complex for basketball, netball, soccer, weightlifting, outdoor hockey and field games. The learning/coaching circumstances demand high-quality surfaces, volumes and levels of lighting: highly tuned athletes need high-technology architecture.

The largest volume contains a metal "fuselage" for basketball and netball. Large steel portal frames provide the structure, with insulated corrugated steel stairs forming the enclosure. Internally, the steel is punctured to give acoustic absorption, while at the human contact level, smooth ply facing minimises the danger of player contact. A sprung timber floor ensures the necessary "bounce" demanded by all performers.

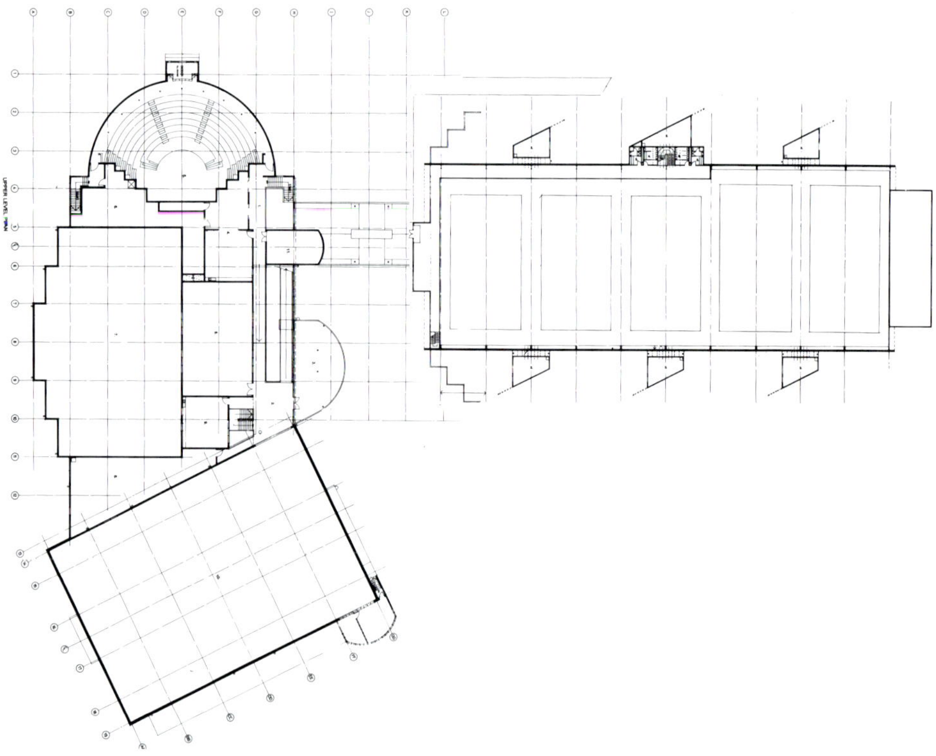

1

2

3

4

5

1 Floor plan
2 Street elevation
3 Main entry
4 Theatre interior
5 Weight training/gymnasium area
6 Entry facade
7 Internal basketball/netball courts

6

7

Australian Institute of Sport Indoor Training Pool

Design/Completion 1981/1983
Bruce, Australian Capital Territory
ACT Capital Works Department
10,000 square metres
Steel frame
Fibre cement panels, metal deck and solar heating

The swimmers wanted a "fast tank" as a training centre for the country's best talent. The government wanted a cheap building—a basic shed containing the tank and a swimming workshop comprising two pools: a 25-metre training pool and a 50-metre pool able to be divided into two 25-metre areas.

The framework is a stick-like welded steel structure. A mobile gantry (as in a factory) moves a bulkhead for varying lap lengths. Components of structured tensioning maintain the truss camber and, from the outside, express what lies within. The skin consists of fibre cement panels, colour-layered inside and out in a gradation of wet greens. Outside, where the top edge meets the sky, the colour echoes the faded green of the Canberra hills. Inside, the deepening colours below the water surface mimic the sunlight's weakening penetration.

1

2

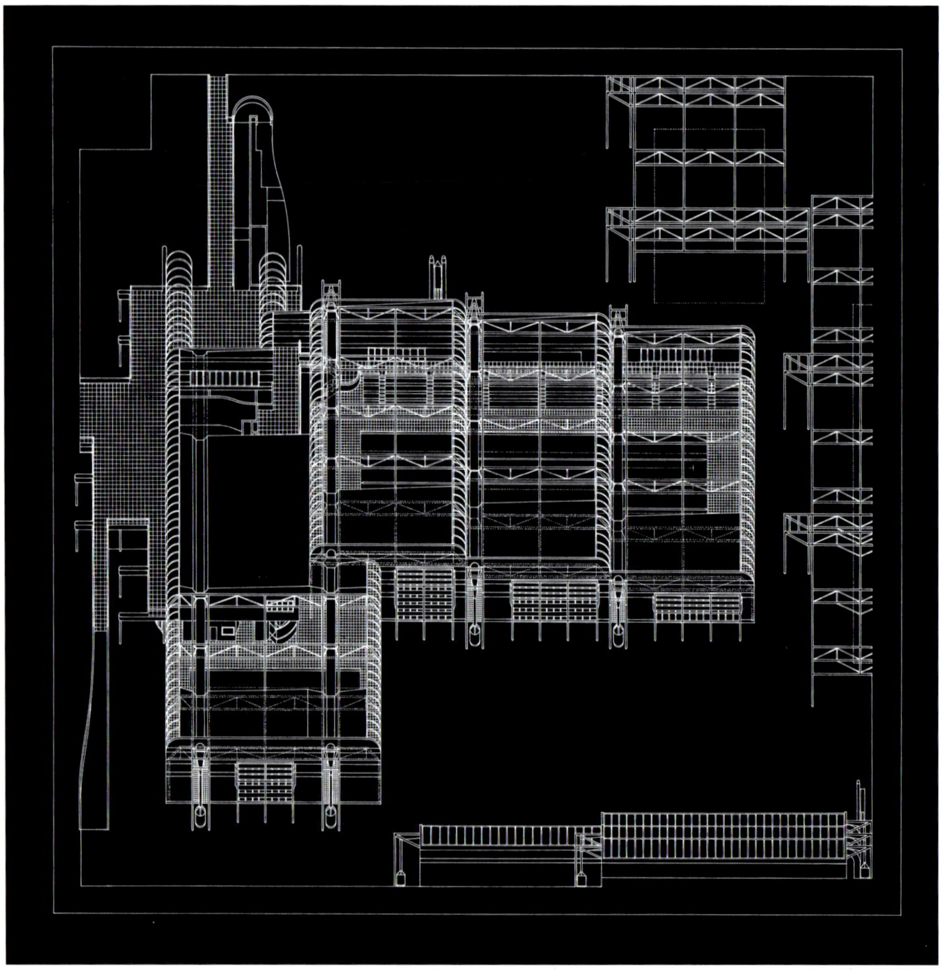

3

4

1 Facade detail
2 Exterior view
3 Axonometric study
4 Steel trusses over pool
5 Facade facing netball courts

5

Australian Defence Force Complex

Design/Completion 1980/1986

Campbell, Australian Capital Territory

Department of Housing and Construction for Australian Defence Force Academy

Associated architects: Department of Administrative Services Construction Group (ACT Region)

2,500 square metres

Concrete walls

Plaster interiors and metal deck roof

The complex is a skin-and-bones building. A straight spine, appropriate to a military establishment, runs the length of the structure, providing both a source of light and a means of access to marshalling facilities for physical education and cadet recreation. The support structure is bound into the masonry skin, giving visual expression inside as a means of scaling the interior. The building's brick exterior is horizontally banded to link it formally to other Academy buildings. Curves or segments broken out of the regular plan pattern emphasise the principal entrance as the contrasting element.

Inside, formal games "boxes" line each side of the spine. Those with observation openings or open spectator areas are closest to the entrance. Further along the spine are the more enclosed boxes, which become "destination". A symmetrical sunscreen structure acts as a transitional, somewhat transparent set or backdrop for the parade ground.

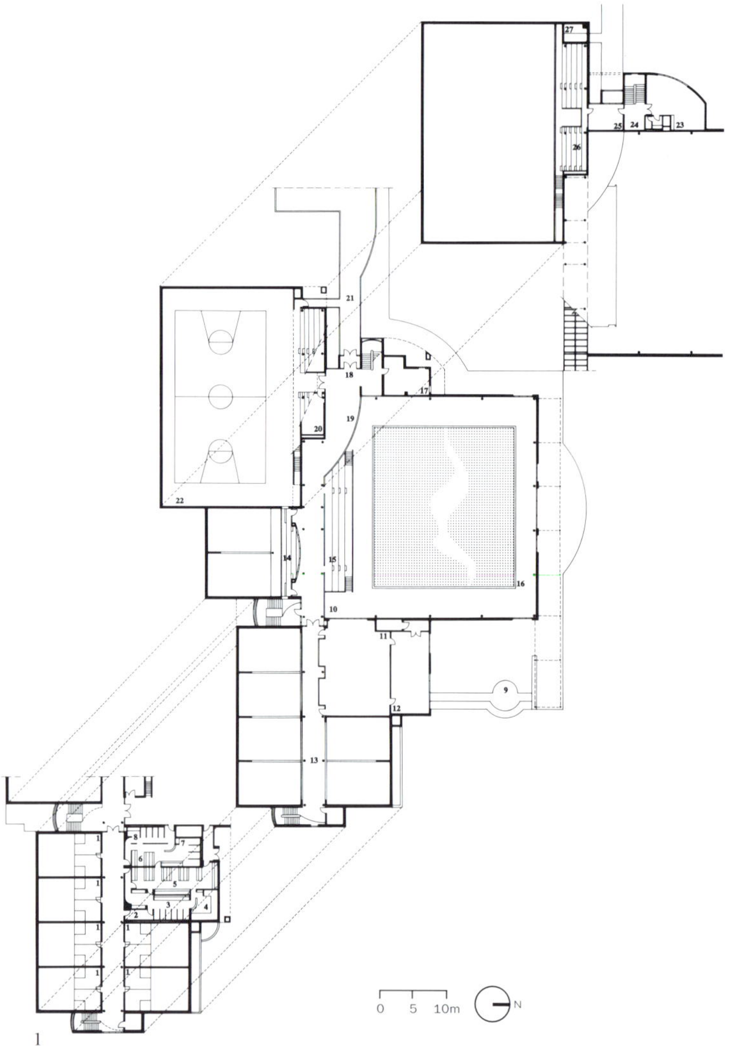

1

2

1 Floor plans
2 Building landscape
3 Top-lit passageway
4 Main facade
5 Swimming pool

3

4

5

Melbourne Cricket Ground Great Southern Stand

Design/Completion 1988/1991
Jolimont, Victoria
Melbourne Cricket Club
Associated architects: Tompkin Shaw & Evans Pty Ltd
81,300 square metres
Post-tensioned concrete frame supporting cantilevered steel box girders with precast concrete plates
Precast concrete, glass

The Great Southern Stand at the Melbourne Cricket Ground holds some 50,000 spectators for both Australian Rules football and international cricket matches. Clear sightlines, close proximity to the action, comfortable seating, adequate services, food and drink facilities, good companions and a win for the team are all significant aspects of any visit. There should be a sense of arrival at the outside ticket box, a celebratory progression to one's designated seat, and the anticipation of spectacle. Highly-tuned athletes are expected to perform miracles on a piece of turf that holds many mysteries and matches prospect with memory.

The architecture offers the vision of a gathering place akin to a Colosseum, where the crowd becomes part of the game. Critical advice is offered to both players and umpires as occasion and temperament demand.

I call it Melbourne's living room.

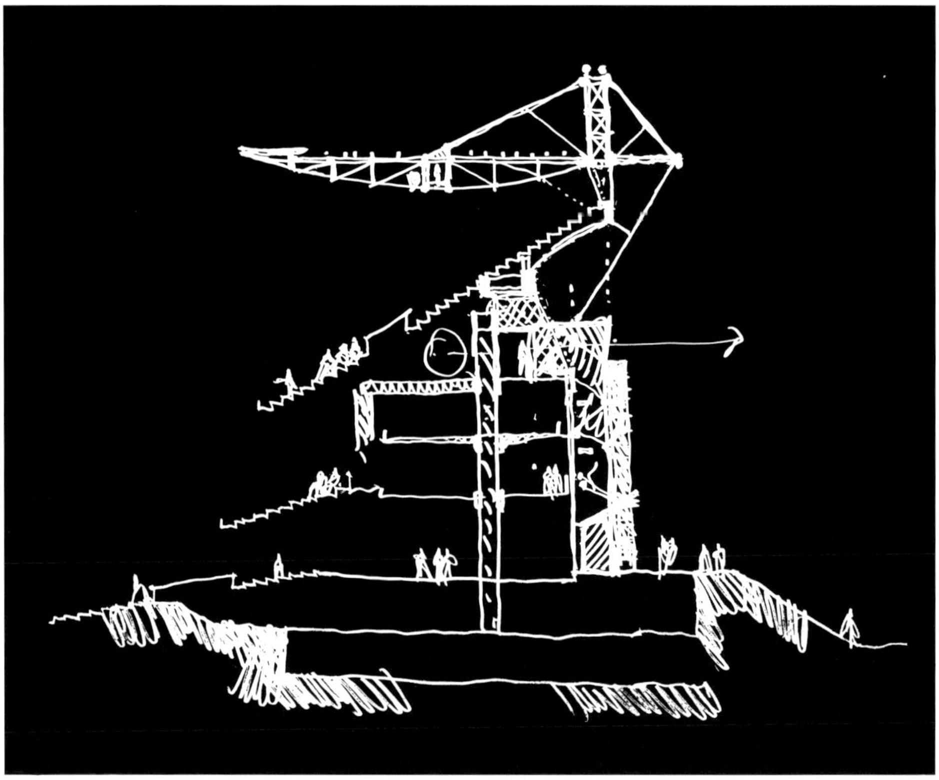

1

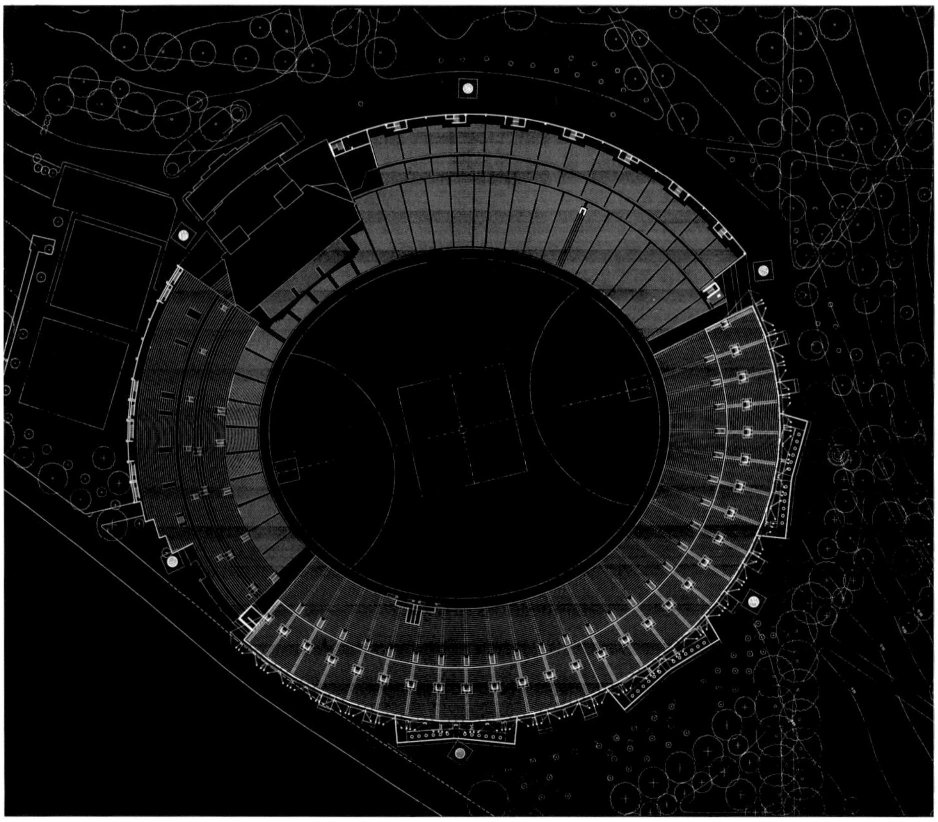

2

1 Design sketch: section through grandstand
2 Concourse level plan: new and old together
3 Aerial view of Melbourne Cricket Ground

3

4 Circulation ramps
5 Ramp elevation: the outer edge
6 Internal elevation
7 Axonometric view

4

5

TYRRELL'S WINES
KOOKABURRA
HONDA
Ansett Australia
EASTON SPORTS
FOSTERS
MAGNA
Budget
Australia's Telecom
DIADORA
BMW

6

7

8

9

10

11

8 Grandstand seating
9 Steel roof truss detail
10 Top deck: seating and structure
11 Arrival

Royal Melbourne Tennis Club

Design/Completion 1976/1977
Richmond, Victoria
Royal Melbourne Tennis Club
Architects: Daryl Jackson Evan Walker
1,460 square metres
Off-form concrete and steel deck

On a tight, inner-urban site, a small garden, a sloping covered terrace and a three-level clubroom introduce the "royal game". Two in situ concrete courts are roofed by a canopy of tubular steel trusses which provide filtered natural light. The architecture is raw, brutally expressed and as "unconventional" as the game itself

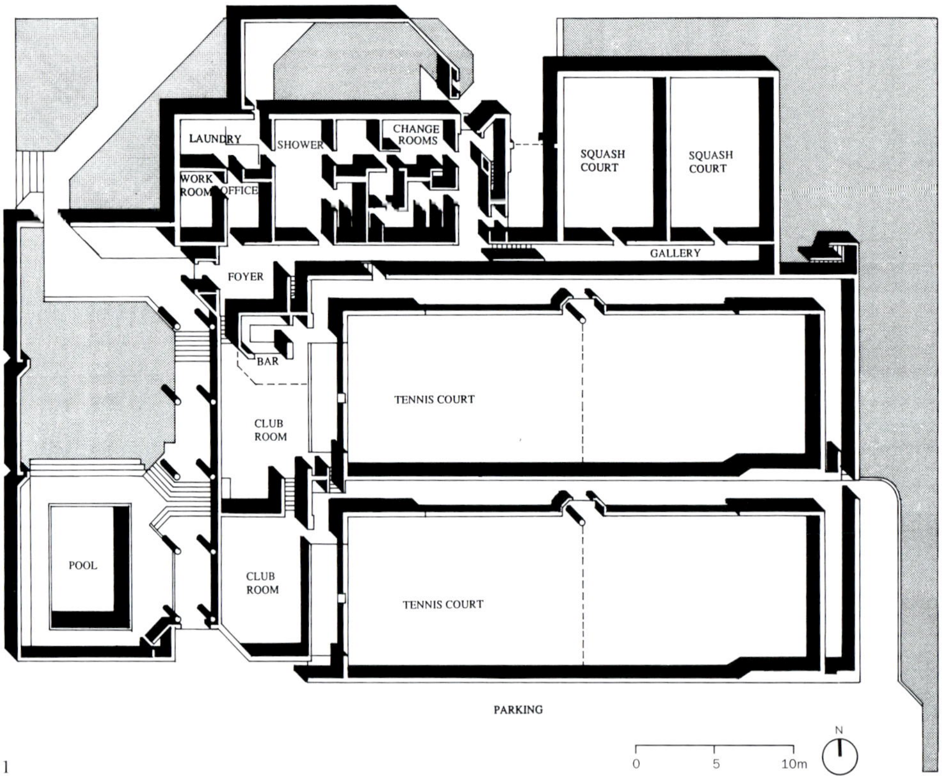

1

2

3

1 Ground-floor plan
2 Covered walkway
3 Gallery overlooking tennis courts
4 Clubroom
5 Indoor tennis court

4

5

The Gabba Master Planning Study

Design/Completion 1993/1995
Woolloongabba, Queensland
Brisbane Cricket Ground Trust
15,000 square metres
Steel-framed grandstand with in situ drop panel concrete slabs
In situ concrete wall panels, aluminium-framed glass and teflon fibreglass fabric roof

A two-tier stand with a central area for dining and club entertainment constitutes the cross-section. One side of the stand faces the action (football and cricket matches); viewlines, proximity to the play and comfortable seating are the key requirements. The steel structure becomes an element for the tectonics of cantilever, guyed masts and backstays. The canopy of fibreglass protects spectators from sub-tropical rain and sun. Its umbrella form, spiky and stick-like, is in deliberate contrast to the concrete plinth of the base and the solid form of the steel elevation. The "Gabba" is a significant part of inner suburban Brisbane.

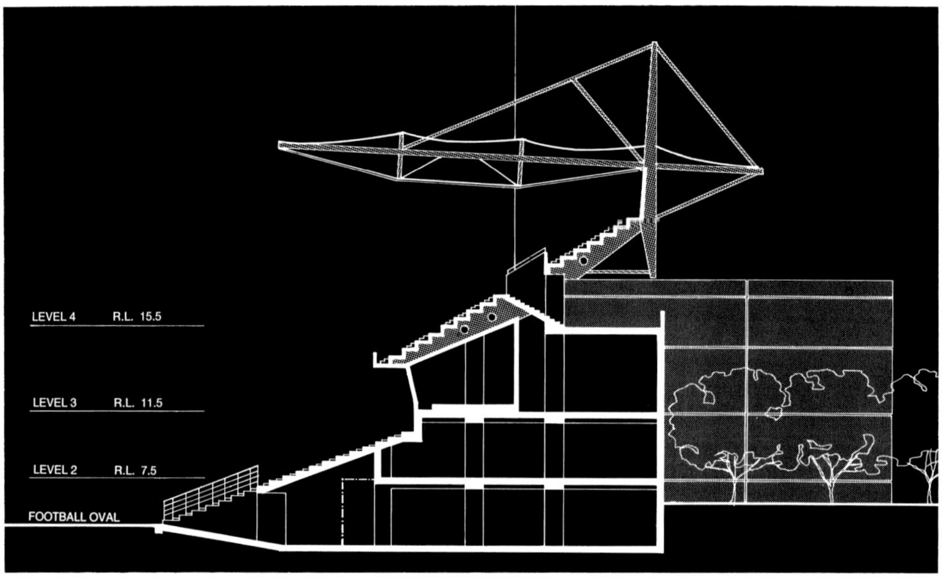

1

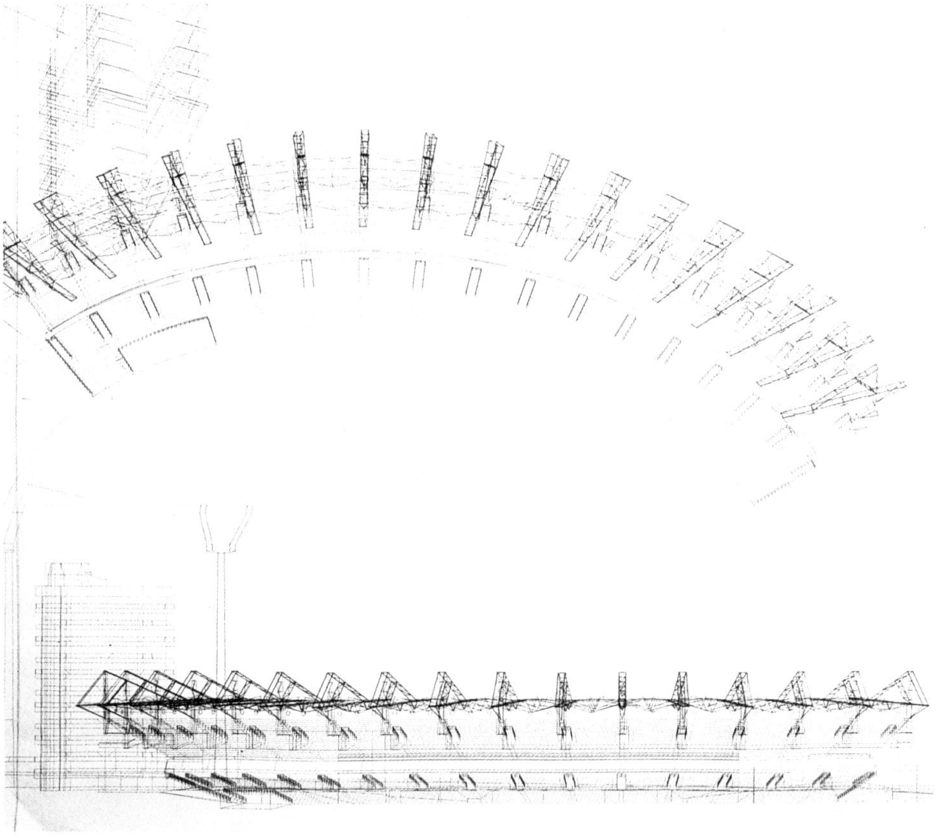

2

1 Section through grandstand
2 Axonometric and elevation of stand
3 Perspective
4 Steel-framed roof trusses

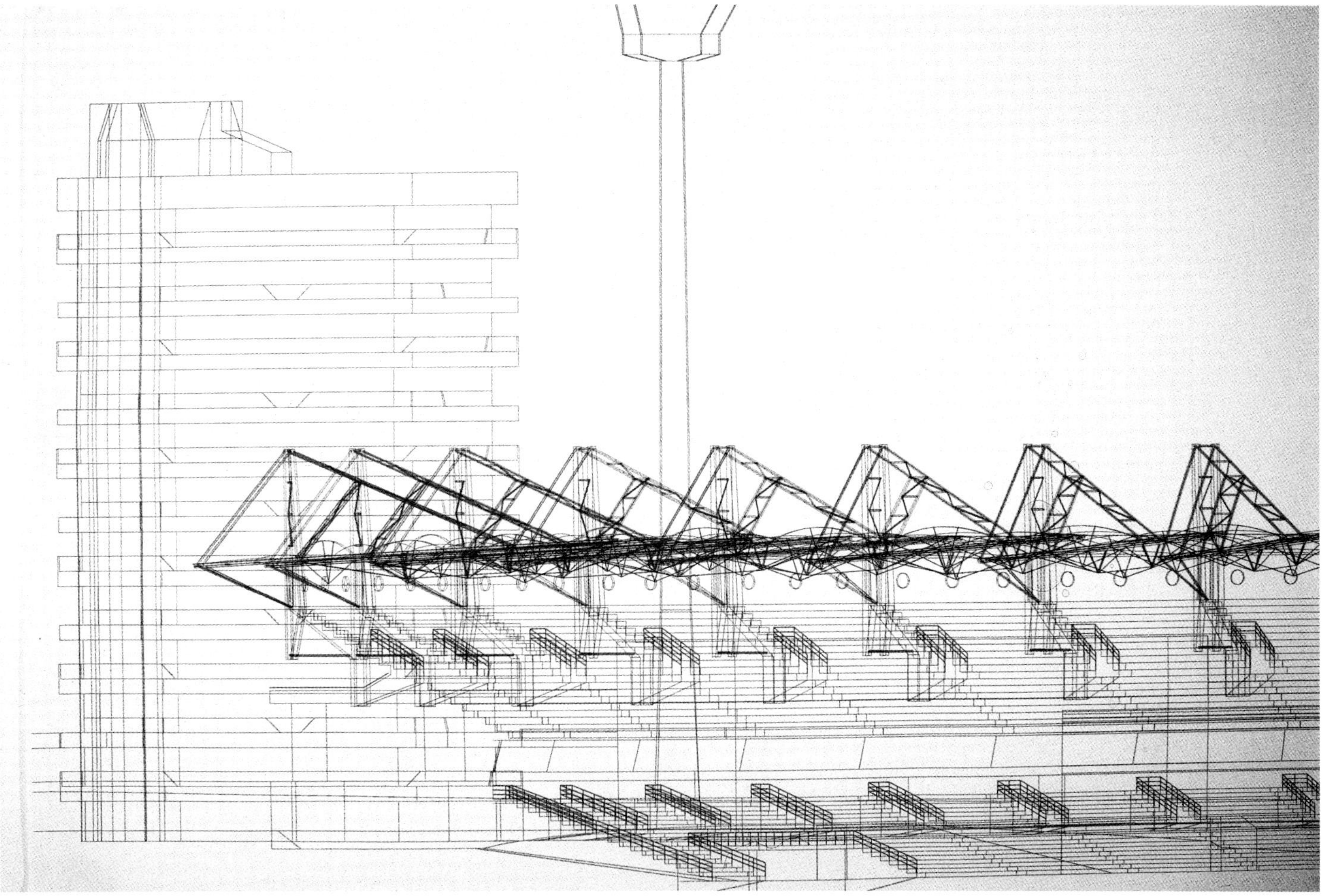

3

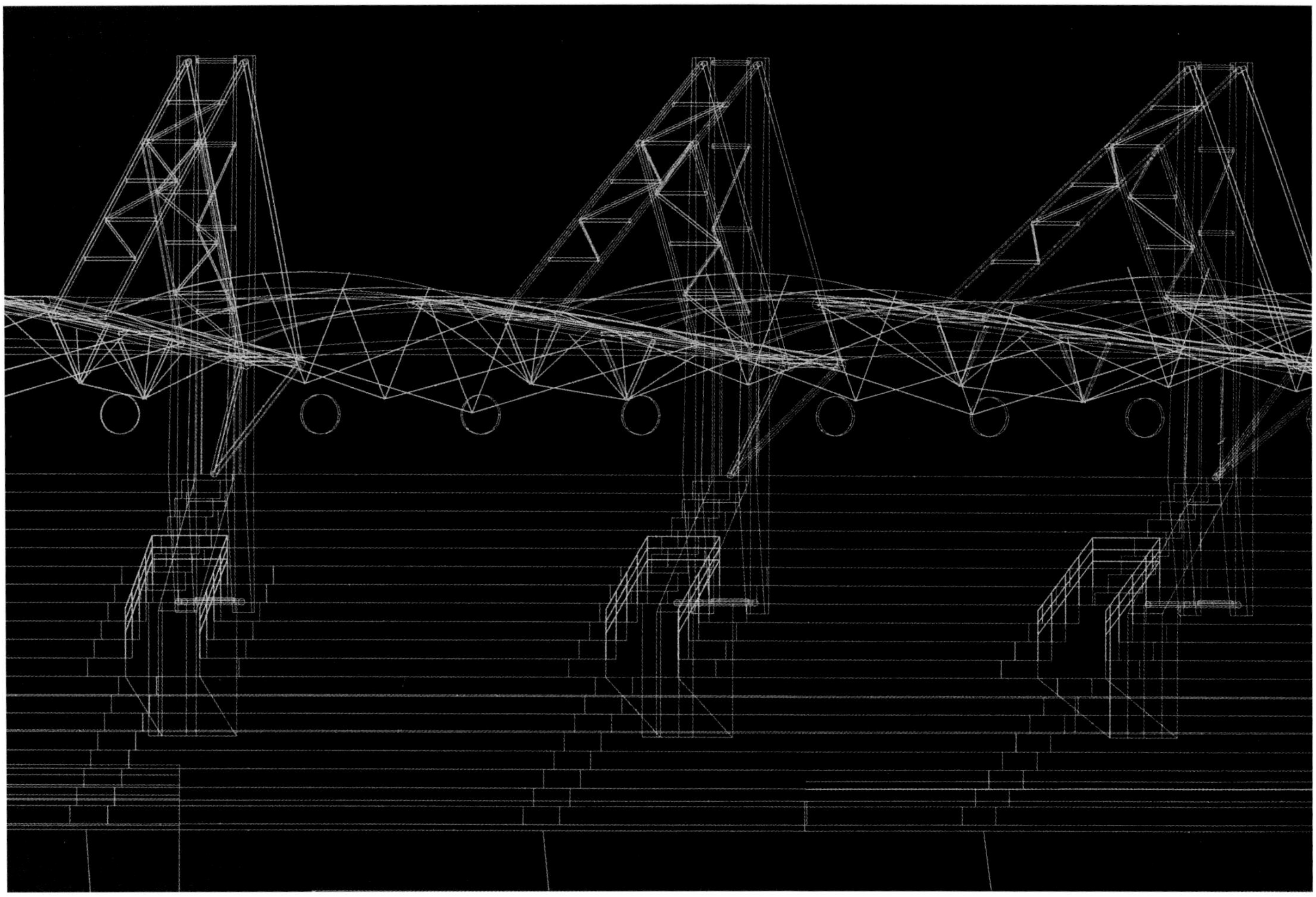

4

Tuggeranong Pool

Design/Completion 1988/1993
Tuggeranong, Australian Capital Territory
ACT Capital Works Department/ACT Sports and Recreation Department
Architects: Daryl Jackson Alastair Swayn Pty Ltd
7,500 square metres
Steel frame structure
Fibre cement, brickwork, metal roofing

The optical illusion that a building is sinking on one side surrounds an architectural project with a certain amount of excitement.

The site for Tuggeranong Pool and Recreation Centre is at the northern end of one of Canberra's new "satellite town" centres, in a sparse Australian landscape. The fibrous cement sheet construction is colour-coded: bright yellow entrance; red for the pool sheds; blue for the building housing the creche, cafe and weight-training and aerobics rooms. From outside, the arched roofs of the sheds mirror the surrounding Brindabella Mountains, while internally they form an acoustic volume to receive the noise of those in the pools, whether competing seriously or having fun.

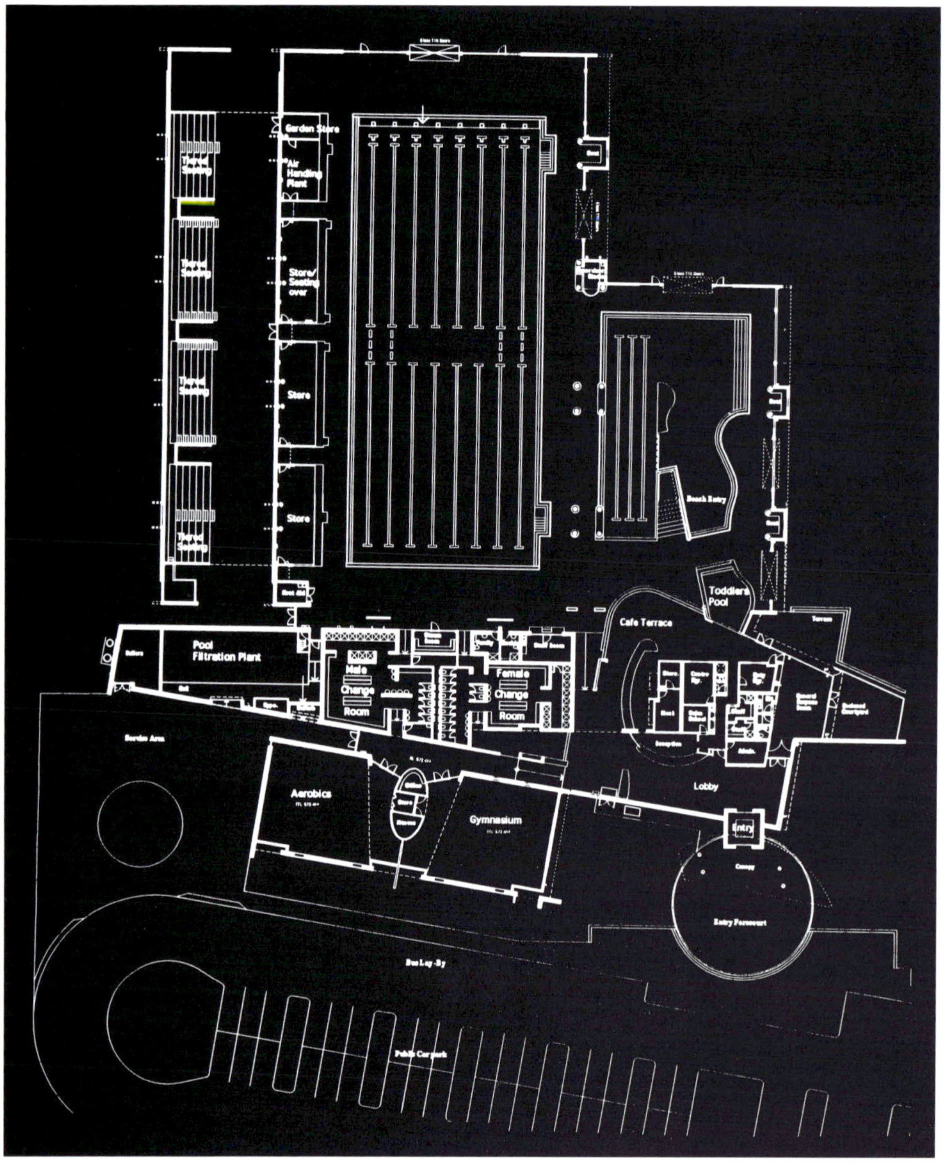

1

2

1 Ground-floor plan
2 Entrance facade
3 Entrance canopy
4 Exterior view
5 Interior of pools
6 Building landscape
7 Pool interior showing steel roof structure

3

4

5

6

7

WA Indoor Sports Centre

Design/Completion 1985/1988
Mt Claremont, Western Australia
State Government of Western Australia
Associated architects: Peter Hunt, Perth
14,700 square metres
Steel frame structure incorporating curved exposed steel trusses
Concrete floors, metal deck roof and fibre cement sheet cladding

Two large arches are brought together on each side of a central facilities spine to enclose a swimming and diving hall and a 4,000-seat games area. On the exterior, the curved roof forms echo the rounded dune hills of City Beach. From within, their taut bowed profile suggests an athleticism which contrasts with the stasis of water held in the pools. The spine locates athletes' changing rooms at one level and spectator amenities at another. The linear system of assembly reveals the parts, suggesting extendability, yet holding the composition in place.

1

2

1 Entrance facade
2 Tensile roof support detail
3-4 Sections
5 Ground-floor plan

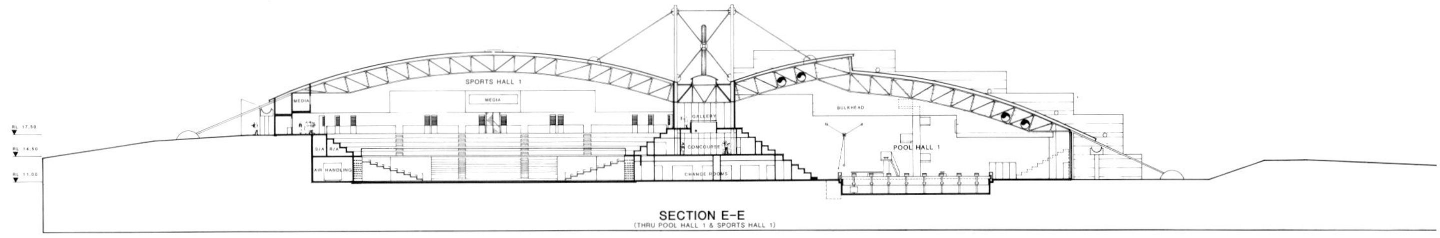
SPORTS HALL 1
MEDIA
GALLERY
CONCOURSE
CHANGE ROOMS
AIR HANDLING
BULKHEAD
POOL HALL 1
SECTION E-E
(THRU POOL HALL 1 & SPORTS HALL 1)

3

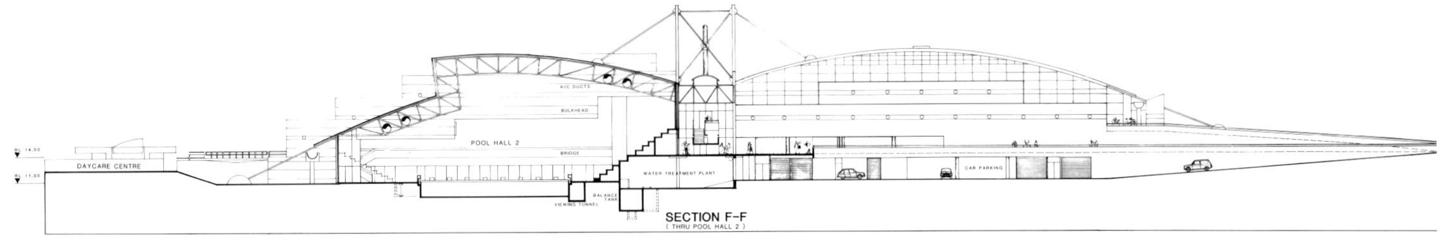
A/C DUCTS
BULKHEAD
POOL HALL 2
BRIDGE
DAYCARE CENTRE
WATER TREATMENT PLANT
BALANCE TANK
VIEWING TUNNEL
CAR PARKING
SECTION F-F
(THRU POOL HALL 2)

4

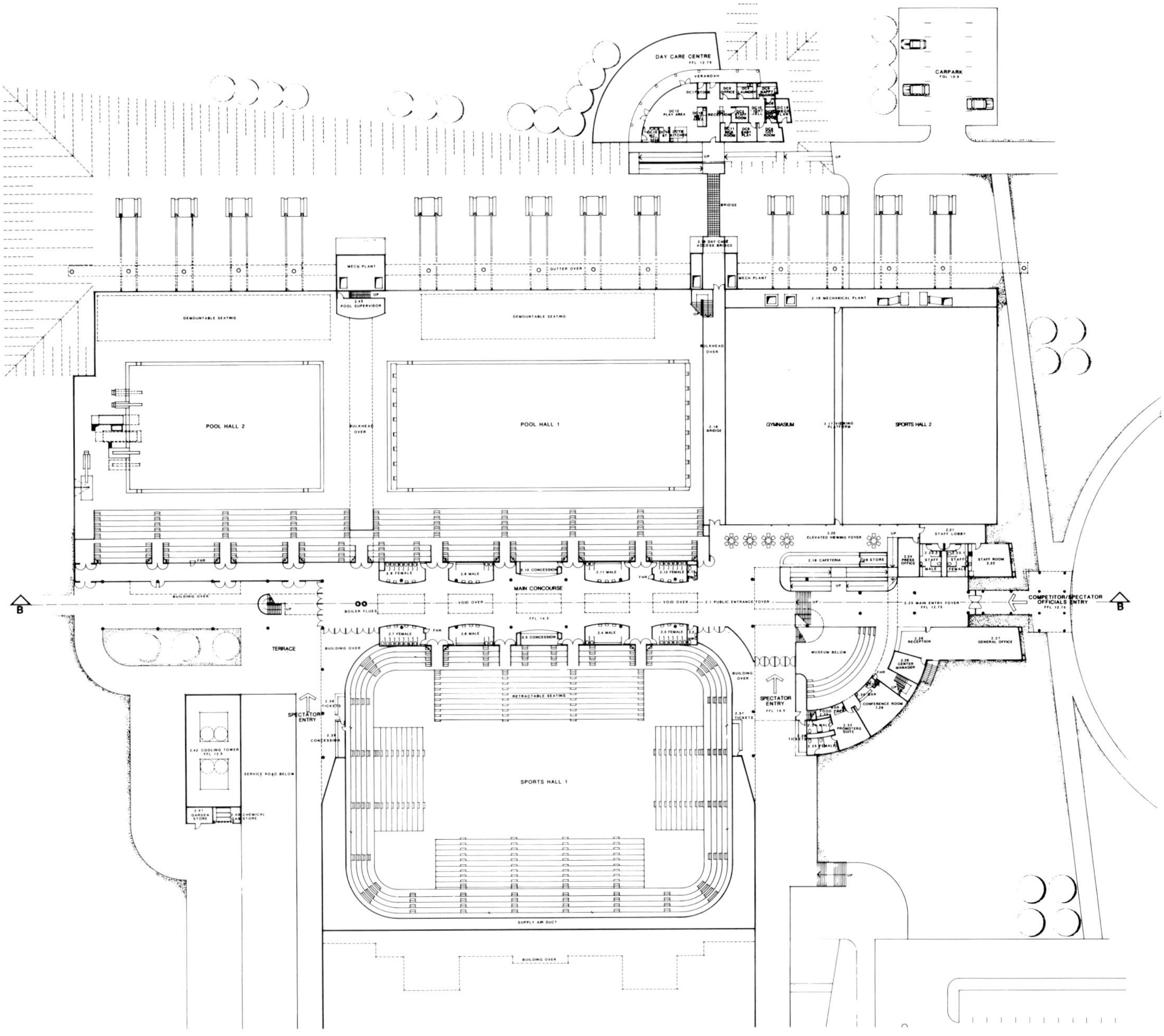
DAY CARE CENTRE
VERANDAH
CARPARK
BRIDGE
MECH PLANT
GUTTER OVER
POOL SUPERVISOR
DEMOUNTABLE SEATING
DEMOUNTABLE SEATING
POOL HALL 2
BULKHEAD OVER
POOL HALL 1
GYMNASIUM
SPORTS HALL 2
ELEVATED VIEWING FOYER
STAFF LOBBY
STAFF ROOM
CAFETERIA
MAIN CONCOURSE
VOID OVER
BOILER FLUES
PUBLIC ENTRANCE FOYER
MAIN ENTRY FOYER
COMPETITOR/SPECTATOR OFFICIALS ENTRY
BUILDING OVER
TERRACE
RECEPTION
GENERAL OFFICE
MUSEUM BELOW
CONFERENCE ROOM
SPECTATOR ENTRY
SPECTATOR ENTRY
TICKETS
RETRACTABLE SEATING
VOID OVER
SPORTS HALL 1
COOLING TOWER
SERVICE ROAD BELOW
GARDEN STORE
CHEMICAL STORE
SUPPLY AIR DUCT
BUILDING OVER

5

6 Roof detail over swimming pool
7 Roof detail over gymnasium
8 View of swimming pool and stand
9 Axonometric

6

7

8

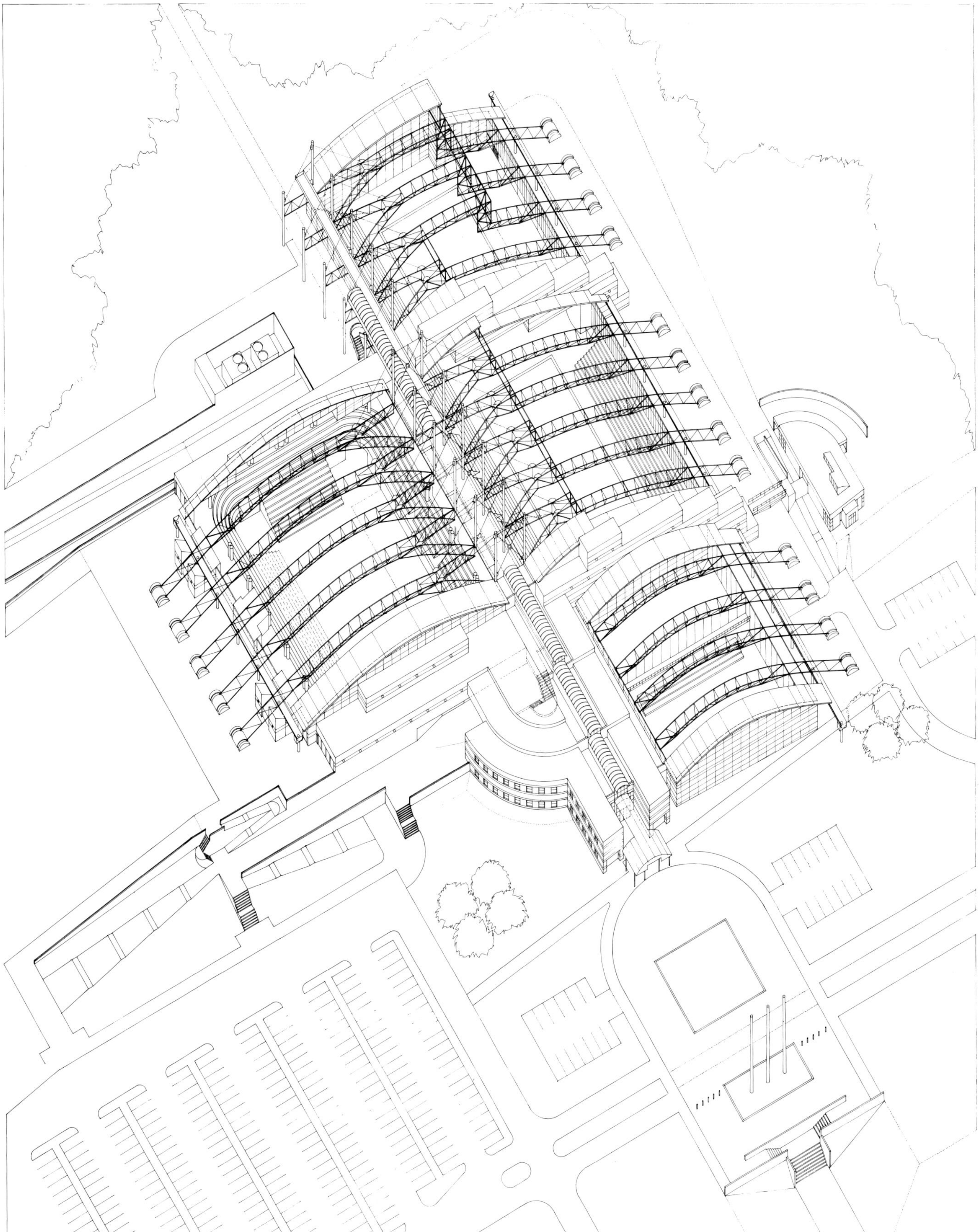

9

SELECTED AND CURRENT WORKS

Public

Footscray Library

Design/Completion 1991/1993
Footscray, Victoria
City of Footscray
1,500 square metres
Concrete floor slabs, precast concrete walls, metal deck roof on structural steel frame

Three high walls of concrete and an open glass shopfront enclose a double-storey library space. Within the box, a centre segment is removed to create an outdoor courtyard. The concrete and steel structure contrasts with a glass frame-wall, while a long streetfront veranda slices across the facade.

1

2

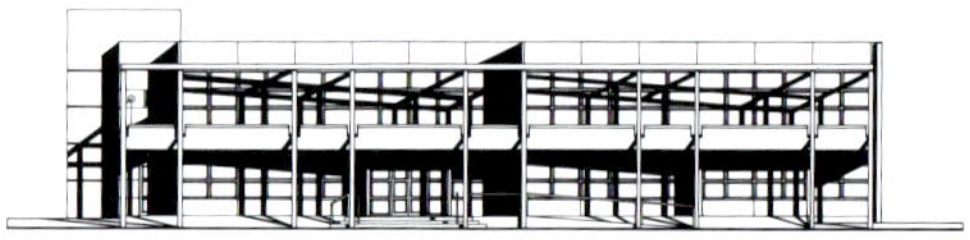

3

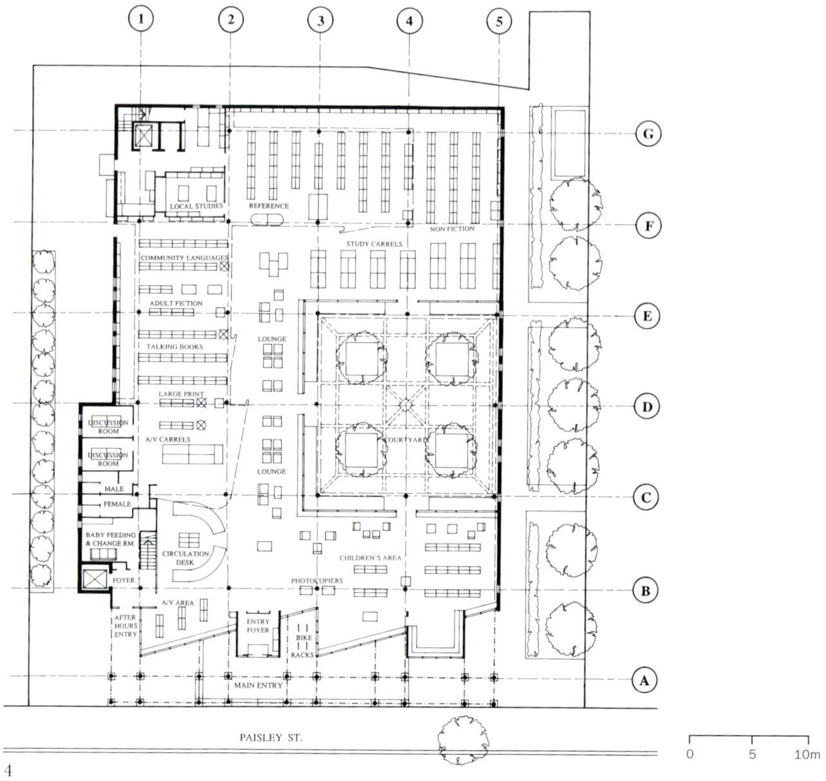

4

1 View along Paisley Street
2 Detail of steel structure
3 Paisley Street elevation
4 Ground-floor plan
5 View along Paisley Street
6 Side elevation showing entrance canopies

5

6

Frankston Civic Centre

Design/Completion 1992/1994
Frankston, Victoria
City of Frankston
Post-tensioned concrete floor slabs, precast concrete walls, metal deck roof on structural steel frame

An 800-seat community theatre, a function centre and a regional library are the principal public ingredients of this complex. Three decks of commercial car parking and a children's toy library provide important supplementary functions. The library is constructed on a large site with three street frontages, each street providing a point of address.

The composition is dominated by a castle-like fly tower oriented to occupy the central area of the site.

The lowest level of the library faces the city as a large open volume, with the function centre and theatre sharing a common foyer which occasionally serves as a gallery. Through-block access is achieved via a north–south public staircase which links the on-site activities as will as dramatising the progression between the lower and upper parts of the city.

Materials consist of sand-coloured concrete tilt slab walls, sea-green fibre cement panels and a white metal deck roof.

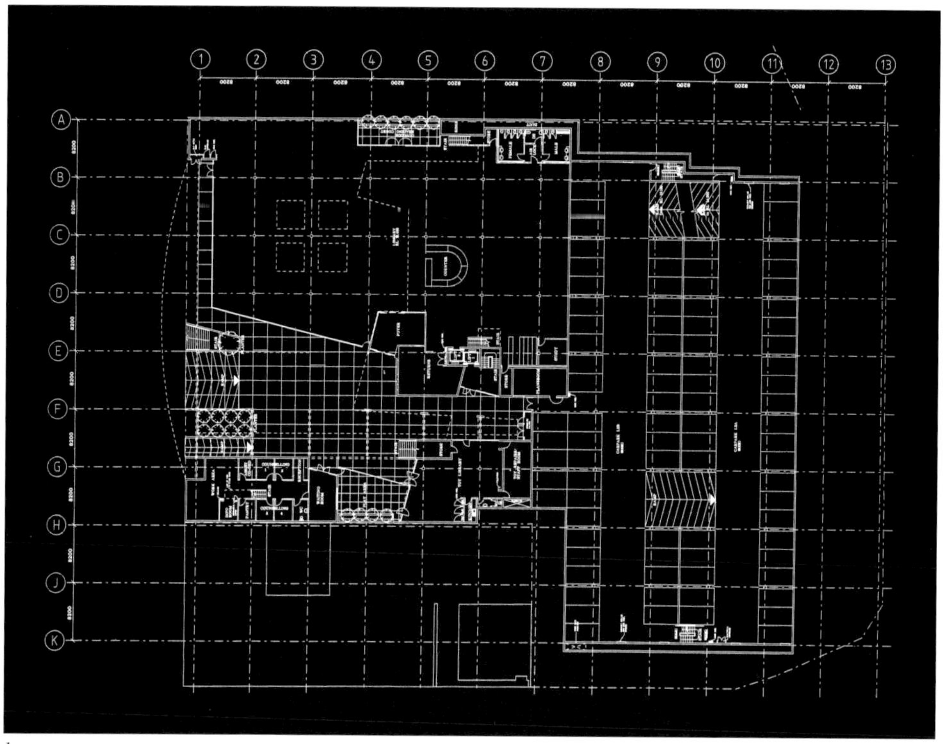

1

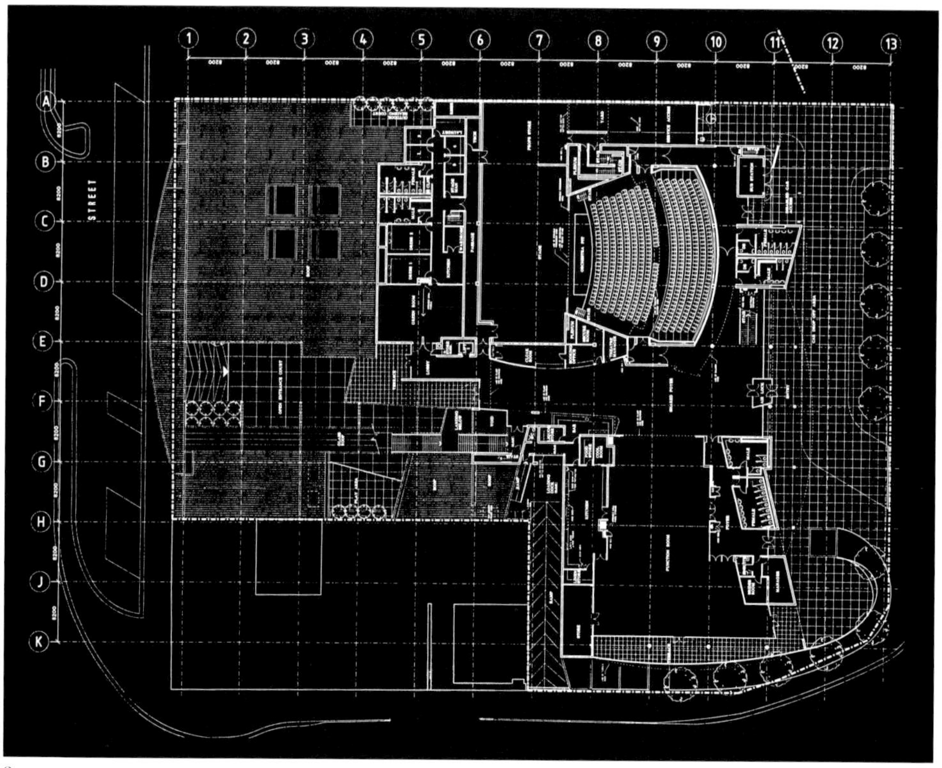

2

1 Ground-floor plan
2 Level 4 plan
3 Section
4 Playne Street elevation

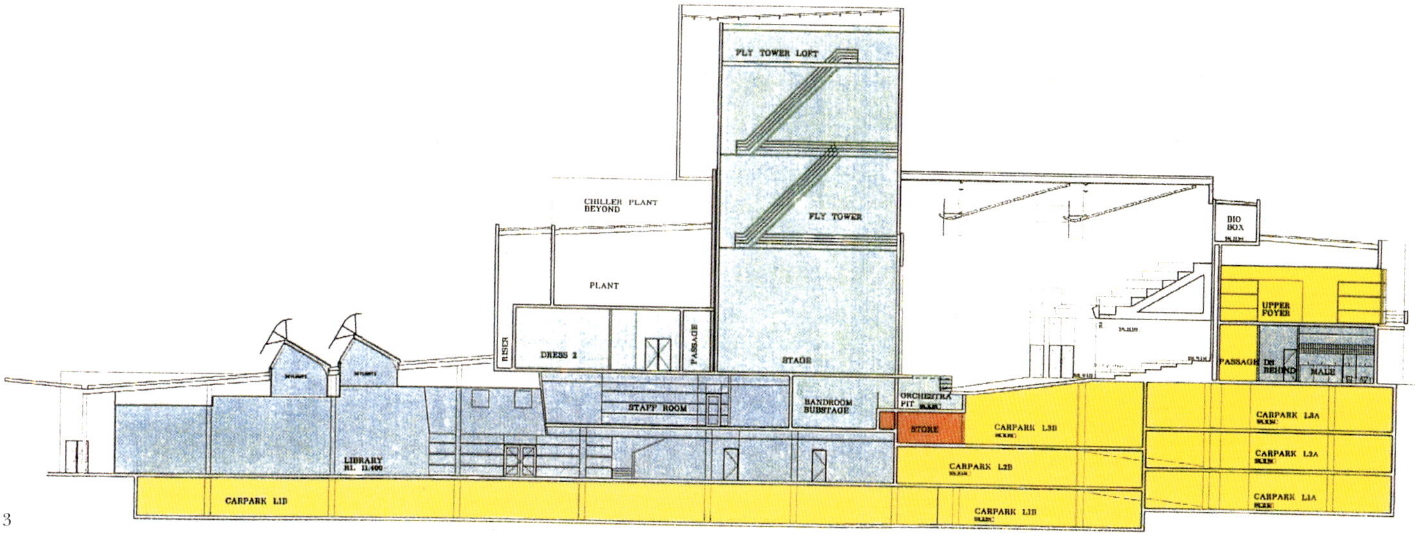

3

4

Australian Chancery, Riyadh

Design/Completion 1985/1987
Riyadh, Saudi Arabia
Overseas Property Group, Department of Administrative Services
Associate architects: Meldrum Burrows
7,950 square metres
Reinforced concrete frame, concrete floor slabs, load-bearing concrete blockwork
External walls of hollow concrete blockwork, reinforced concrete roofs

Foreign embassies in the desert capital of Saudi Arabia may not express their national architectural characteristics. They must accord with "Central Nadj" style which is characterised by thick walls and roofs, small courtyards and shade gardens. This style reflects the demands for privacy and protection from intense daytime heat, rapid cooling at night, and heavy, if infrequent, rain.

Two elements were required: a chancery and a residence. They are linked to provide a complex arrangement of courts and enclosures using the Arab souk as typological source. The sequence of volumes assembled across the site creates a series of varied, friendly spaces. The courtyard negatives appear to be cut from the one mass, instead of different masses combining to form enclosures. The light and shade, planar density and mass achieve the necessary feelings of security, comfort and familiar aesthetic necessary for Australians living on foreign soil.

1

2

1 Floor plans and sections
2 Chancery entrance: layered walls providing shade
3 Atrium space

3

4

5

6

7

4 Chancery entrance
5 Courtyard
6 Swimming pool courtyard: water and sun control
7 Courtyard wall detail
8 Axonometric study of the labyrinth

8

Penguin Visitor Centre, Phillip Island

Design/Completion 1986/1988
Phillip Island, Victoria
Director of Fisheries and Wildlife
2,177 square metres
Visitor centre: stud frame, colorbond custom-orb cladding, fabric tent-structure roof
Viewing platforms: reinforced concrete

The Penguin Visitor Centre is at the rocky western point of Phillip Island.
The building marks the way to the nesting fairy penguins, which come up the beach to burrow in the dunes at twilight.
The Visitor Centre incorporates and extensively modifies three existing buildings (formerly pine-clad pioneer huts). It is dominated by the central tensile fabric roof, a floating wing-like form which hovers above the orientation area.

The program required that the building accommodate up to 3,000 people on a typical summer evening. The scale of the building provides a presence which relates to, yet protects, the penguins' natural habitat. Elevated timber decks keep visitors above the dunes and away from the penguins. Concrete viewing platforms control the crowd and give the penguins a chance to make it from the water to their burrows without being rushed.
Architecture mediates the experience of observing natural wildlife.

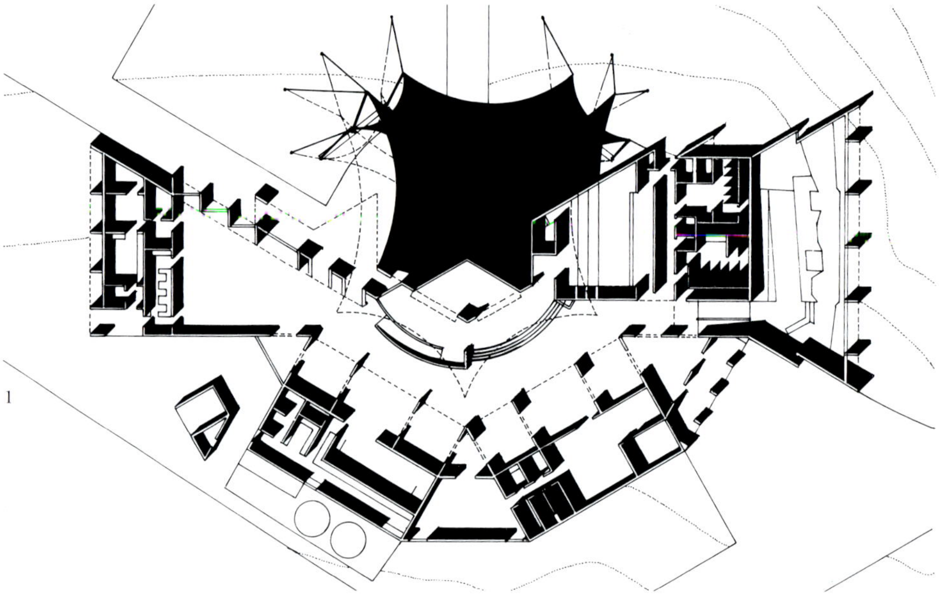

1

2

1 Ground-floor plan
2 View of building from sand dunes
3 Tensile fabric roof structure
4 Entrance courtyard

3

4

Department of Land Administration Offices

Design/Completion 1991/1993
Redlands, Western Australia
Department of Land Administration, Western Australia
Associate architects: Peter Hunt Architects, Perth
21,000 square metres
Reinforced concrete frame
Red brick external cladding and precast concrete wall panels

Commissioned to regenerate employment in this outer Perth suburb, the new offices are planned as three interconnected pavilions, all fronting a former main street, now converted to pedestrian plaza.

The typology and the financial opportunities are closely controlled formulae characteristic of a design-construct competitive bid. Red brick is an emblem of Redlands. The banded lighter-coloured, upper-level enclosing walls suggest a "reducing" of mass as the buildings melt into the sky.

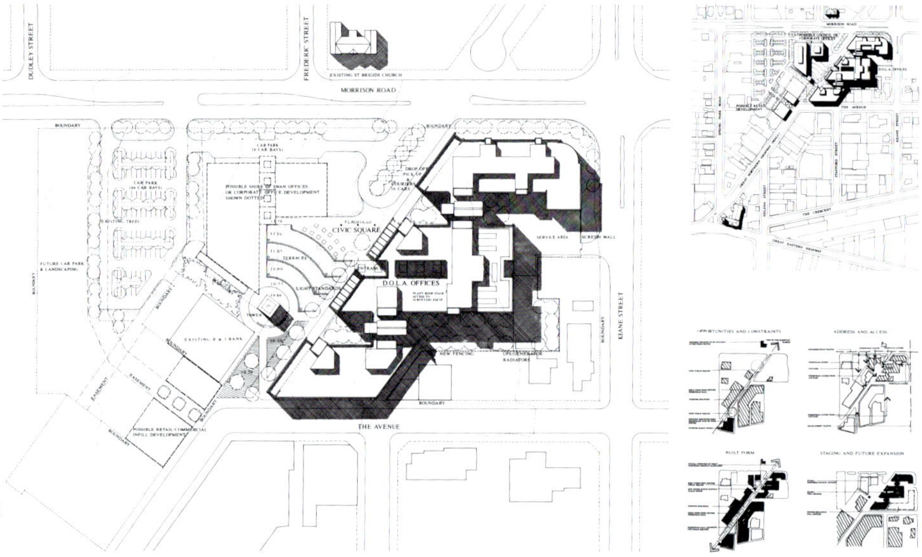

1

2

1 Site and location plan
2 Street facade
3 Axonometric
4 Beneath canopy
5 Interior arrival hall
6 Glass awning

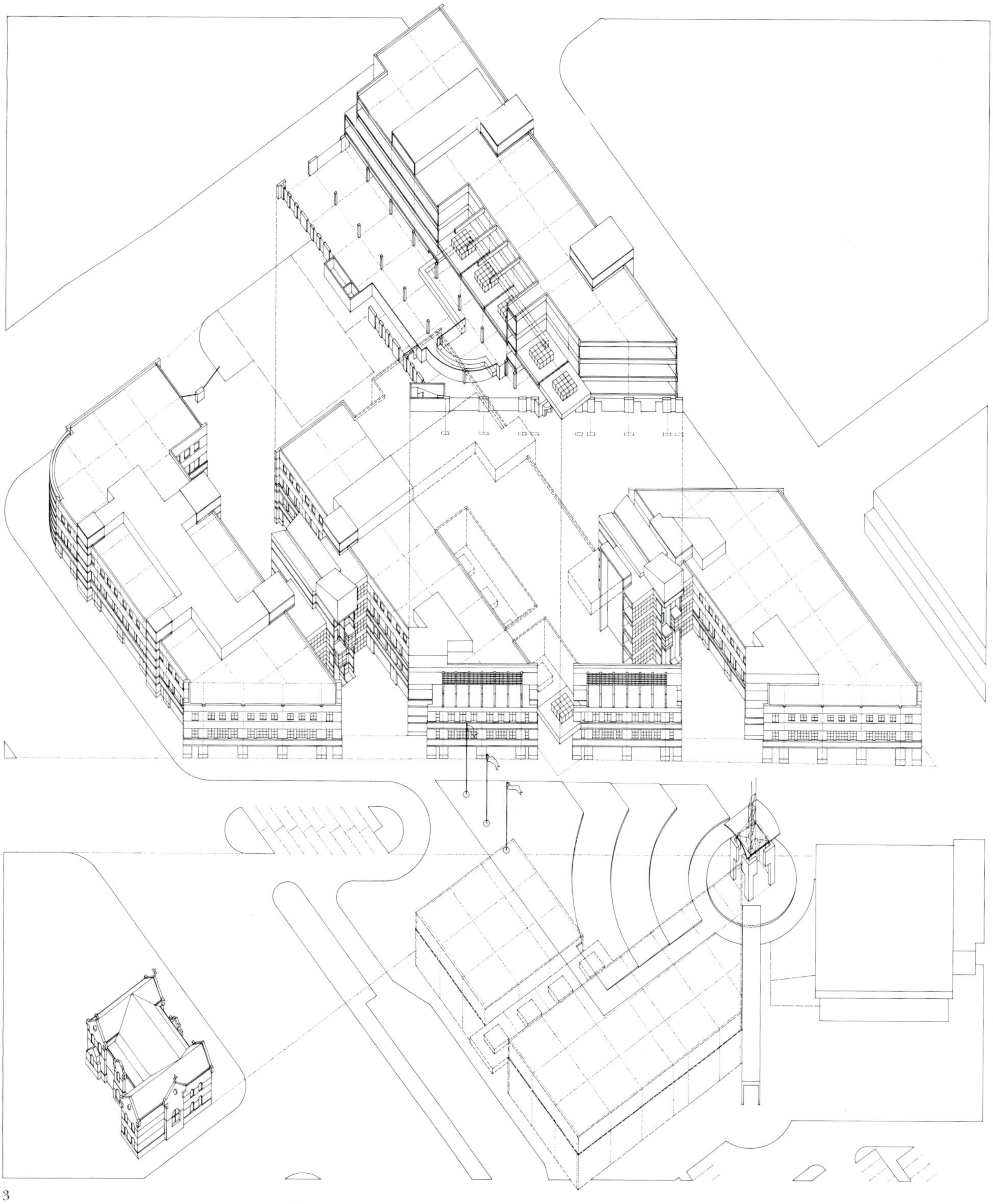

3

4

5

6

Walter and Eliza Hall Institute

Design/Completion 1982/1986
Parkville, Victoria
The Walter and Eliza Hall Institute of Medical Research
Associate architects: Godfrey Spowers
21,210 square metres
Reinforced concrete frame
Cream brick and GRC external cladding, metal sunshades

This is a building for highly skilled scientists, their support teams, animals and, above all, their ideas and experiments. Each scientist requires natural light, a workbench, write-up space, equipment and a high level of services. Shared facilities include autoclaves, fume exhaust stations and animal housing.

There are four typical laboratory floors, logically sandwiched between support services at ground and roof levels. Deep within the building, large vertical chimneys meet up with services, leaving the outer edges, with their light and view, available for the research teams. The workshop has a spartan aesthetic of exposed equipment ducts, pipes and wastes.

Mechanical support systems are enclosed in a curved, blue-panelled skin at each end of the structure and across the roof. Horizontal floor beams penetrate this skin and make reference to the balconies of the adjoining 1940s hospital.

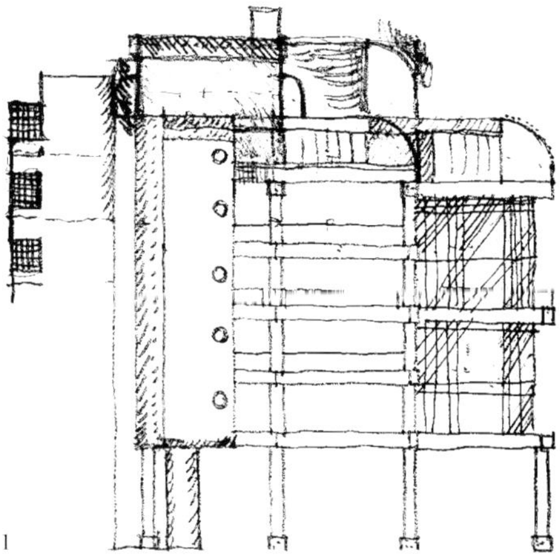

1

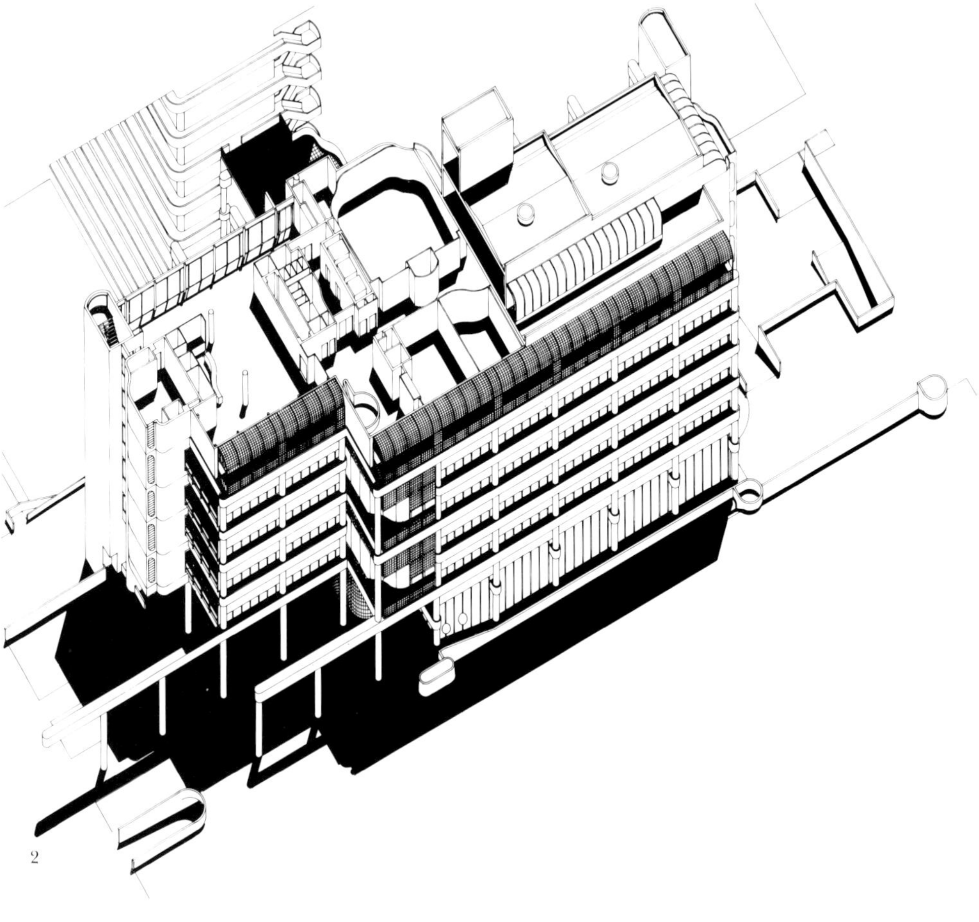

2

1 Design sketch
2 Axonometric
3 Entrance facade
4 Exterior view

3

4

5

6

5 Staircase upper
6 Entry foyer
7 Elevation sketch
8 Laboratory interior
9 Roof detail
10 Laboratory interior

7

8

9

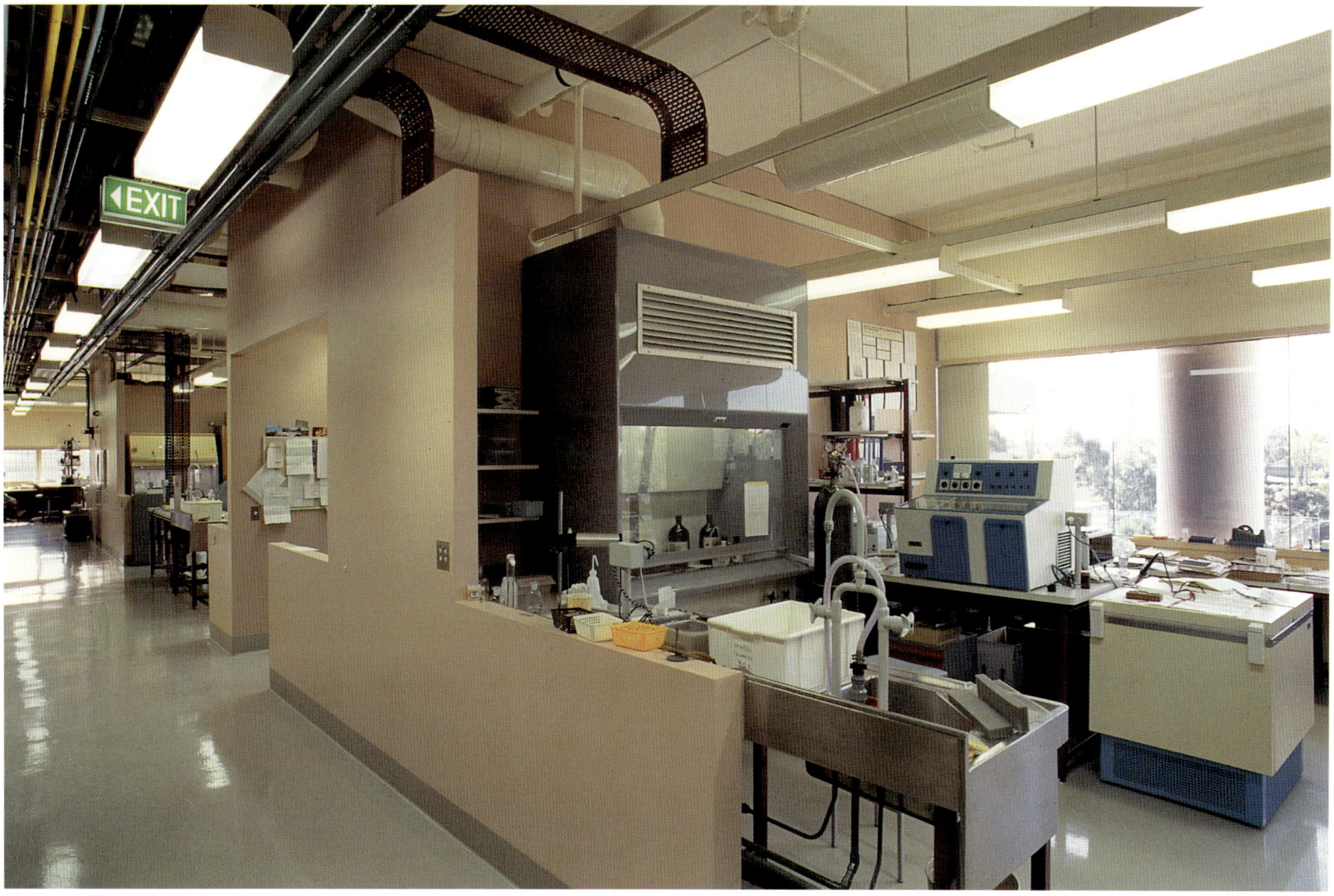

10

Royal Melbourne Hospital

Design/Completion 1990/1995
Parkville, Victoria
The Royal Melbourne Hospital
Associate architects: Di Carlo Potts Health Planners
15,457 square metres
Reinforced concrete frame, concrete floor slabs
Brickwork, vitreous enamelled metal panel cladding, dry wall partitions

Health planning is now a demanding field in its own right—balancing capital costs against recurrent management outlays, balancing needs against wants within each department and, above all, addressing the ever-expanding technologies which materially affect medical procedures. But hospitals are also expected to symbolise care and offer hospice.

Phased redevelopment of the 1940s Modern hospital demanded new facilities for emergency, cardiology, radiology and coronary care departments, operating theatres and the sterile processing unit. The new work evidences an urban attachment to the old, so forming a continuity and expressing the inherent interdependencies. White enamelled steel panels, cream brick and white cement render strike up a dialogue to offer resemblance without replication.

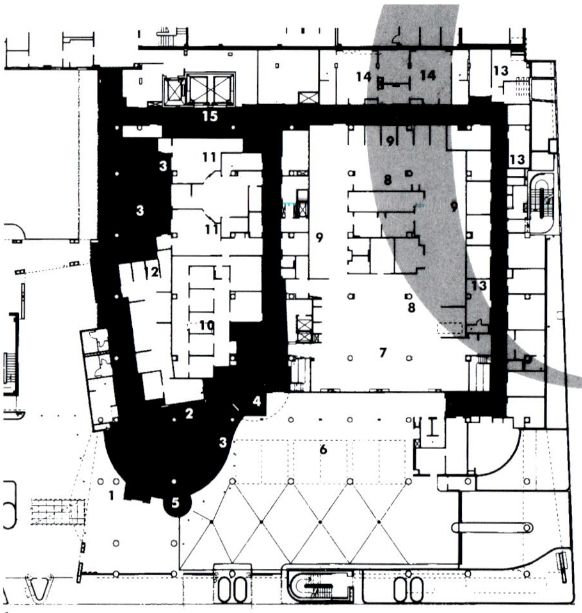

Ground floor plan
1 entry emergency and admissions
2 reception
3 waiting
4 triage
5 security
6 ambulance
7 resuscitation
8 nurse station
9 emergency beds
10 clinical examination rooms
11 x-ray rooms
12 admissions
13 offices
14 procedure rooms
15 patient lifts

■ **primary circulation**

1

2

1 Ground floor plan
2 Facade detail
3 Exterior view
4 Aerial view: corner of Royal Parade and Grattan Street
5 Royal Parade elevation

3

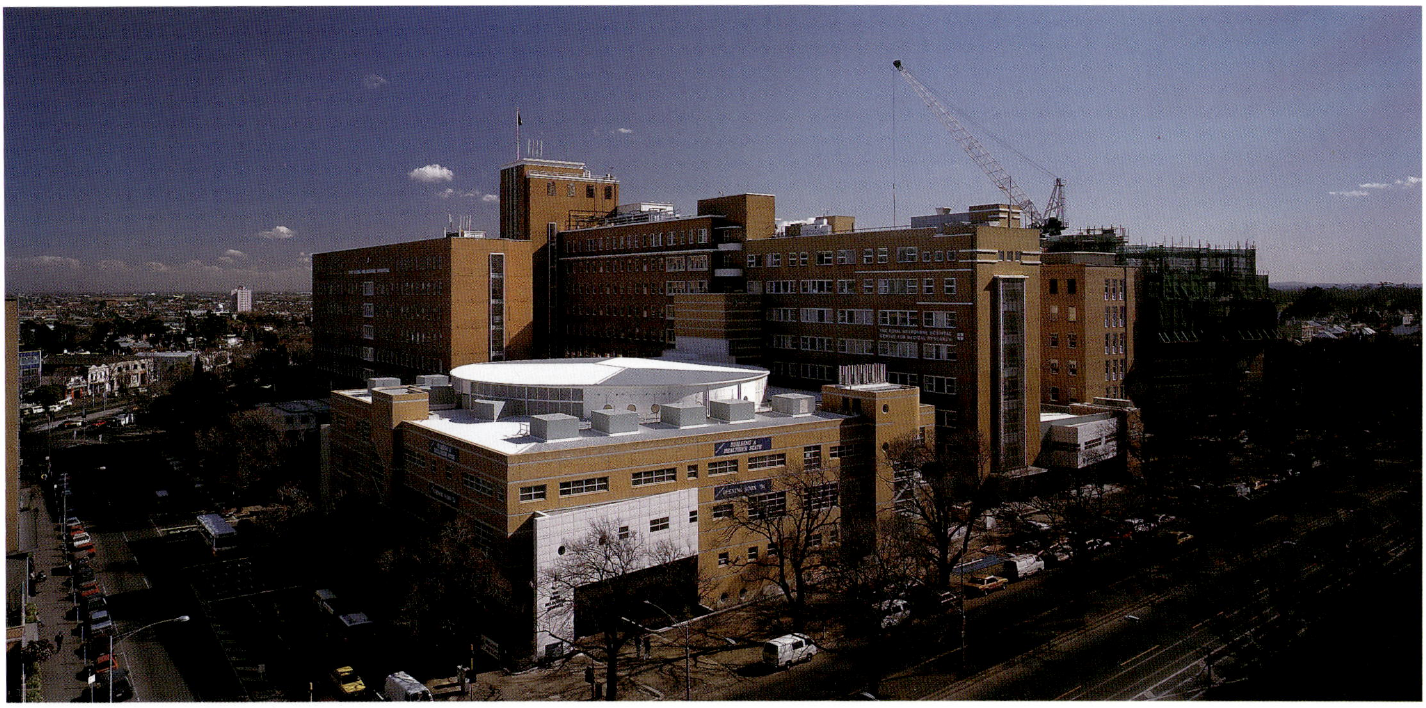

4

5

Australian Bicentennial Exhibition

Design/Completion 1986/1988
Australian Bicentennial Authority
Kenworth pantechnicons, fabric structure tent roofs, portable steel framework

In January 1988, a fleet of 70 vehicles carrying structures, exhibitions and staff began a tour of 34 country and city centres around Australia as part of the Bicentennial Travelling Exhibition. The exhibition comprised an innovative tent theatre, exhibition arcades and various other tents for displays and entertainment. The light, floating, conical fabric structures and their stick-like supports demonstrate an economy of form and spirit, and reveal the structural principles and methods of assembly. The system had to be easy and reliable to erect, dismantle, and transport.

Continued

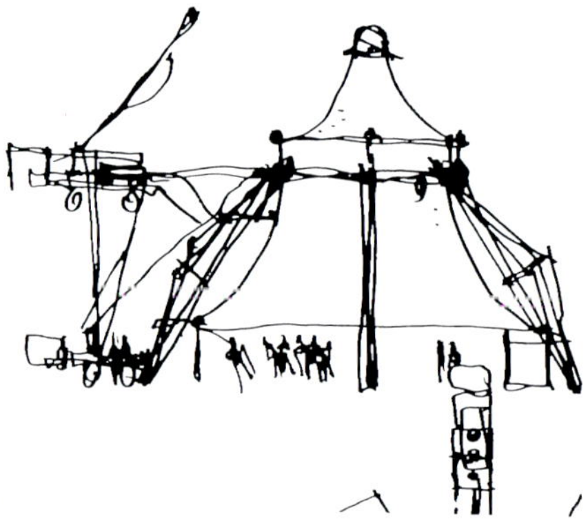

1

1 Study sketch
2 Assembled exhibition
3 Fabric structures and front-end vehicle
4 Design studies

2

3

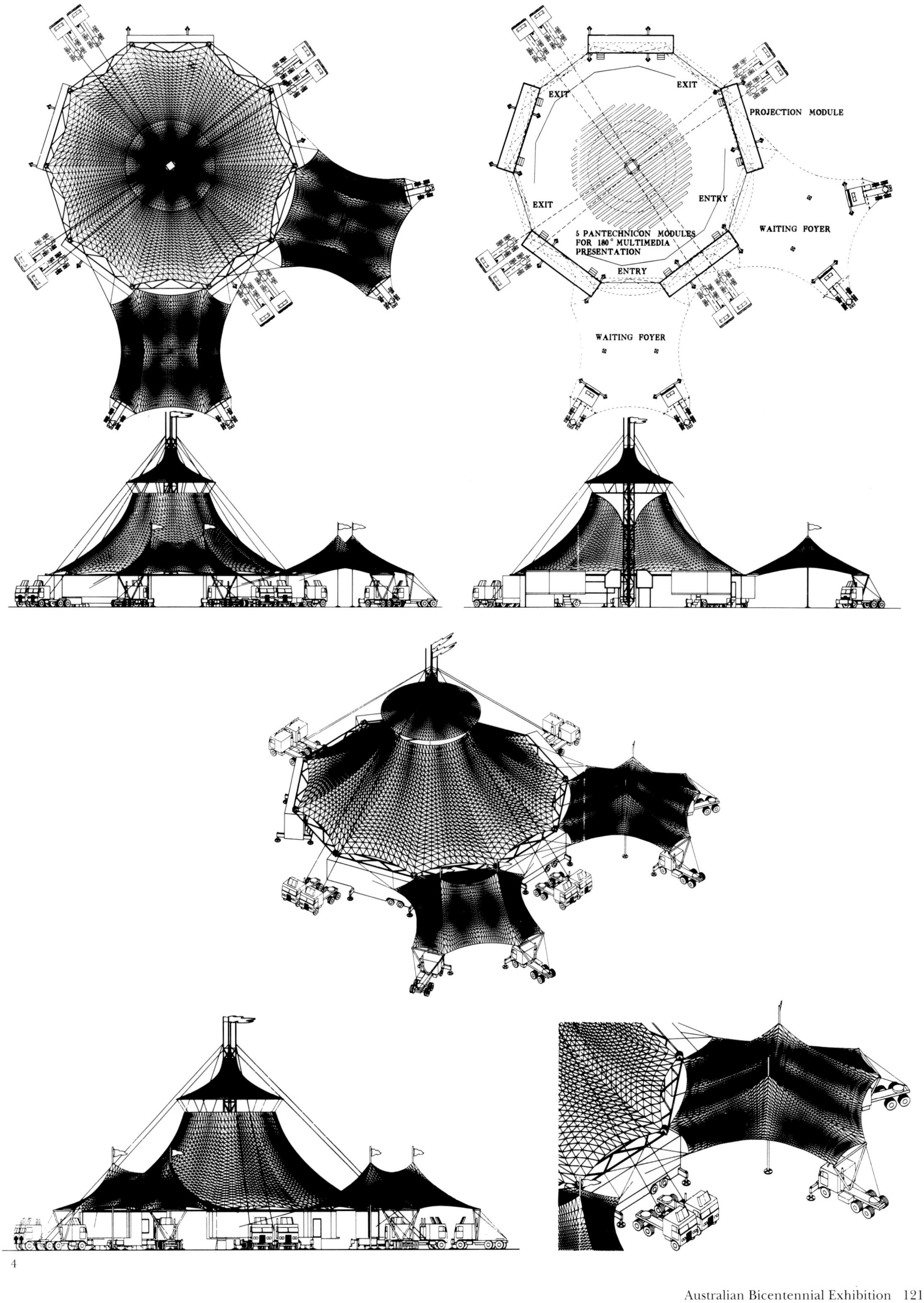
EXIT
EXIT
PROJECTION MODULE
EXIT
ENTRY
WAITING FOYER
5 PANTECHNICON MODULES
FOR 180° MULTIMEDIA
PRESENTATION
ENTRY
WAITING FOYER

4

5 Exhibition area
6 Theatre
7 Entertainment sound shell

At each exhibition site a tent city was erected using the road vehicles to assemble, anchor and tension the fabric structures supported on masts. Vehicles were elevated on hydraulic outriggers to enable levelling on undulating sites, and large, circular cast aluminium base plates were used to spread loads on a variety of subsoil conditions. Small-bore ground anchors were used on the more exposed sites as a precautionary measure against inclement weather. A team of up to 60 workers could erect the exhibition in two days.

5

6

7

Singapore Embassy

Design/Completion 1981/1985
Yarralumla, Australian Capital Territory
Singapore High Commission
3,750 square metres
Concrete, cement render, plaster interiors, metal deck roofing

Canberra's foreign embassies are designed to reflect national traditions. But historic styles, when literally reproduced, create a Disneyland effect. The modern State of Singapore, a combination of three Asian cultures with a British colonial overlay, rejected this approach. It wanted to express its 20th-century identity as city-state banker, trader and manufacturer.

The idea was to introduce a degree of sculptural tension to illustrate the interaction of disparate cultures. Singapore's climate (and Australia's) is symbolised in lattice sunshades, overhanging roofs, double posts and veranda iconography.

The building steps up the sloping site in three parallel arcaded wall planes that extend out into the gardens and provide a link with the curving hill and eucalyptus trees of the site. The sweeping first floor and roof edges form an arc (a segment of the equatorial circle locating Singapore). This second geometry complements the land contour and road edge, and opposes the parallel wall planes which it intersects and penetrates.

1

2

1 Entrance facade
2 Interior staircase
3 Interior foyer
4 Axonometric study

3

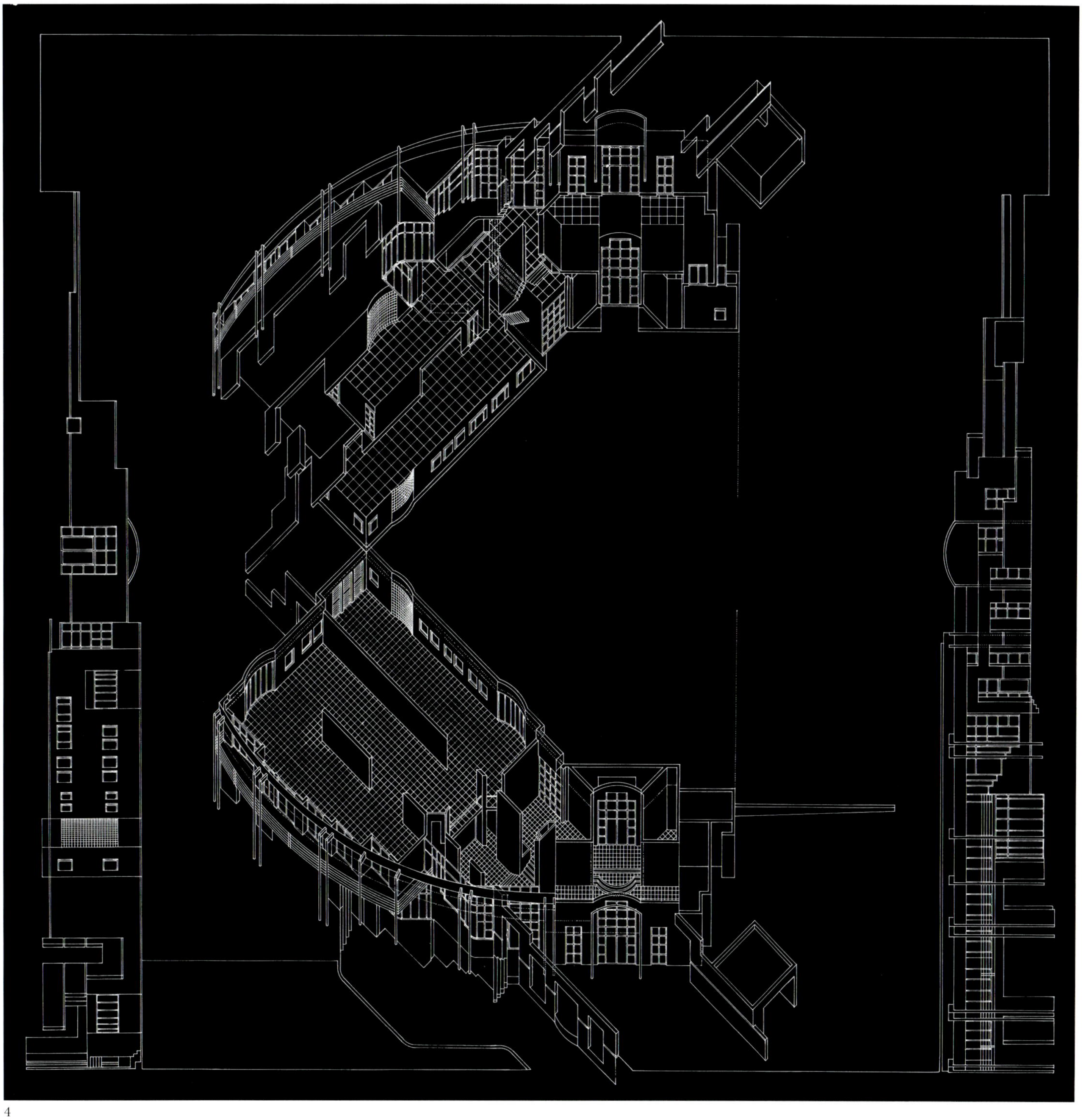

4

McLachlan Offices

Design/Completion 1978/1980
Barton, Australian Capital Territory
National Capital Development Commission
Architects: Daryl Jackson Alastair Swayn Pty Ltd
15,260 square metres
Concrete frame, flat plate floors
Glass, metal infill walls, metal deck roofing

Originally planned in 1974, these offices were built in 1978. Pedestrian movement, separate identities for each department, flexibility for expansion and change, and open and closed office spaces were all planning considerations. The building idea is structured by a theoretically limitless field of columns into which inner courts are carved, and around which exterior form is designated. It is an architecture of indeterminacy, with field and flat-plate floor planes capable of being manipulated in the present and extended in the future.

Each floor increases in size, making a stepped profile that is undercut where it meets the ground and extended where it reaches towards the sky. The long edge beams constitute an imposed topography of layered floor platforms which the columns inhabit as "figures".
The circulation system of bridges, service pods and divisional entrances cuts through the field of columns and positively separates the perception of office space into route and destination, with the idea of "place" being an amalgam of both.

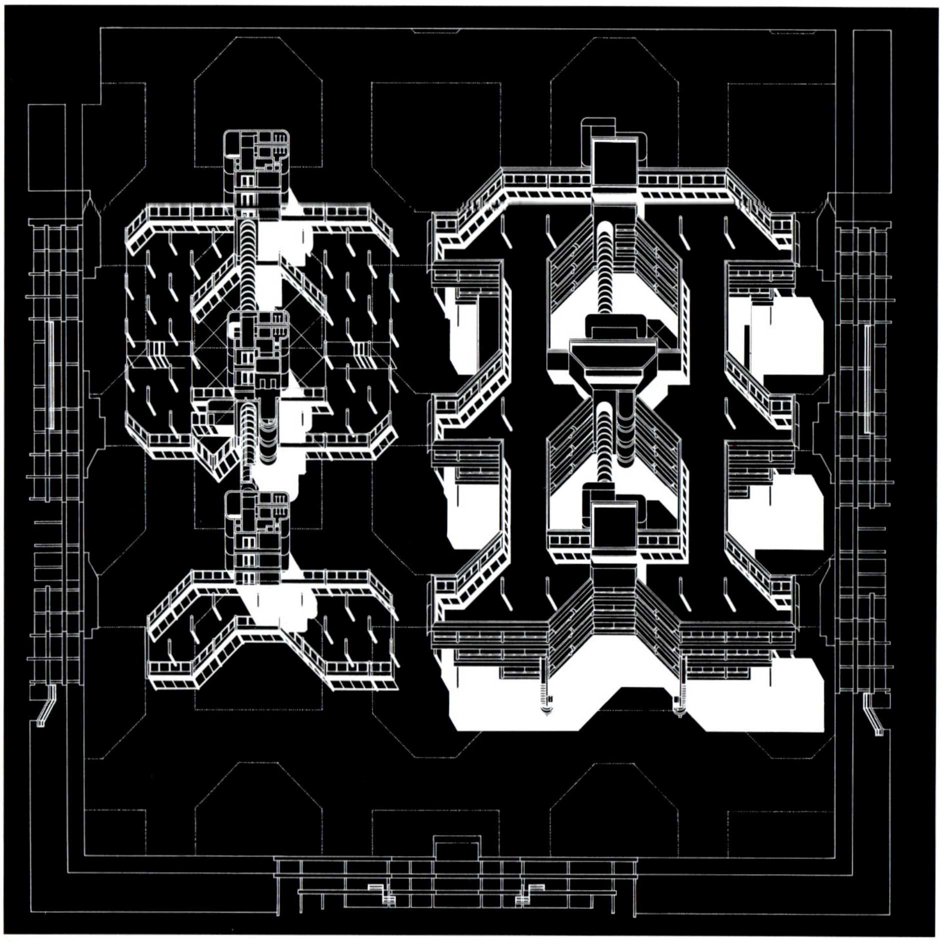

1

2

1 Axonometric view
2 Glazed passageway
3 Street exterior
4 Front view
5 Concrete stairwell

3

4

5

SELECTED AND CURRENT WORKS

Commercial

120 Collins Street

Design/Completion 1986/1991
Melbourne, Victoria
Foxhina Pty Ltd
Associate architects: Hassells Pty Ltd
65,700 square metres
Reinforced concrete core, concrete columns and steel beams supporting concrete slab on metal deck formwork
Reconstituted granite, polished precast cladding, aluminium and glass curtain walls

The new construction required an independent expression with formal reference to the old (the Victorian church and office building retained on Collins Street). The tower is set to the rear corner of the site and is connected to the streets by a low-scale atrium and cloister spaces. These fill in the street edge, offering a street address and accommodating church offices, professional suites and shops. The tower has a tripartite reading of base, middle and top, stepping inward as it rises up to create a skyline profile that expresses the lift and service cores.

Precast panels define the corners and frame elements of the curtain wall in a positive/negative composition of edge and centre.

1

2

1 Street view
2 Foyer interior
3 City view

3

4 Communications tower
5 Urban image
6 City elevation
7 Plan and elevation

4

5

6

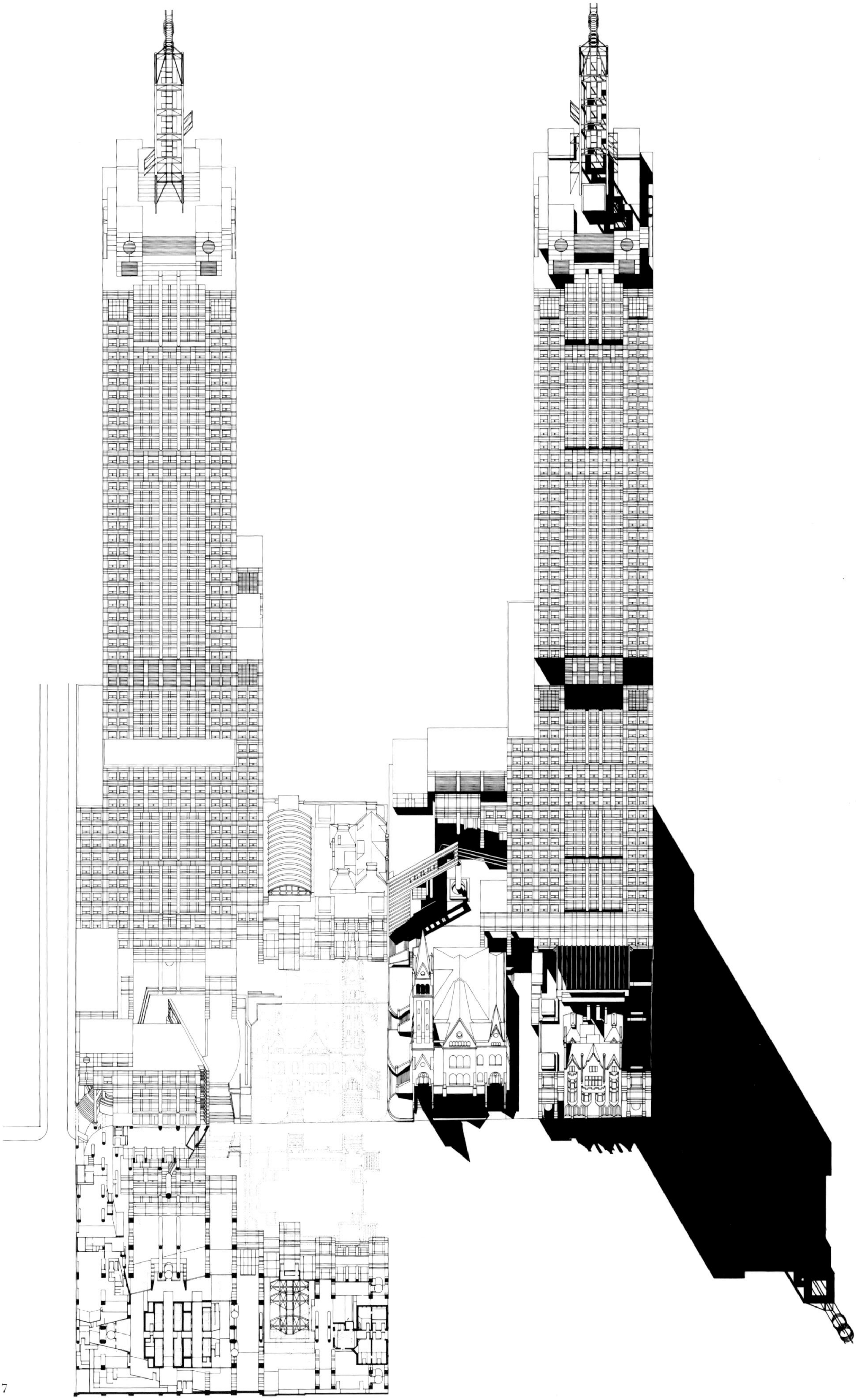

7

Commercial Union

Design/Completion 1985/1991
Melbourne, Victoria
National Commercial Union Ltd
Associate architects: Peter Hunt Architects, Perth
33,880 square metres
Steel structure, reinforced concrete core, concrete floor slabs on metal deck formwork

This is a two-stage development with dual street frontages: the first 10-storey stage to accommodate circulation and connections for the second 22-storey stage. The building has excellent views over the Flagstaff Gardens to the north and the docks and city to the west and south. The eastern elevation is stepped to provide views over the gardens for people deep inside the building.

The top levels, dedicated to staff facilities, are terraced for outdoor gardens. The Latrobe Street facade evokes the security and permanence of Commercial Union as a major insurance company. A solid outer frame of precast panels with punched windows contrasts with the recessed and curved inner curtain wall. The outer frame also insulates the building from its mirrorglass neighbours.

1

2

3

1 Office interior
2 Ground-floor foyer
3 City view
4 Axonometric study

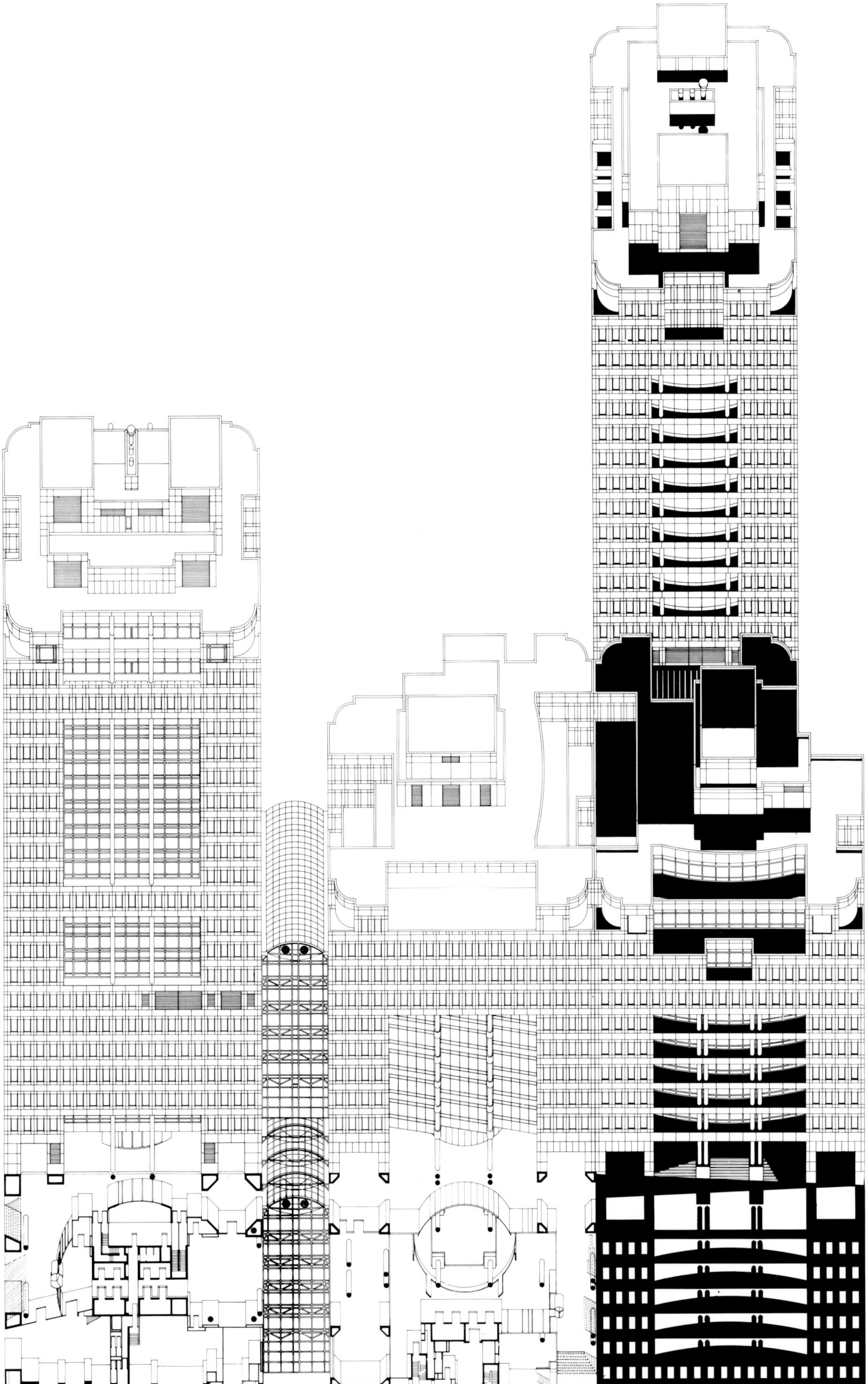

4

Seymour Powell, London

Design/Completion 1989/1991
London, UK
Seymour Powell Pty Ltd
Architect: Daryl Jackson International Pty Ltd
1,200 square metres
Installation within existing hall
Glass, aluminium, maple

An old Methodist chapel in West Kensington is converted to house industrial design consultancy Seymour Powell.

The theme of transportation is prevalent in the design, consistent with work of the consultancy. Frameless glazed partitions supported by steel cables and yacht shackles create a series of cellular workstations. Stressed skin mezzanines above the ground floor and in the basement, reached by "ship's ladders", provide extra work space. Further extending the theme, a sailcloth canopy stretches over the garden from the side wall.

1

1 Workshop
2 Connecting stay
3 Entry door
4 Studio floor

2

3

4

IBM Southgate

Design/Completion 1990/1994
Melbourne, Victoria
IBM Australia Ltd
9,000 square metres
Tenancy fitout, internal partitioning and workstations
Granite cladding to entrance foyer

IBM's new Marketing Centre is housed in the top 10 floors of the Southgate complex in Melbourne. The aim of the design is to provide a space in which customers can learn how to use IBM equipment. A new plaza level lobby displays granite banding and a light installation as a way of representing IBM's philosophy. On the floors above, the new stair is an installed piece of "cool theatre" with minimalist partition; high-quality floating aerofoil screens are a further element.

1

2

3

4

1 Display centre
2 Steel plate stairs
3 Staircase
4 Display centre
5 Entry foyer

5

Flight Bays, Sydney International Airport

Design/Completion 1992/1992
Mascot, New South Wales
Spotless Catering Services Ltd
Architects: Daryl Jackson Robin Dyke Pty Ltd
350 square metres
Steel suspended light structure
Laminate, timber, glass, copper to joinery, carpet, tiles to floors

Food, flying and farewelling the friends with a drink, are now an integral part of a modern air terminal. These installations are intended to represent the idea of flight. The aerofoil-shaped lighting canopies and curving bars offer a sense of excitement as well as a necessary identity. Seating extends along the face of the building to adjoining bars and food outlets, affording patrons extensive views of arriving and departing planes. These are places for waiting and gathering, greetings and goodbyes.

1

2

1 Arrivals cafe
2 Cocktail bar, arrival level
3 Bar

3

Hyatt Hotel, Canberra

Design/Completion 1986/1988
Yarralumla, Australian Capital Territory
Hotel Canberra Ltd
Architects: Daryl Jackson Alastair Swayn Pty Ltd
32,500 square metres
Reinforced concrete
Brickwork and render, tiled roofs, plasterboard interiors

The Canberra Hotel of 1927 is one of the capital's older buildings. With a symmetrical layout of pavilion and garden courts, it bears traces of Beaux-Arts, Frank Lloyd Wright and Walter Burley Griffin influences.

The new section of the hotel refers to this vocabulary without wanting to recreate it. A central top-lit galleria extends along the principal axis, opening up towards the lake, the original dining room, and the new public rooms to each side of the gallery. Symmetrical room units are placed in the consolidated landscaped setting, confirming the existing form of garden court and freestanding pavilion. The additions are designed with the idea of evolutionary continuity, building onto and within an existing design pattern.

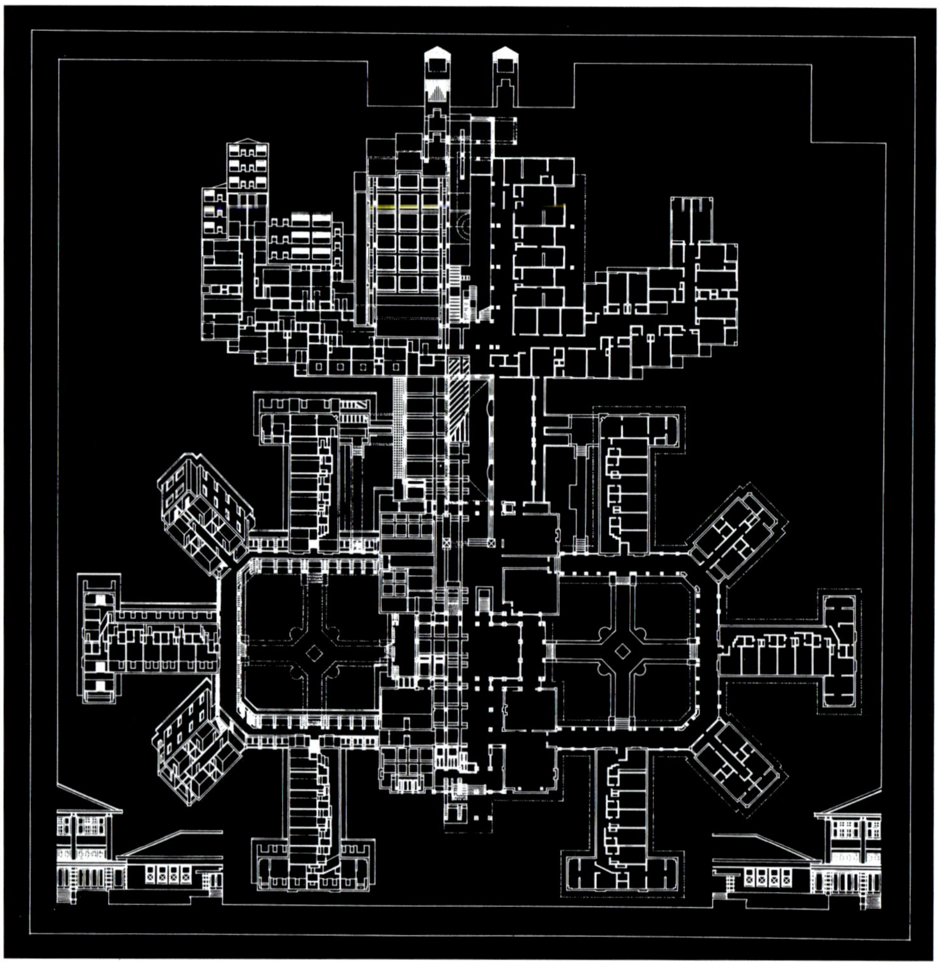

1

2

1 Ground level floor plan/projection
2 Ballroom arrival
3 Staircase to the rooms

3

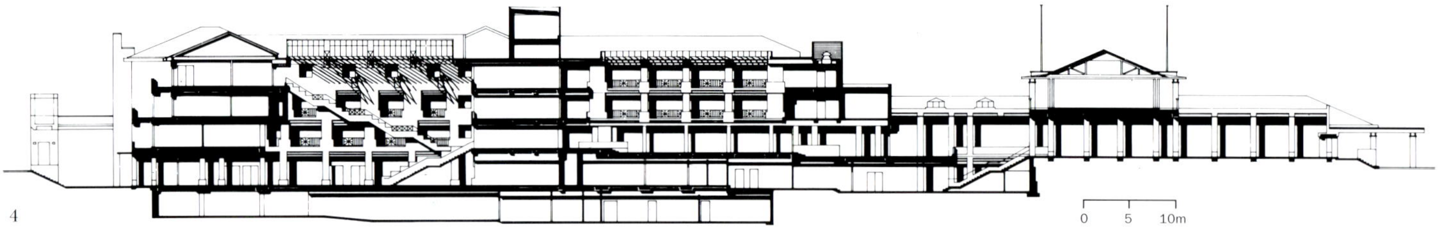

4

5

6

4 Section
5 Gallery
6 Foyer
7 Suites atrium
8 Staircase

7

8

Stonier's Winery

Design/Completion 1989/1991
Merricks, Victoria
Stonier Yuill and Limb Pty Ltd
963 square metres
Steel and timber framework
Colorbond custom-orb external cladding, timber pergolas

A corrugated iron sail-like structure covers the winery, deflecting sun, but not light, from the interior. Form has been determined by function: holding tanks inhabit the high side while the lower side houses service quarters. A vine-covered timber pergola encloses the walkway—a place for visitors to meet and for summer wine tastings.

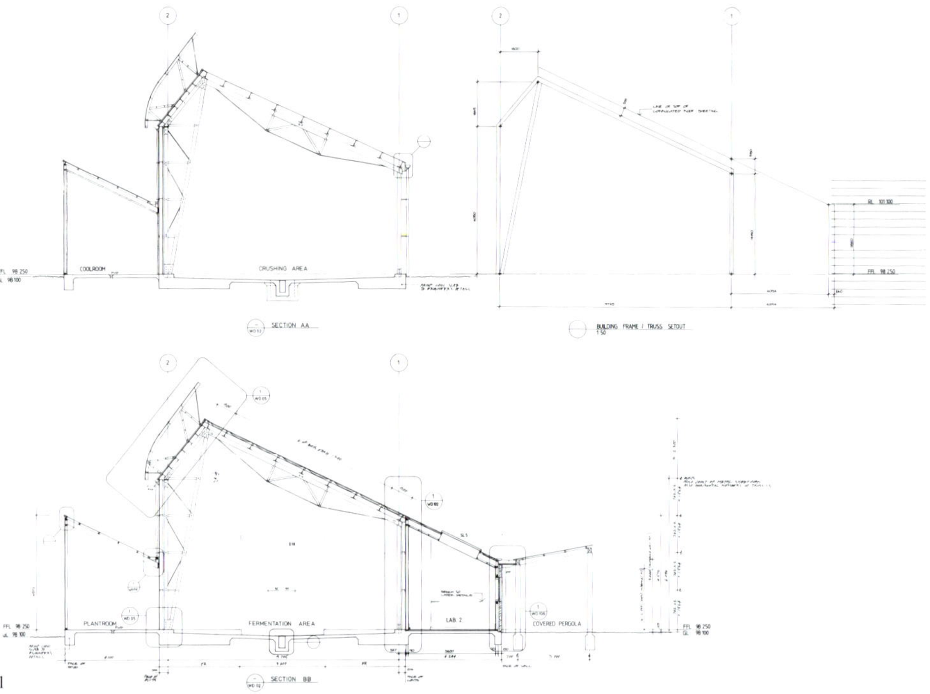

1

2

3

1 Sections
2 Exterior approach
3 Light and sun control
4 Ventilation
5 Interior
6 From the vineyard

4

5

6

European Serviced Offices, Budapest

Design/Completion 1991/1992
Budapest, Hungary
Irodahaz KFT and Simon Property
Architects: Daryl Jackson International Pty Ltd
in association with Mel Yepterv (Budapest)
Atrium: local stone and marble
Zinc roofs, epoxy stone walkways, cast plaster

A late 19th century apartment block in Budapest is converted into a modern, serviced office building. Built around a central courtyard, the Neo-Renaissance style structure has been refurbished to include an extra floor in the roof space. Catering facilities, a gymnasium, and a sauna are also included on the lower ground floor.

A single-membrane PVC roof is extended over the courtyard to create an atrium. By day it serves as a reception area and is drenched by natural light. At night, uplights in the marble floor bounce light off the polyester coating, illuminating the area as a function/exhibition hall.

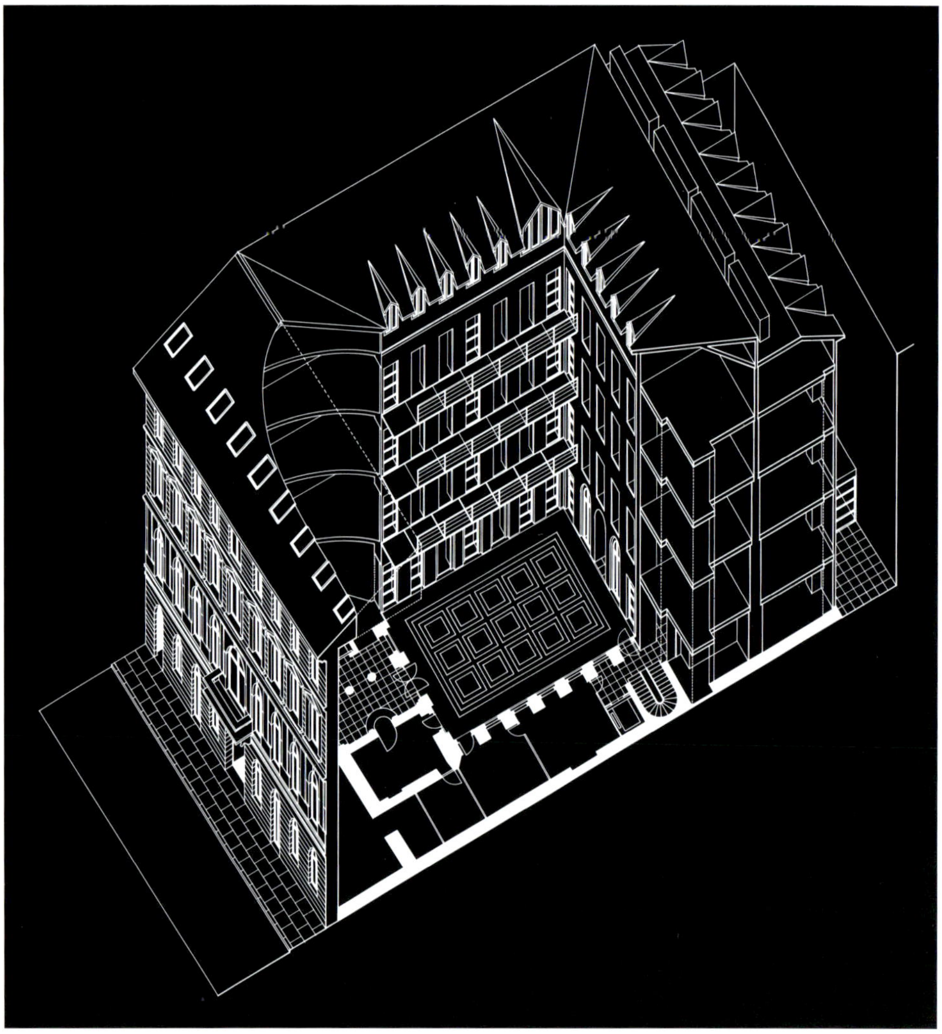

1

2

1 Cutaway axonometric
2 Building facade
3 Arrival
4 Entry
5-6 Fabric roof

3

4

5

6

Cape Schanck National Golf Club

Design/Completion 1985/1988
Cape Schanck, Victoria
National Golf Holdings Ltd
1,892 square metres
Limestone block with colorbond corrugated iron roof

A dramatic, windswept, undulating series of sand dunes characterises the course. The club building is intended as contrast: a fortified establishment of severe limestone walls, gable roof and outstanding views. The interior demanded a number of segregated areas for dining, games, bars, changing, and for the separation of men and women. A formal entrance court receives visitors, drawing them through a long gallery leading to a central staircase overlooking the ocean.

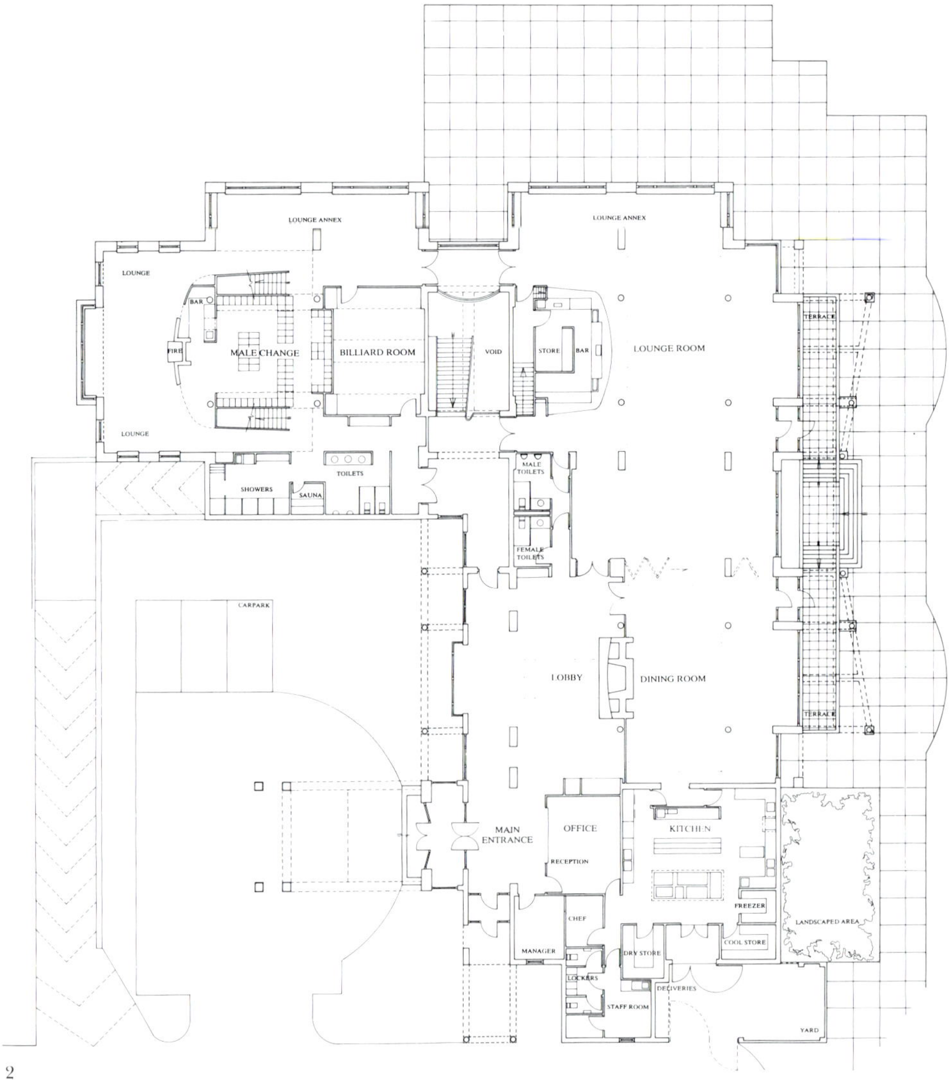

2

3

1

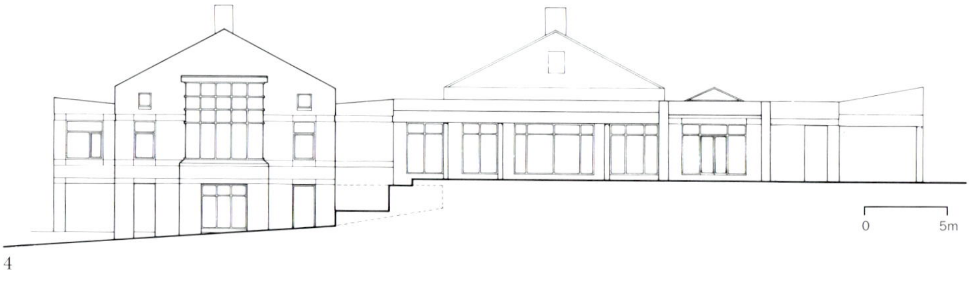

4

1 Staircase detail
2 Ground-floor plan
3 South-west elevation
4 South-east elevation
5 Interior stair
6 Dining room
7 Building in its landscape

5

6

7

Cape Schanck Golf Club

Design/Completion 1985/1987
Cape Schanck, Victoria
Cape Schanck Resort Development
2,068 square metres
Limestone block with colorbond corrugated iron roof

The building is strategically placed, overlooking the 18th hole and undulating dunes, with distant views to Melbourne.

The entry through the layered limestone walls works as gateway to the course as much as to the building itself. The building creates an edge condition that separates car park and arrival from the course beyond. The splayed walls of the entry court embrace and indicate the building's functional components: pro-shop to the east and golf club to the west.

Viewed from the course, the building becomes an object in the landscape, a beacon and home base to golfers. Diagonals and curves are used in plan and section to project spaces into landscape. The planar, orthogonal layers of limestone wall form the ordered backdrop of these projections and car park elevation. The expressive devices respond to the windswept dune profile as well as the golfer's stroke.

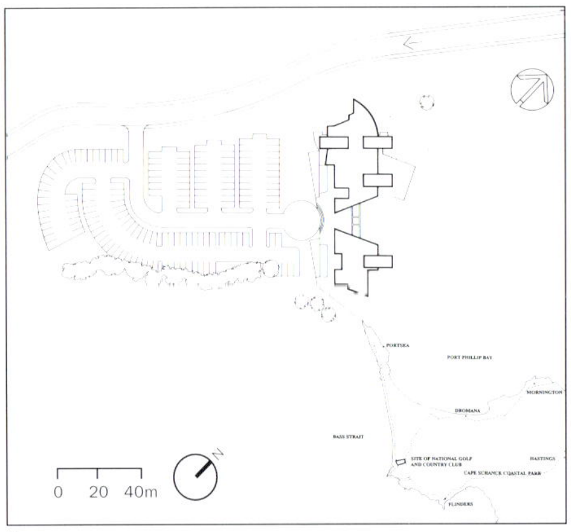

1

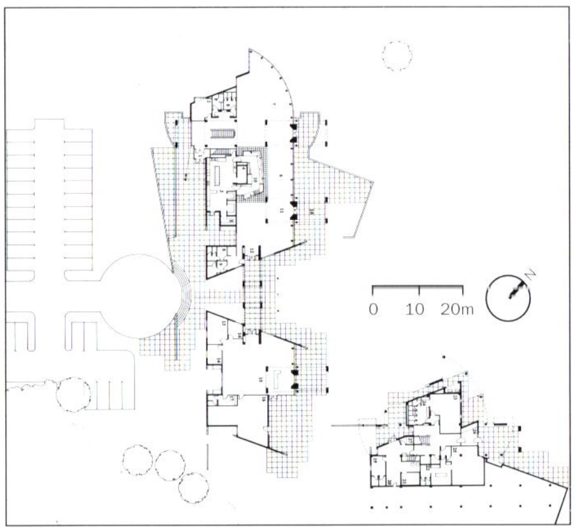

2

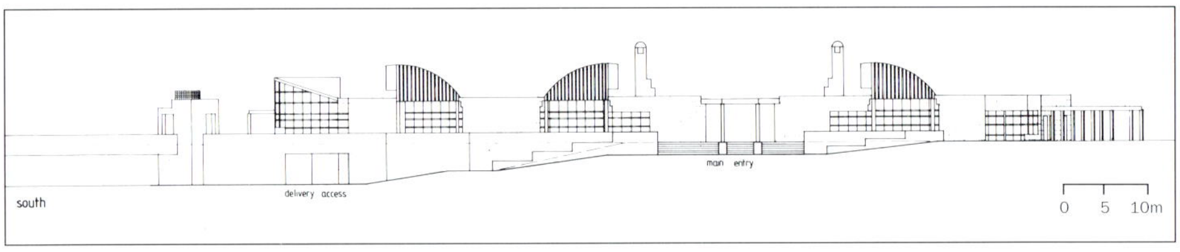

3

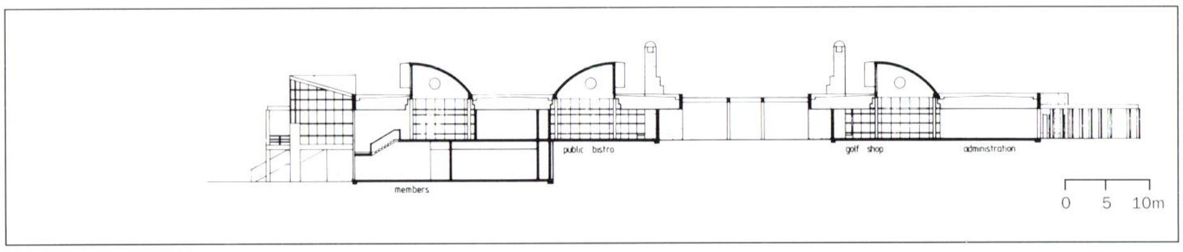

4

5

1 Site plan
2 Floor plans
3 Elevation
4 Section
5 View from the course
6 Sand dune forms
7 Landscape integration
8 Dining room

6

7

8

Esprit de Corps

Design/Completion 1981/1983
Abbotsford, Victoria
Esprit de Corps
2,030 square metres
Brickwork, steel framework and steel frame windows with grey glazing

Here, three existing 19th century factory elements are reused for office/design/distribution/sales, and further warehouse/workroom space is added.

A basic aim was to retain the building's original forms. The three separate brick boxes are linked by a positive/negative arrangement, with new areas being posed as transparent "opposition" to the old solid structures. Three shades of grey and the natural shine of corrugated iron play off against the terracotta brickwork.

A second organising axis for the new "inserts" is a design device that orients the view past the building towards the river and the park beyond, and distinguishes the new from the existing. The new parts make references to the old in the window type and size, and the roof monitors. Old and new are related by a composition of opposites.

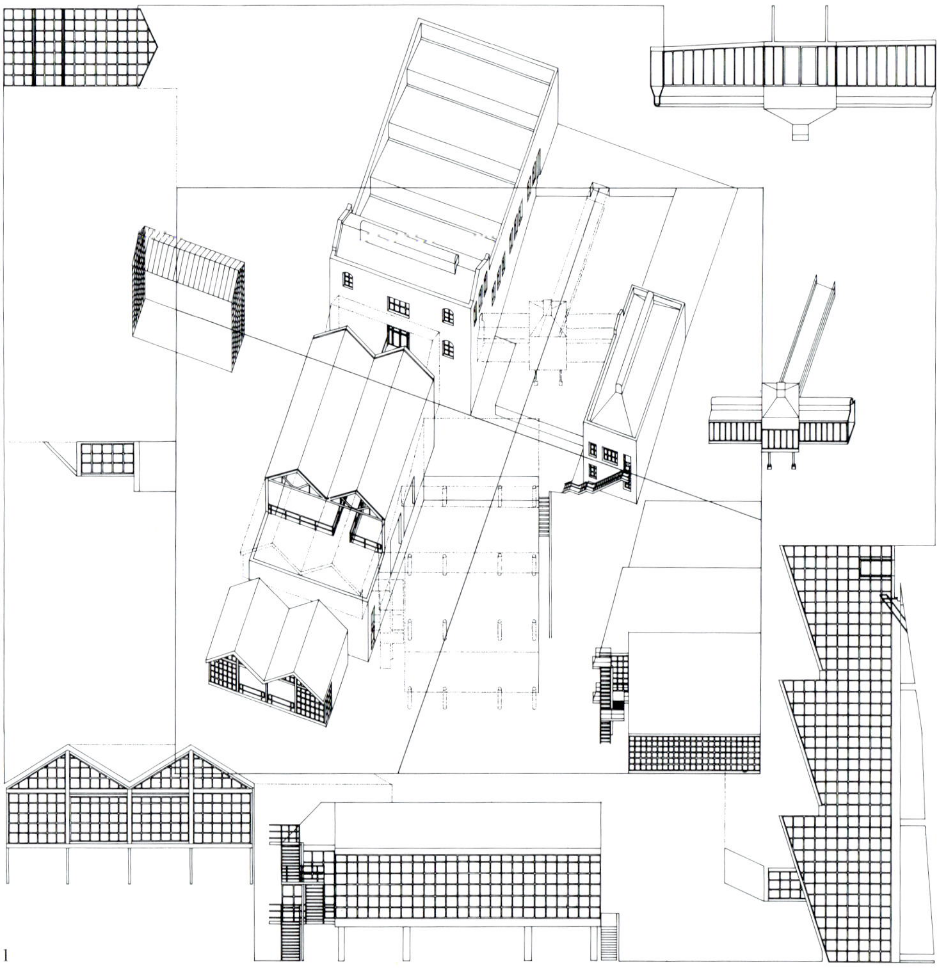

1

2

3

1 Axonometric study
2 River end gables
3 Glass and brick
4 Ground-floor plan
5 Elevation
6 Warehouse interior
7 Approach
8 Foyer
9 Interior bridge

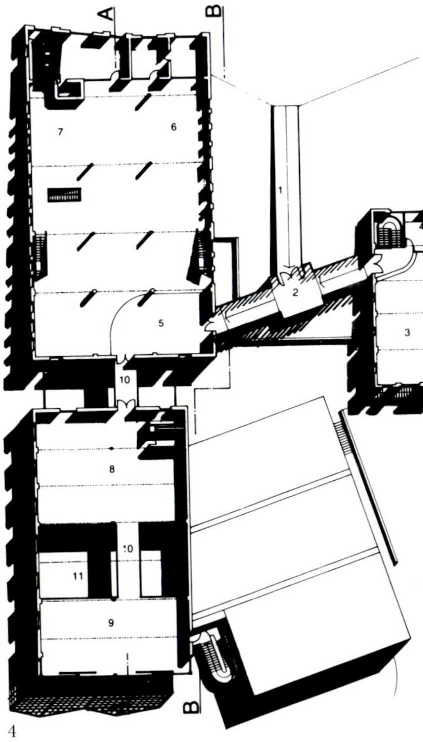

4

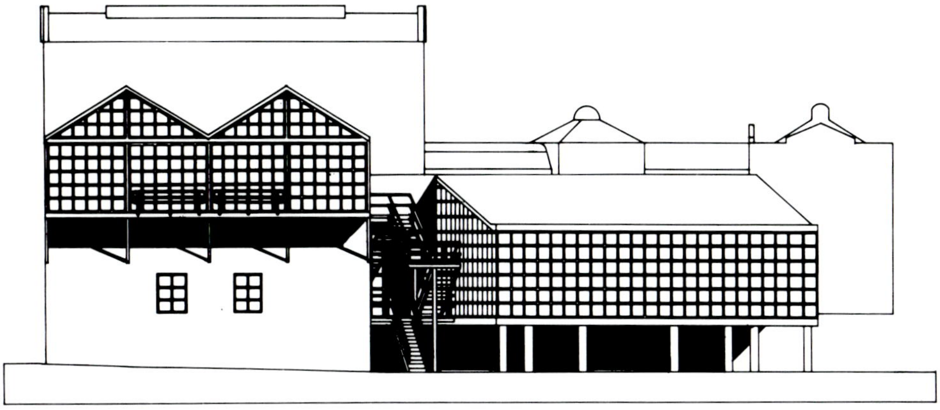
5

6

7

8

9

Centenary House

Design/Completion 1990/1993
Barton, Australian Capital Territory
John Curtin House Pty Ltd
Architects: Daryl Jackson Alastair Swayn Pty Ltd
7,000 square metres
Concrete frame and precast panels, glass curtain walls, metal deck roofing

Speculative offices for government tenancies with fixed rents generate a need for flexibility, efficiency and economy. This is a taut, incisive assembly of cut, precast concrete panels attached to an in situ frame. The sharp edges are important to the expression, conveying a "house of cards" idea. Pieces of precast rotate away from the facade to support balconies, while the main entrance is recessed within. Cable-tied steel framing supports thin pressed steel sunshading.

1

2

1 Street elevation
2 Boardroom
3 Services elevation
4 Entrance
5 Corner detail
6 Street elevation

3

4

5

6

SELECTED AND CURRENT WORKS

Houses & Housing

Abrahams House

Design/Completion 1977/1979
Brighton, Victoria
Daryl and Christine Abrahams
720 square metres
Sand-coloured concrete block and grey bleached timber

House sites in Melbourne with direct access to the beaches of Port Phillip Bay are rare. Here a tiny street frontage fans out to overlook the beach, with its grassy dunes in the foreground, a middle ground of yachts in the marina, and a distant water/sky horizon. The house is designed to bridge water and land elements (the roof profile taking on a dune form), as well as harmonising with the neighbouring standard tiled pitched roofs. It is a freestanding pavilion building, linked by a courtyard to a small studio on the landward side.

The ground floor sequence is open and informal—spaces flow together for easy entertainment and relaxation. Upstairs, the rooms are cellular and enclosed: parents' and children's study/bedrooms are separate areas, linked by the stair and skylit roof. The natural colours of the materials (grey bleached timbers and sand-coloured masonry) evoke a timelessness so often experienced in buildings associated with the seaside.

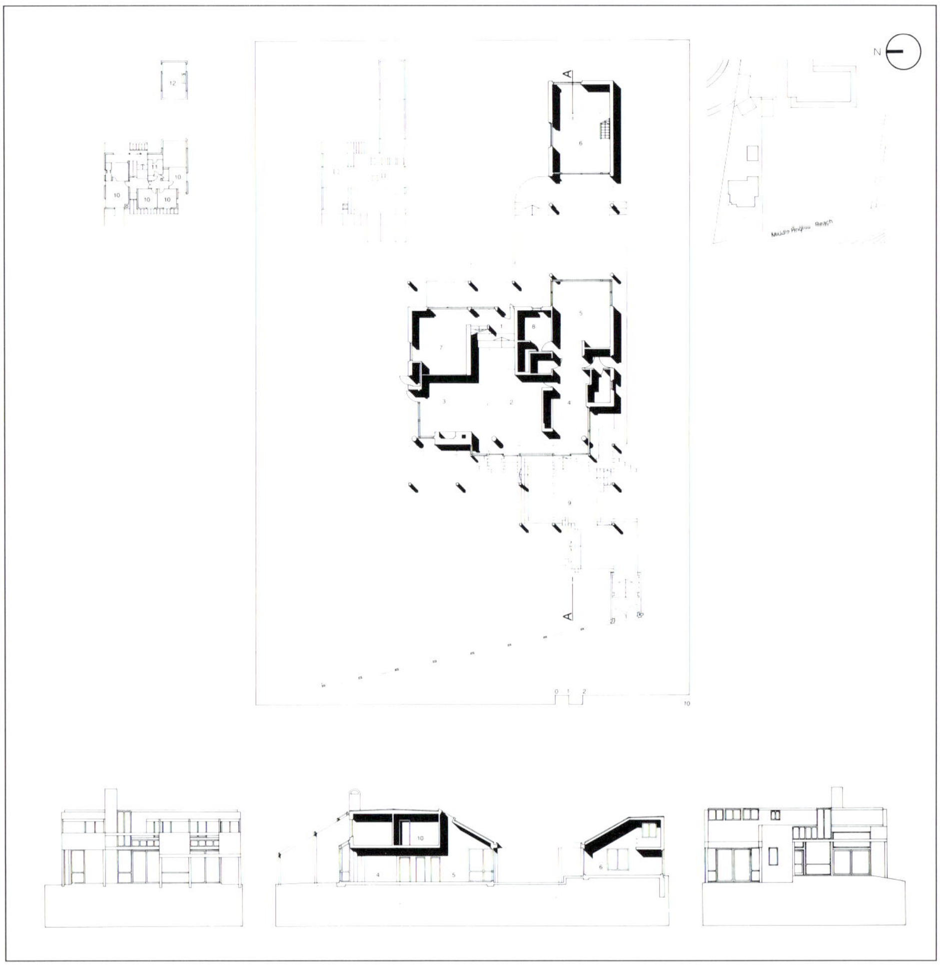

1

2

3

4

5

6

7

1 Plans, elevations and section
2 From Port Phillip Bay
3 Exterior
4 Skylight detail
5 Timber sunshade detail
6 Interior staircase
7 Living room

Cox House, Hawthorn

Design/Completion 1980/1983
Hawthorn, Victoria
Laurie and Julie Ann Cox
525 square metres
Bagged and painted brickwork with timber lattice sunscreens supported by a detached steel frame

This house is in a neighbourhood of mature gardens. It is a cubist exercise of volumes pulled apart to suggest separate needs and uses. Entrances to the lower floor living areas are curved to represent the arc of opening out or revelation, and are protected by the tighter boxes of bedrooms above. Large columns support an upper mass, which suggest the solidity and security of the enclosure. Three stairs (one from the external first floor terrace to the pool) provide alternative access paths, to allow residents to possess the house over time.

The pool/court, overhung by a detached line of lattice sunscreens, is an integral part of the site, marking the midpoint of house/garden. The lattice line, seen as an abstraction, creates a constant: it addresses the sun and makes a linear reference to the city skyline further down the Yarra River.

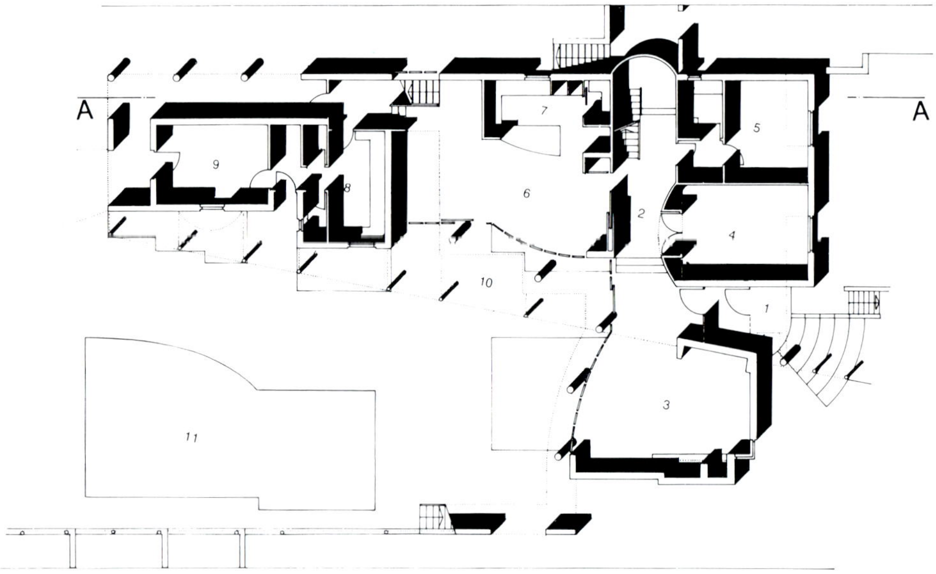

1

2

1 Ground-floor plan
2 Street facade
3 Axonometric study
4 Elevation
5 Section
6 Pool and courtyard

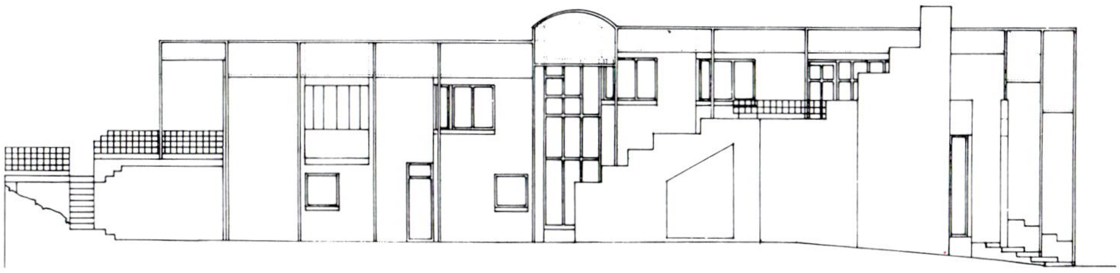

4

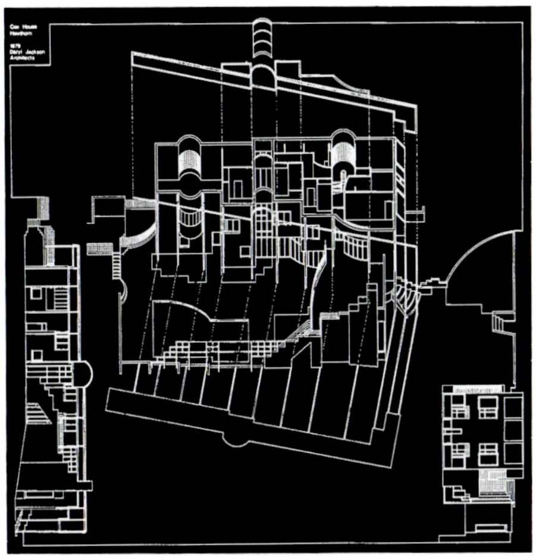

3

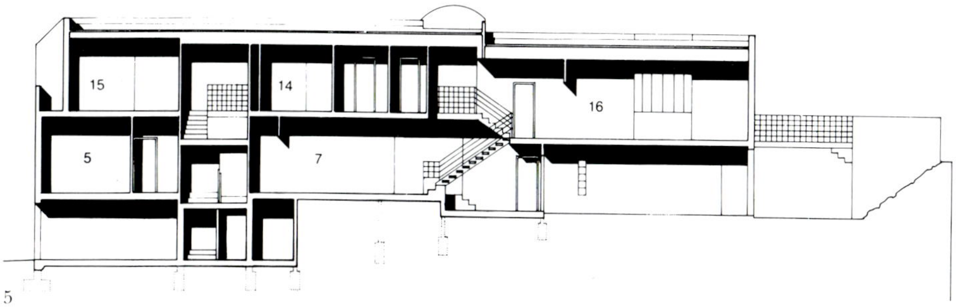

5

6

Cox House, Portsea

Design/Completion 1986/1987
Portsea, Victoria
Laurie and Julie Ann Cox
450 square metres
Timber frame
Red cedar weatherboard cladding, metal deck roofing

Portsea is the bayside holiday village traditionally favoured by Melbourne residents. There are social rules at Portsea which affect its architecture. This house reviews the traditional captain's cottage. It is a one-sided site, looking out to the sea and the sun, with a steep cliff face of tea-tree behind. The available land is a ledge cut by an access path to the boat sheds below. Part of the house is cut off from the main area and located lower down, giving the children a space of their own and allowing the composition opportunity for another layer of mass.

1

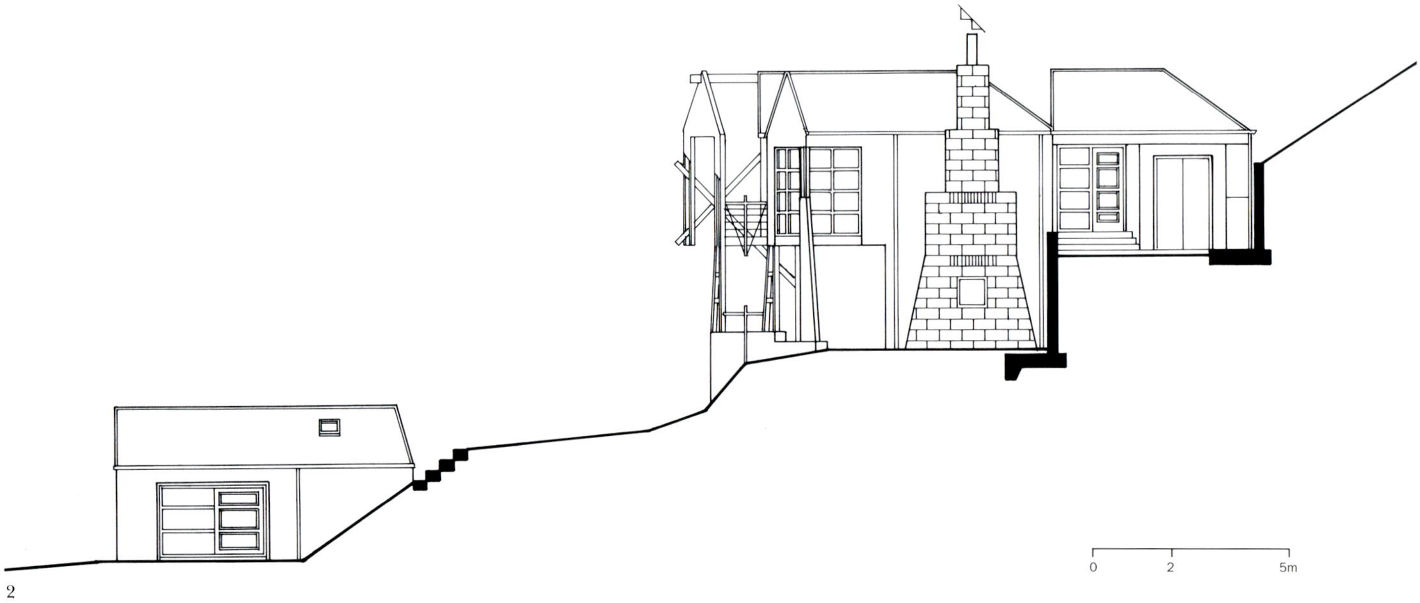

2

1 Timber frame sunscreen
2 Section through site
3 Plans
4 Living area overlooking the sea
5 Freeform kitchen

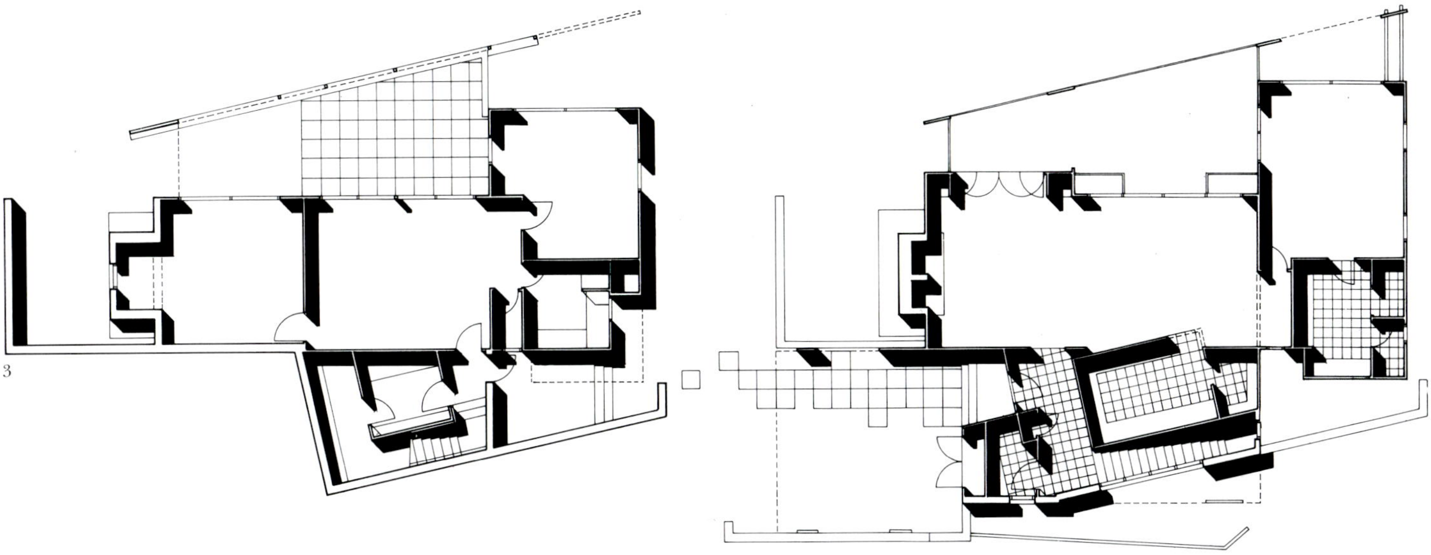

3

4

5

Engehurst Competition

Design 1980

Upon reflection, The Completion of Engehurst problem has been more pleasurable to contemplate than complete.

There is inherent complexity: to intervene and complete what seems to have been a continual embalming of the original Verge fragment since 1832.

The categories of interest encountered with Engehurst come to mind like subject heading from an old library. What currently exists contains allusions to and permutations of: adventure... mystery... humour... and true romance—loved, love lost—and loved again?

The Verge fragment is merely that; the promise of what it was to come never eventuated. Today Verge's proposition is real only in terms of surreal assemblage. Hence our joy at coining the term 'deja Verge': of intended references to the original Engehurst front; to the metaphysics of de Chirico and the argument of Baird, Graves and Koolhaas.

This is a 'literary' piece of architecture with the plot/scenario/design acknowledging an imagined continuity of time and events, and illustrating past and present urban dreams and symbols.

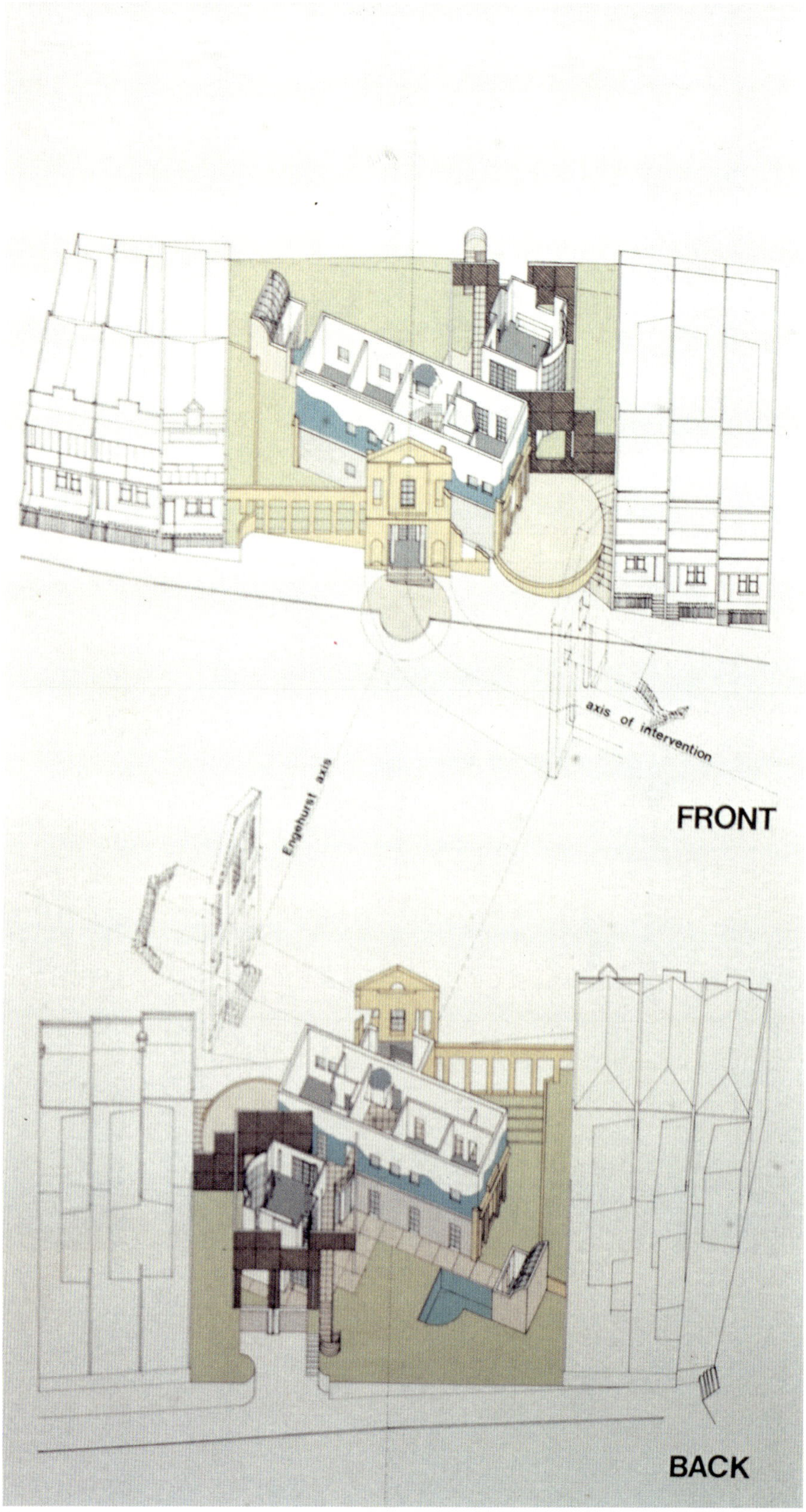

1

1 Axonometric drawings: front and back
2 Elevation and plans

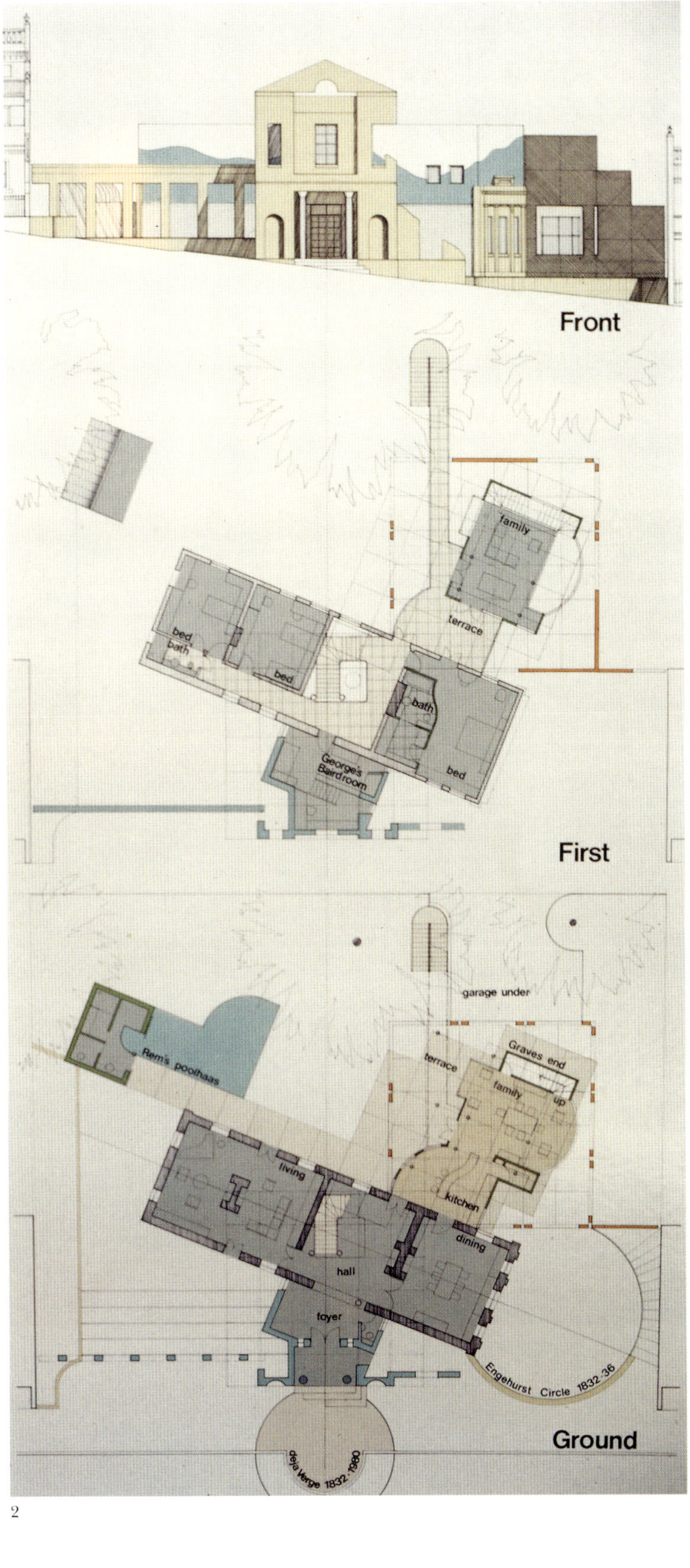

2

The pattern of intervention selectively cuts away the overlay to validate and substantiate the Verge origin, yet conserves built structure. It extracts and resurrects a Verge icon, in the form of the intended portico from the main house, and prescribes a dominant new axis to correlate both existing and new space with the present streetscape.

Astride the new axis, a stair is inserted, illuminated from above by a rooflight. This establishes a place out of which flows the sequence of dwelling spaces. In this place, the ambivalent archetypal notions of the Australian house—formal front and casual back—are brought together.

Through its multivalent layering (Victorian lattice—light filter—verandah?) the new space enclosure at the back reinforces the street axis, accommodates the neighbours and differentiates public from private in a more open form of dwelling endemic to and celebrated in Australian family life. Within this frame varying degrees of interpretation are possible: formal and informal, high style and ad hoc.

If this becomes a 'commentary' beyond the stated confines, then so be it.

Cognition of landscape and orientation to view and sun, complete the hedonistic, pleasurable picture.

In so doing, this completion becomes yet another fragment of consciousness.

Jackson House, Bermagui

Design/Completion 1989/1992
Bermagui, New South Wales
Daryl and Kay Jackson
370 square metres
Timber, corrugated iron, cement render to concrete blockwork, timber-framed windows

The house is a collection of rooms held together by a high wall which folds around the contoured hilltop to create the interior—an open courtyard edged by a large veranda. The rooms are connected only by the exterior, providing a cellular monastic separation. The elevation is a consistently structured section, the skillion reflecting the land contours.

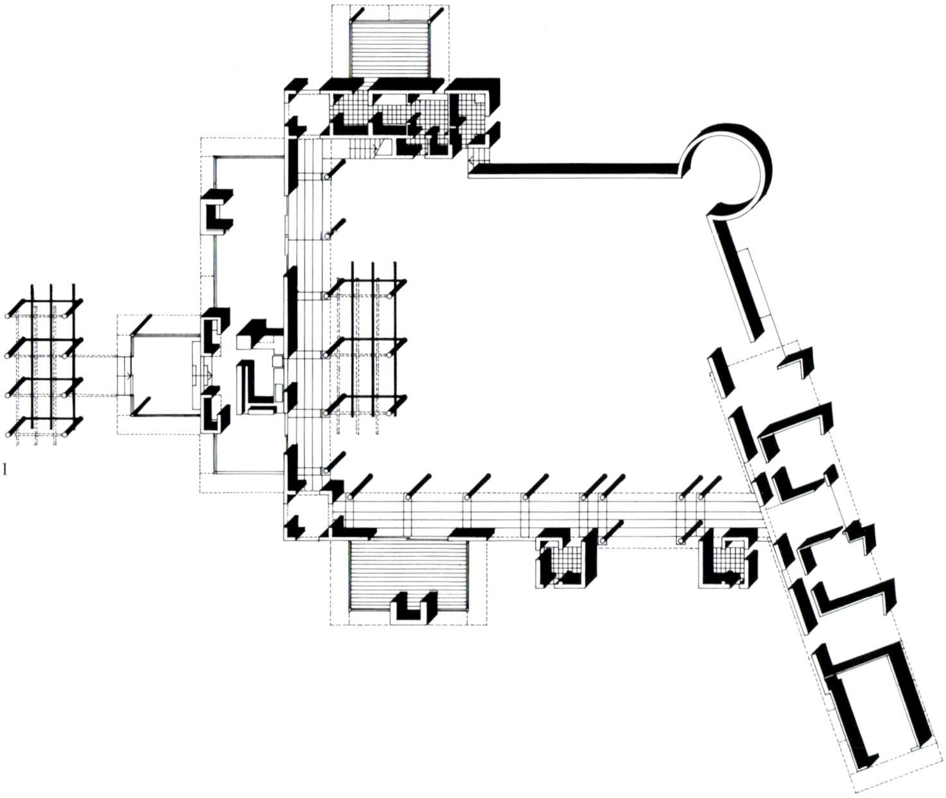

1

2

1 Ground-floor plan
2 Profile
3 Detail

3

4 Courtyard
5 Exploded axonometric
6 Hill from lake
7 Elevation to river

4

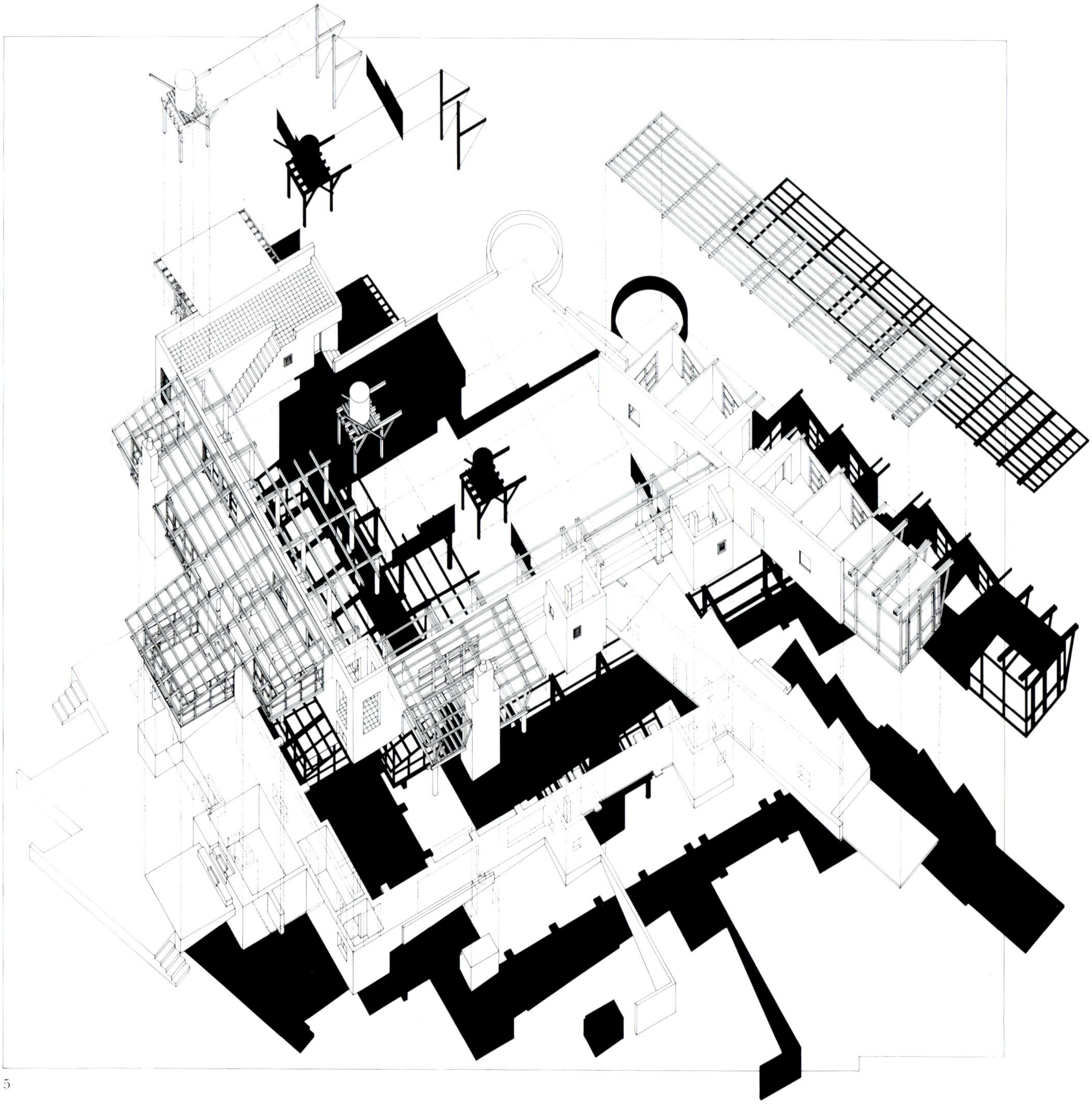

5

6

7

Jackson House, Shoreham

Design/Completion 1976/1977
Shoreham, Victoria
Daryl and Kay Jackson
310 square metres
Timber, corrugated iron

This house has to contend with the landscape; with a pioneer timber slab and mud cottage some 120 years old; and with a marvellous, white pre-Captain Cook eucalypt, all on a hillside dropping away to a creek. The building evokes an Australian understanding of place-making: a solid, not-too-refined corrugated iron and timber exterior, supported on bush poles set down as a structural field.

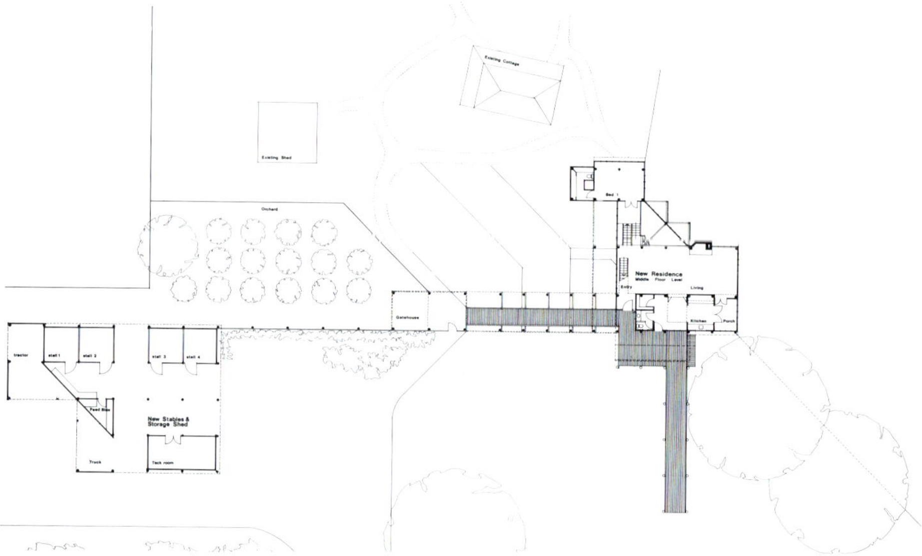

1

2

3

4

1 Floor plan
2 Hillside view
3 Interior
4 Garden
5 Axonometric study
6 Entrance

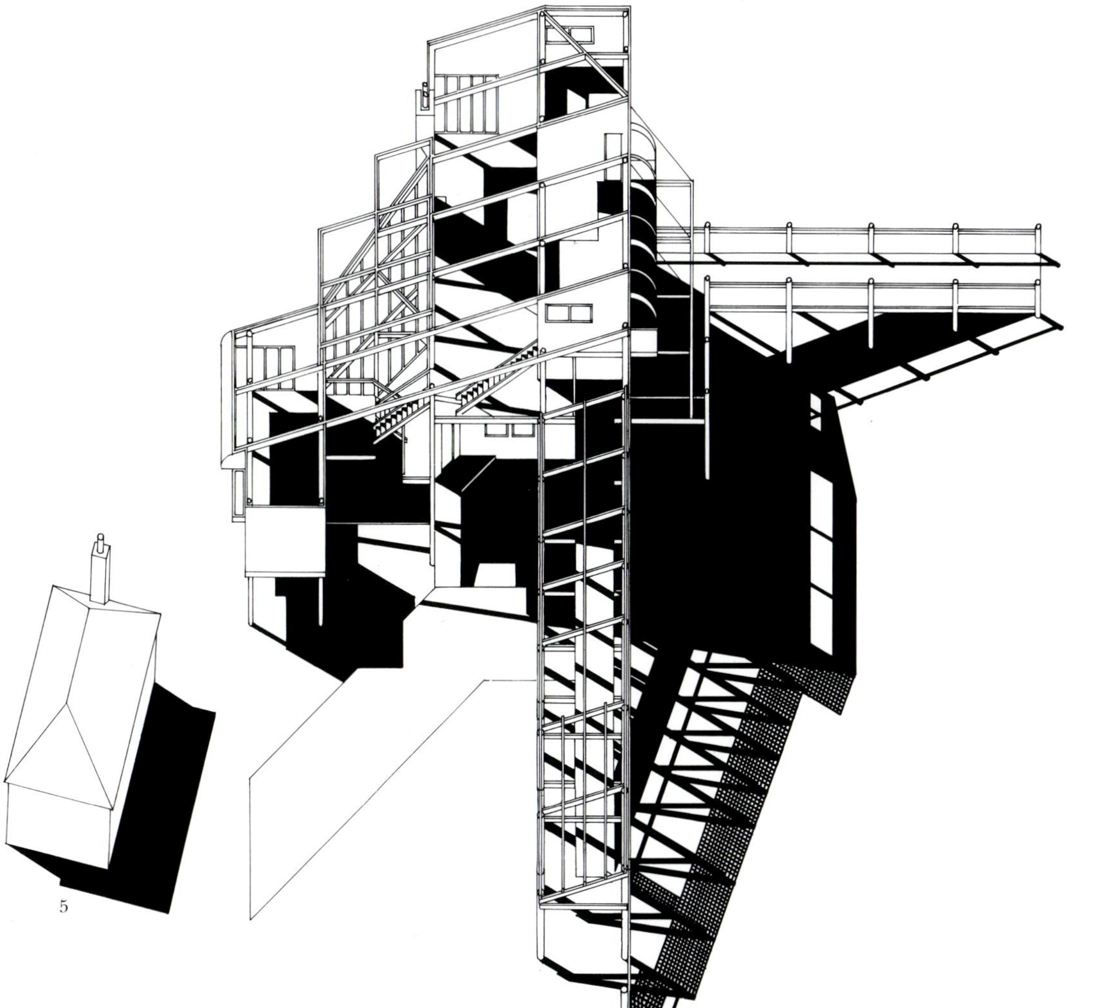

5

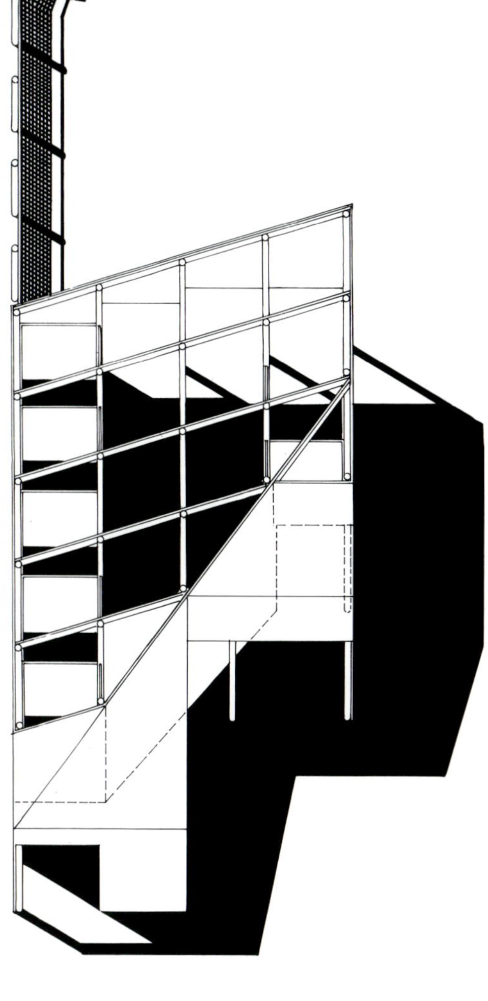

6

Emu Ridge Housing

Design/Completion 1975/1979
Belconnen, Australian Capital Territory
National Capital Development Commission
Architects: Daryl Jackson Evan Walker
12,000 square metres
Concrete frame, concrete brick and metal deck roofing

Public housing is important. This group of apartments ties in to the Belconnen Town Centre and to the Emu Ridge townhouses lower down the slope.

The architecture uses a system of shared staircases, dividing party walls, punched windows and darkly shaded extended balconies. White brick walls are massed to form larger-scale "cubes" which step with the slope. A footbridge to the town centre, which formed part of the composition, has not been built.

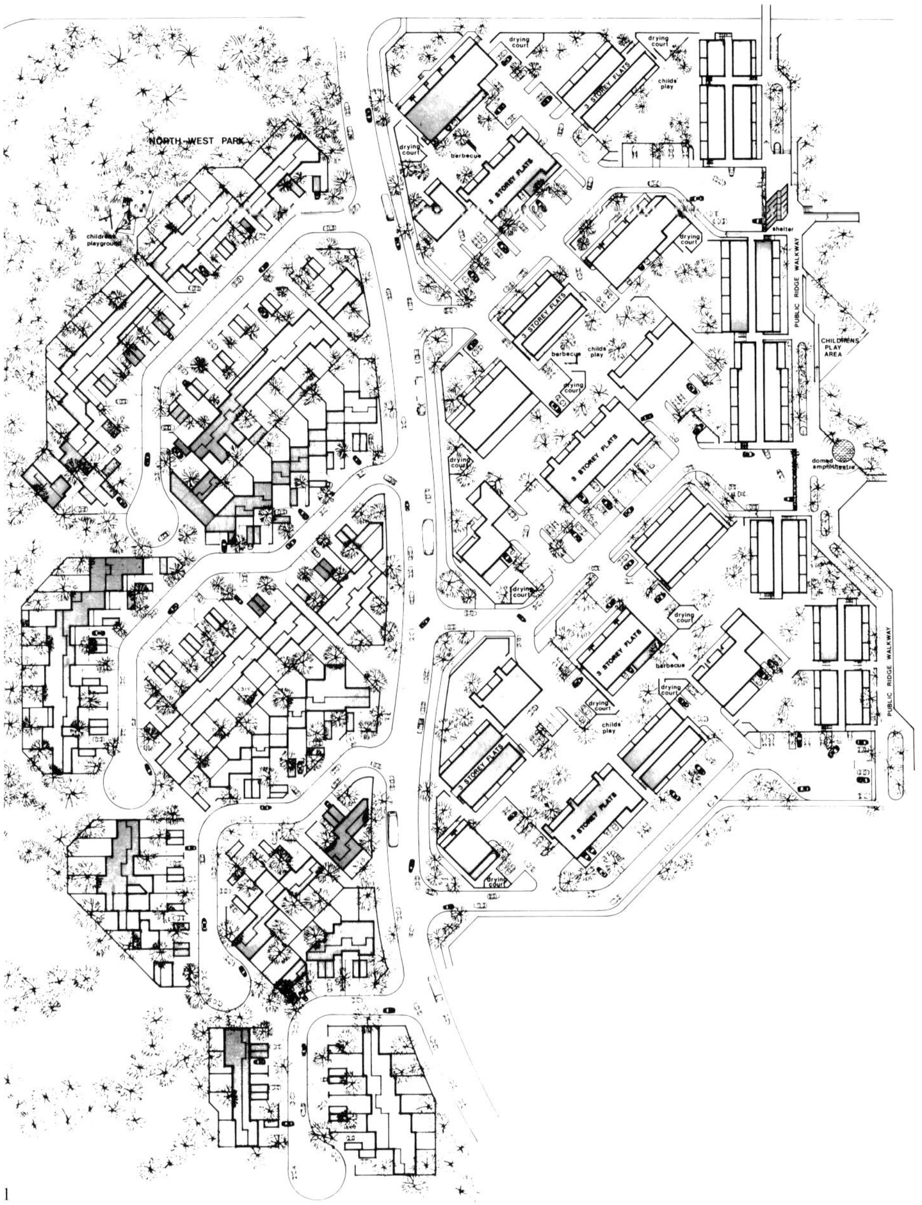

1

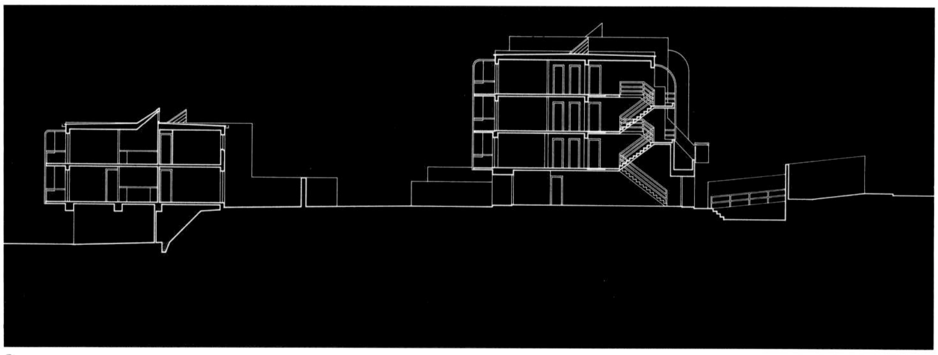

2

1 Overall site plan
2-3 Sections
4 Balcony detail

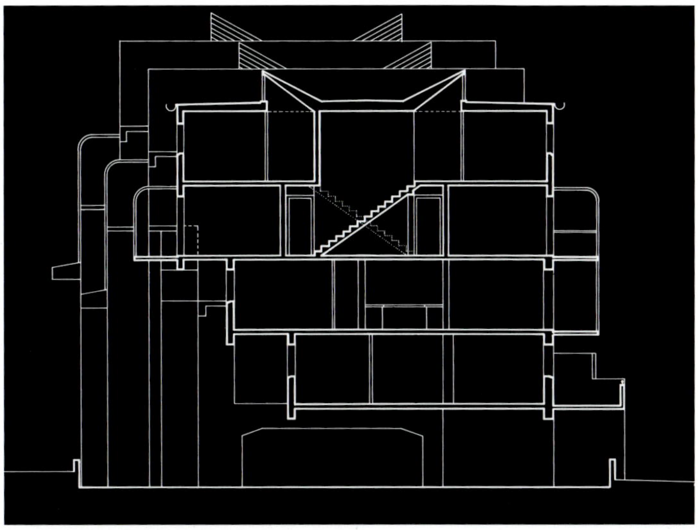

3

4

Belconnen Housing

Design/Completion 1984/1986
Belconnen, Australian Capital Territory
National Capital Development Commission
Architects: Daryl Jackson Evan Walker
Banded red brickwork and green metal deck roofing

There is a mix of housing types in this development. Along the curved road at the top of the hill, a "wall" of apartments bridges across to the street. Lower down the hill, groups of townhouses, each with separate car spaces and gardens, face the view and address the vehicular access street.

The solid red brick walls are banded in white horizontals to establish the idea of platforms on the hill; the sweeping balconies form a counter-curve to the hill and are designed as a "release" from the otherwise controlled and closed form.

1

2

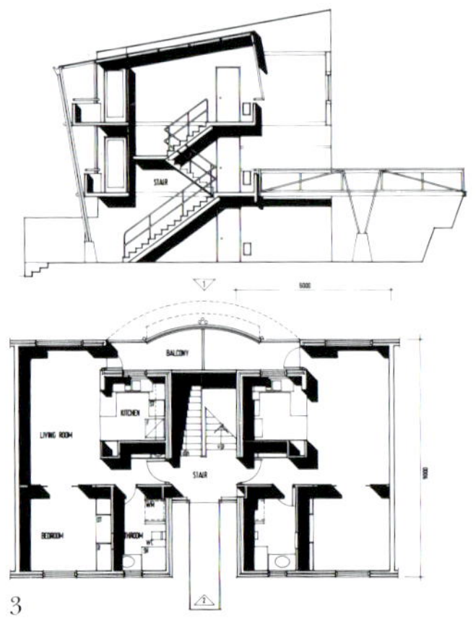

3

4

7

8

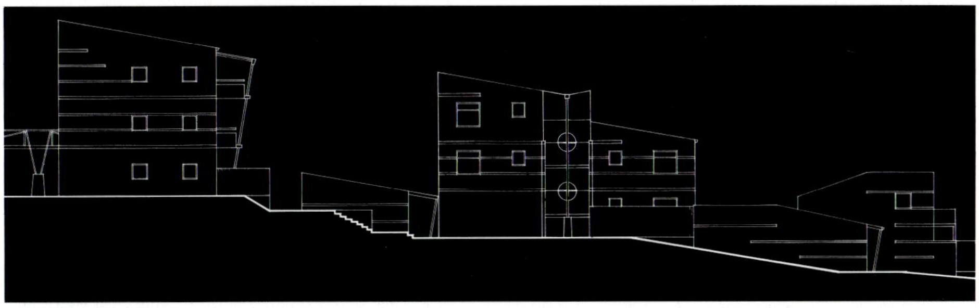

5

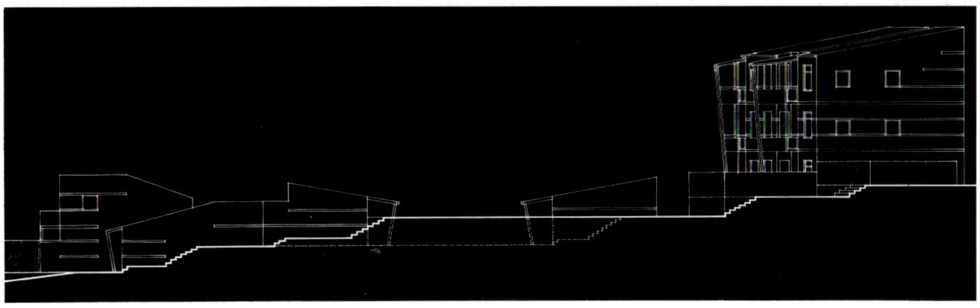

6

1 Site plan
2 Entry bridge
3 Typical section and unit plan
4 Apartments
5 South elevation
6 North elevation
7 Lake view
8 Housing wall

SELECTED AND CURRENT WORKS

Competition/Project

Porta Di Roma, Rome

Design 1987
Rome, Italy
Bond Corporation
Planning study

Imagine a large new town shopping/distribution centre on the edge of Rome, within the Anulare where it intersects the autostrada from Florence. Four major international department stores anchor the specialist tenancies. A covered and shaded street market introduces Italian urbanity: food and fashion, industrial design and regional craftsmanship. Supporting the centre are areas of offices, hotels, housing, gardens and lakes, a sports complex and car parking.

The planning authorities in Rome found it difficult to imagine.

1

1 Master plan
2-3 Aerial view of model

2

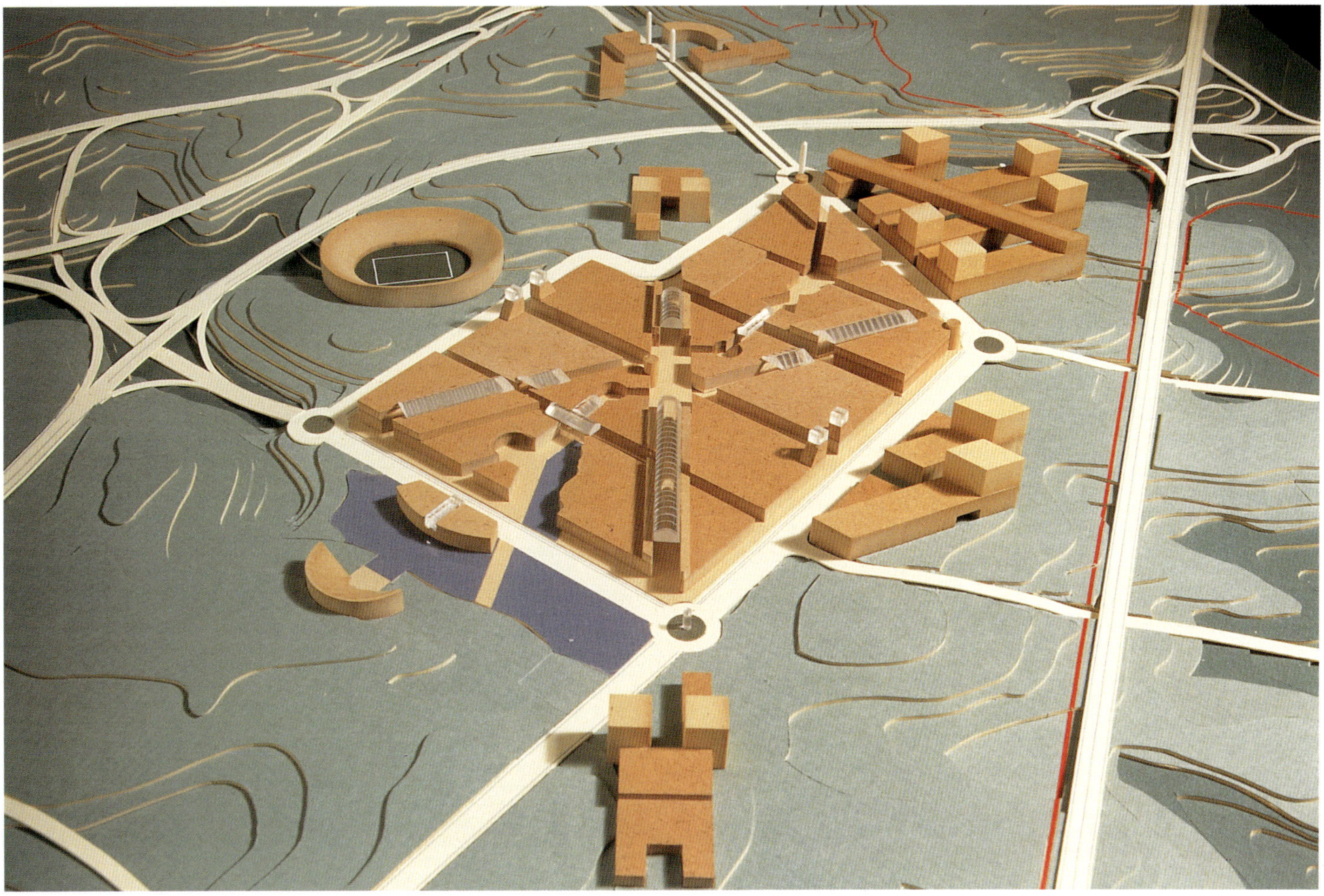

3

Olympic Dockland

Design 1988
Melbourne, Victoria
Melbourne Olympic Committee
Planning study

Seldom do cities have to promote themselves to the extent required for an Olympic bid. Sports complexes are projected or updated and a new residential sector for teams of athletes and the media is required.

Melbourne's docklands, no longer necessary for major shipping and located very close to the city centre, were our ideal venue for a water-based residential and mixed-use precinct in the city's bid for the 1996 Games. Following the Games, the development could be turned over to the general public.

The plan form extended Melbourne's distinguishing grid of 30-metre wide streets and 100-metre square blocks. In the new vision, the roads become canals and the blocks remain. As an overlay idea it entreats with the Melbourne historic plan as emblem: a positive/negative reversal of land to water. The bid was lost to Atlanta.

1

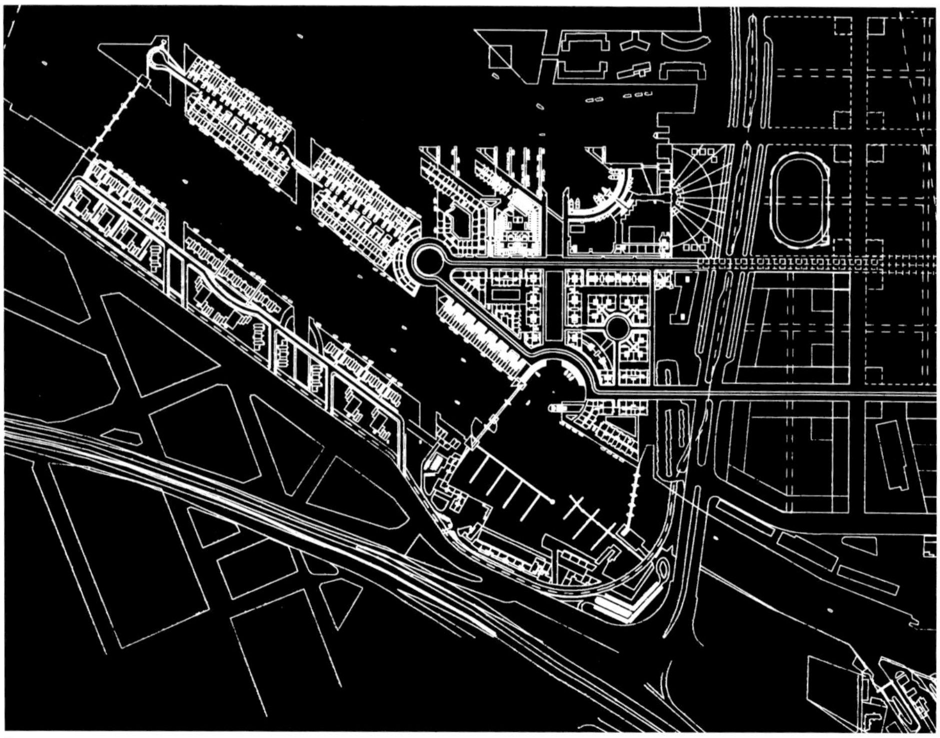

2

1 Plan of Melbourne CBD and context
2 Proposal plan
3 Aerial view of model
4 Plan view of model

3

4

Museum of Scotland, Edinburgh

Design 1991

The project for an addition to the Royal Museum of Scotland, Edinburgh was intended to provide critical cultural vision.

Remaining in accord with the scale and form of the existing museum, the new was to give future prospect, whilst existing for itself. It offers opportunity and complexity via co-existence.

A glazed screen connection between old and new links the Venetian arcade; a restaurant at roof level is a transparent "observatory".

1 Plans and section
2 Elevation
3 Section
4 Axonometric

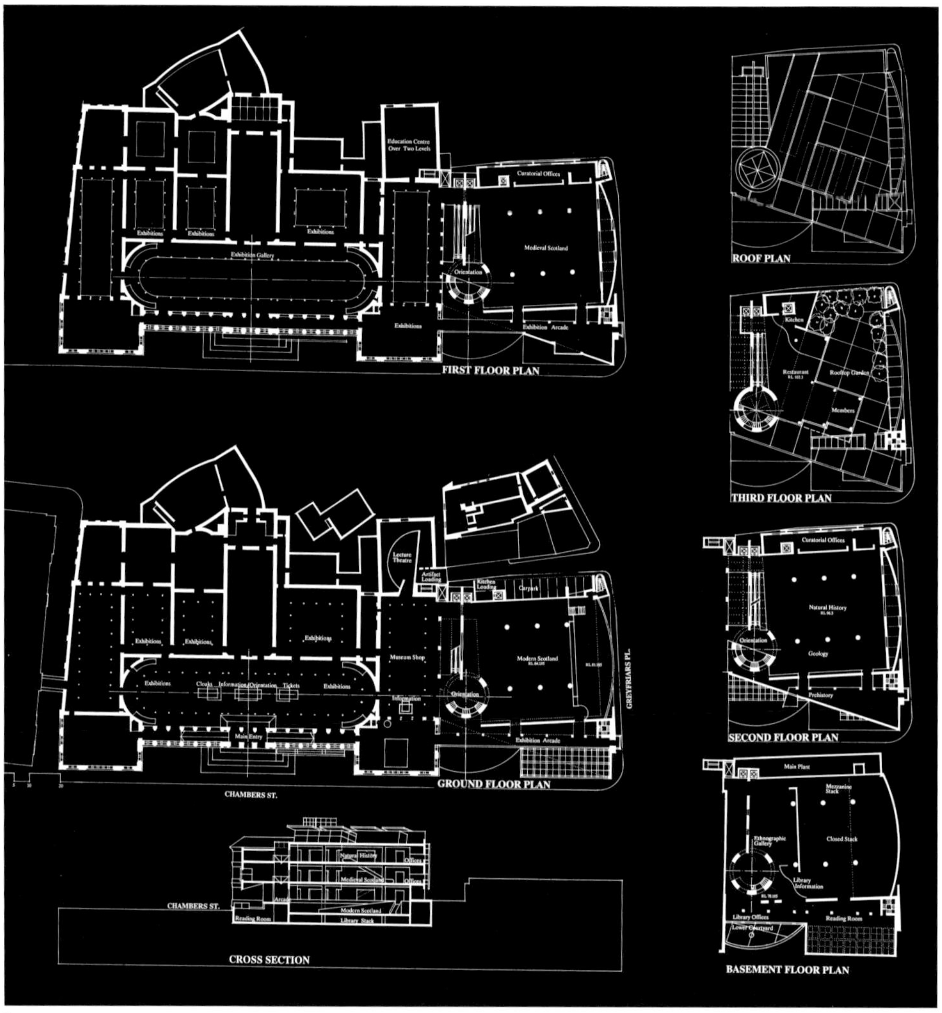

1

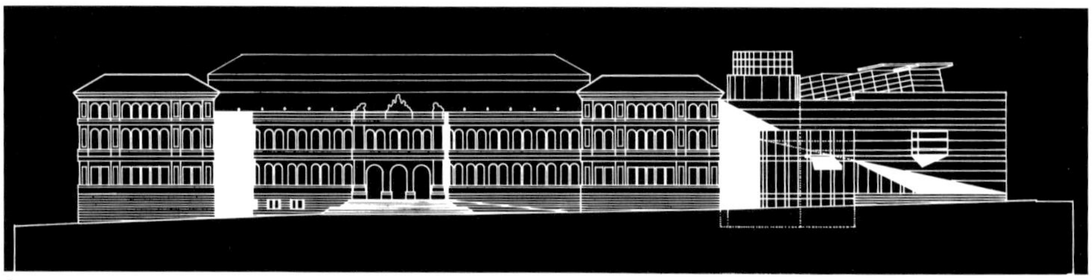

2

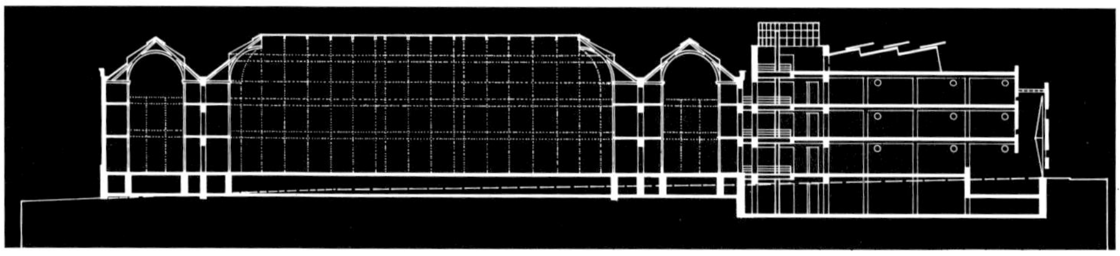

3

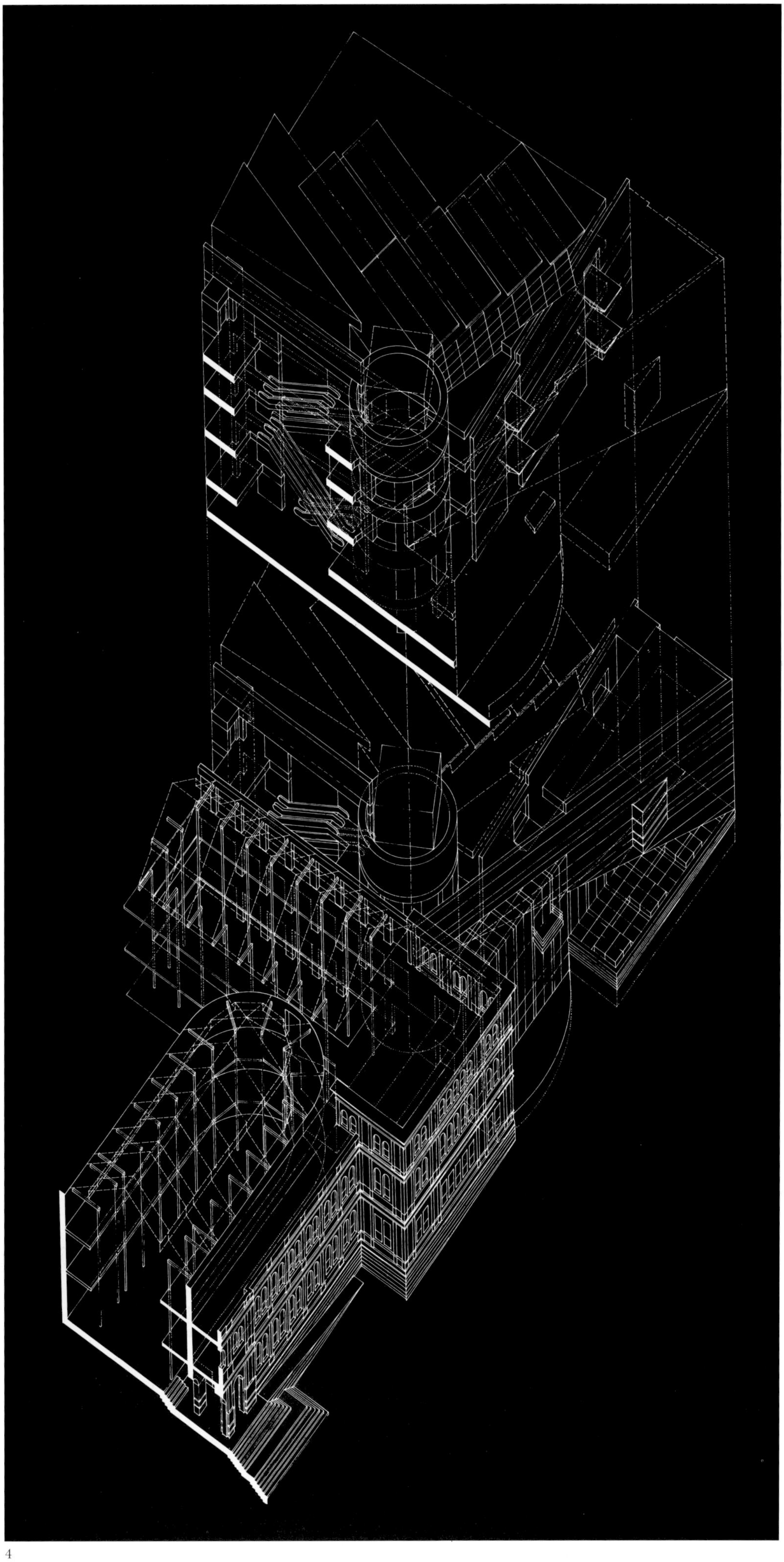

4

Museum of Victoria, Carlton Gardens

Design 1994
Carlton, Victoria
Major Project Unit and the Museum of Victoria
40,000 square metres
In situ concrete frame, metal cladding
Competition entry

The Carlton Gardens Museum Project invents itself within an established, mature 19th century garden. The form of the museum is designed to work in parallel with the Brunelleschi-inspired Exhibition Buildings, constructed in 1879.

An axial, skeletal form opens out to the gardens as in a pavilion with paired, enclosed exhibition halls forming museum courtyards between old and new buildings. The buildings are physically connected via an underground route, allowing them to work together for major exhibitions, yet also work independently.

Entry to the museum is from each street frontage; visitors move through a concourse to a central ticket/information area. Escalators move visitors to upper levels where a "live" exhibit is located above the halls. From this level there are views towards the city and across the gardens.

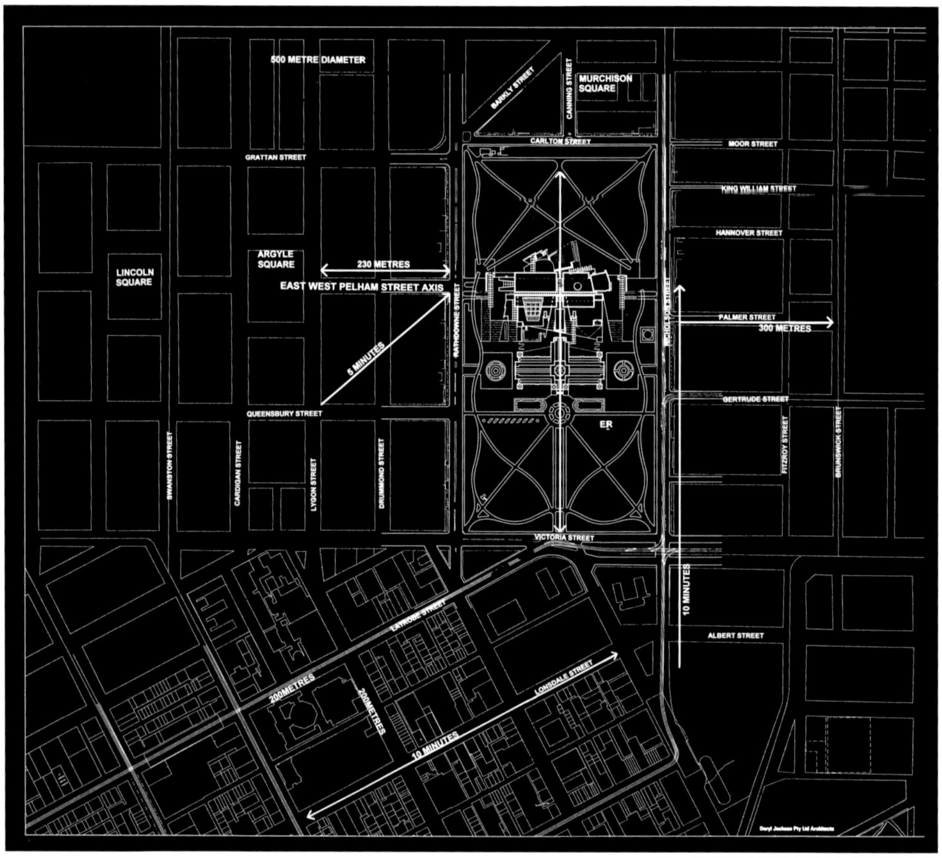

1

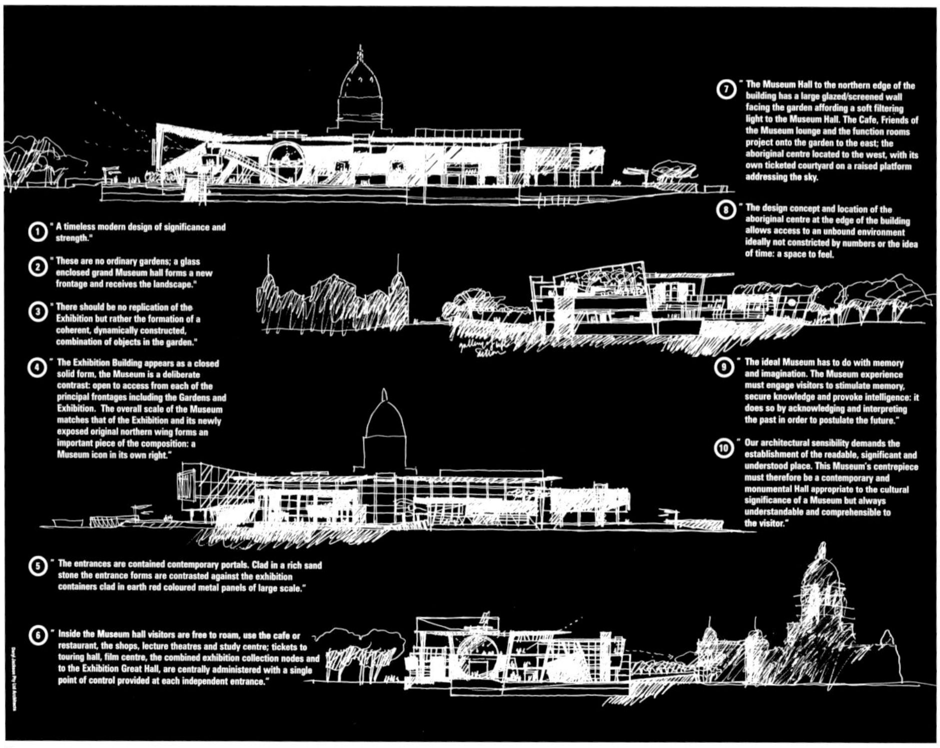

2

1 Site and location plan
2 Design sketches and notations
3-5 Exterior view: model

3

4

5

6

6 South Plaza and Great Hall from museum
7 Floor plan
8 Museum Hall from Nicholson Street entrance
9-10 Sections

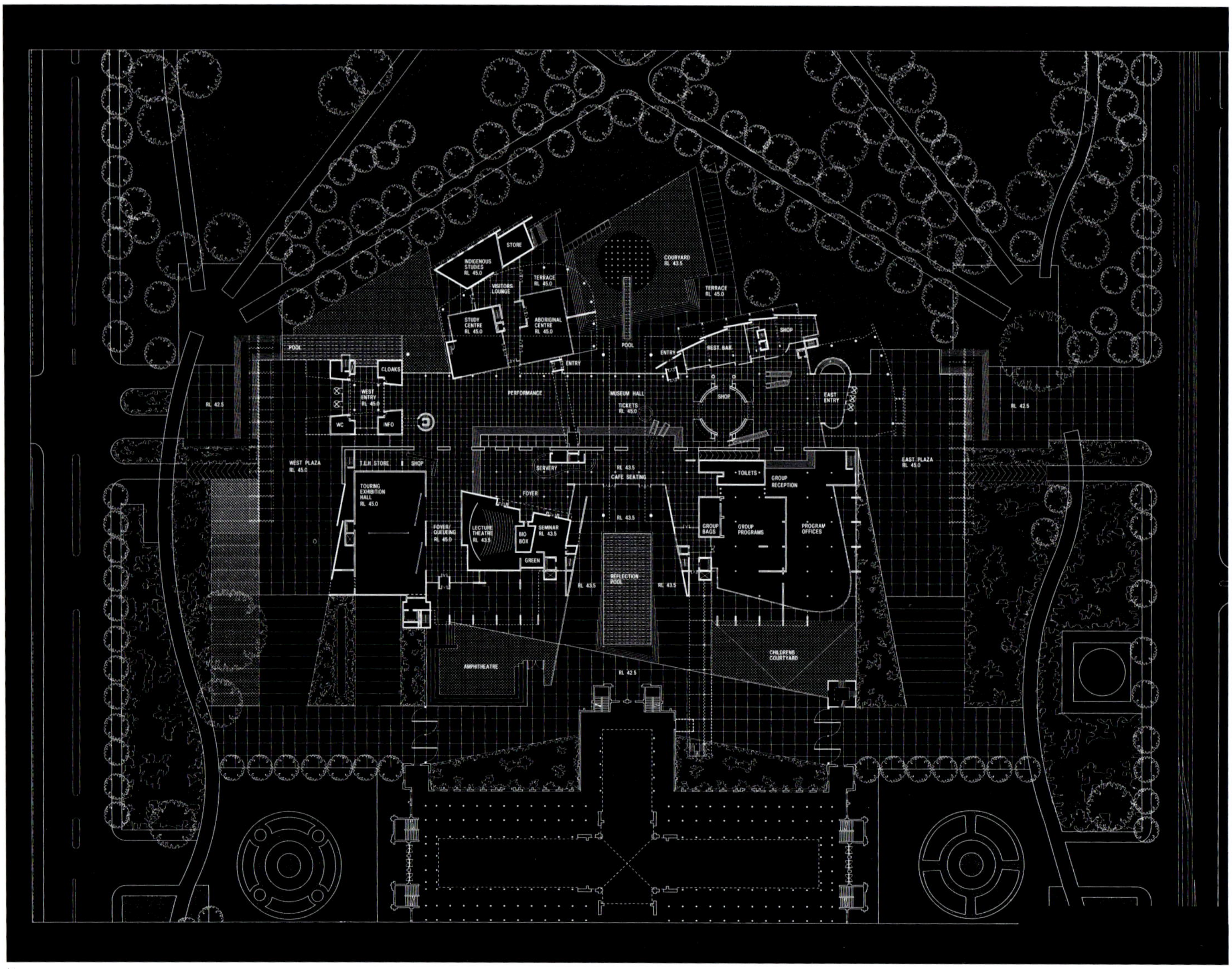

7

8

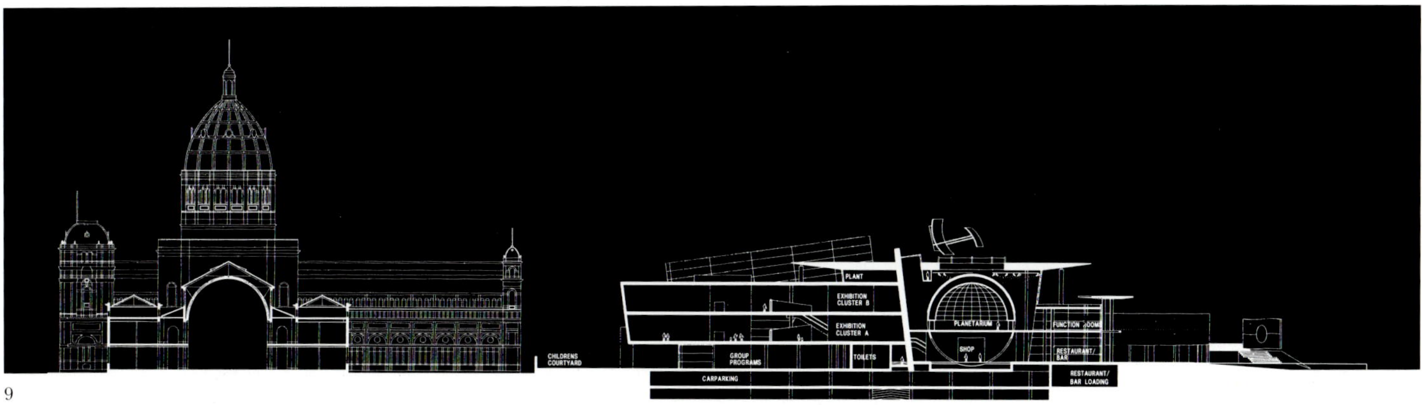

CHILDRENS COURTYARD
PLANT
EXHIBITION CLUSTER B
EXHIBITION CLUSTER A
PLANETARIUM
SHOP
FUNCTION ROOMS
RESTAURANT/ BAR
GROUP PROGRAMS
TOILETS
CARPARKING
RESTAURANT/ BAR LOADING

9

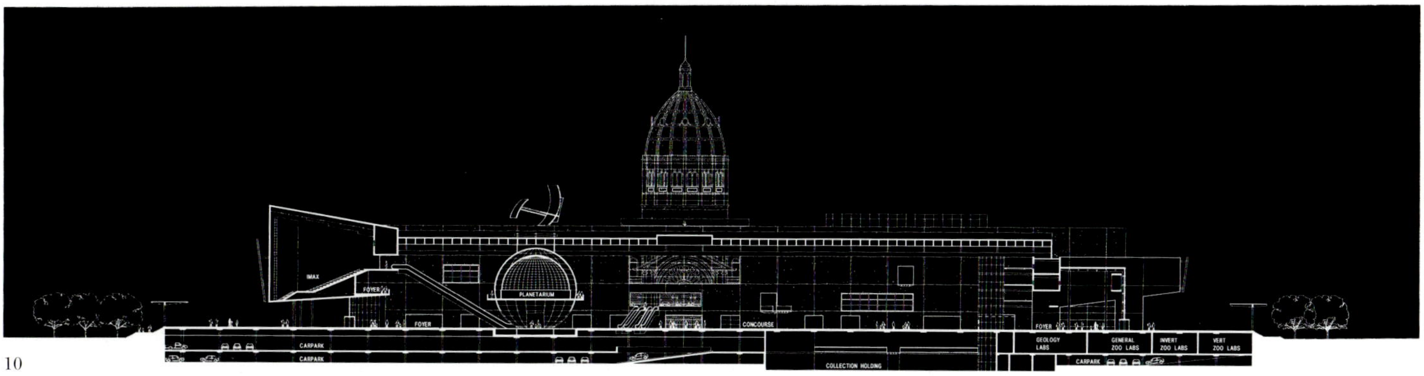

IMAX
FOYER
PLANETARIUM
FOYER
CONCOURSE
CARPARK
CARPARK
COLLECTION HOLDING
GEOLOGY LABS
GENERAL ZOO LABS
INVERT ZOO LABS
VERT ZOO LABS
CARPARK

10

Museum of Victoria, Southbank

Design 1988
Southbank, Victoria
Victorian Ministry for the Arts
60,000 square metres
Concrete frame with post-tensioned floor slabs; precast concrete and metal panel cladding; metal deck roofing

Through reference to its collections, the modern museum is a place of learning and discovery. A museum should also illustrate ideas and concepts which fuel mankind's imagination and allow us to continually transcend past vision. A New Age museum must also be a place of entertainment and social experience.

As object, Melbourne's newest museum consists of a grouping of recognisable parts, each with its own identity, such that visitors can easily identify their journey. A large interior gallery served by escalators links four low-rise public levels and offers vertical progression to the journey. Along the way one can see the thematic ideas which link the content to the architecture. Such information ought to be easy for everyone to understand and read, yet continue to stimulate inquiry. The real objective is to project the collection into the next century, for yet another age of visitors.

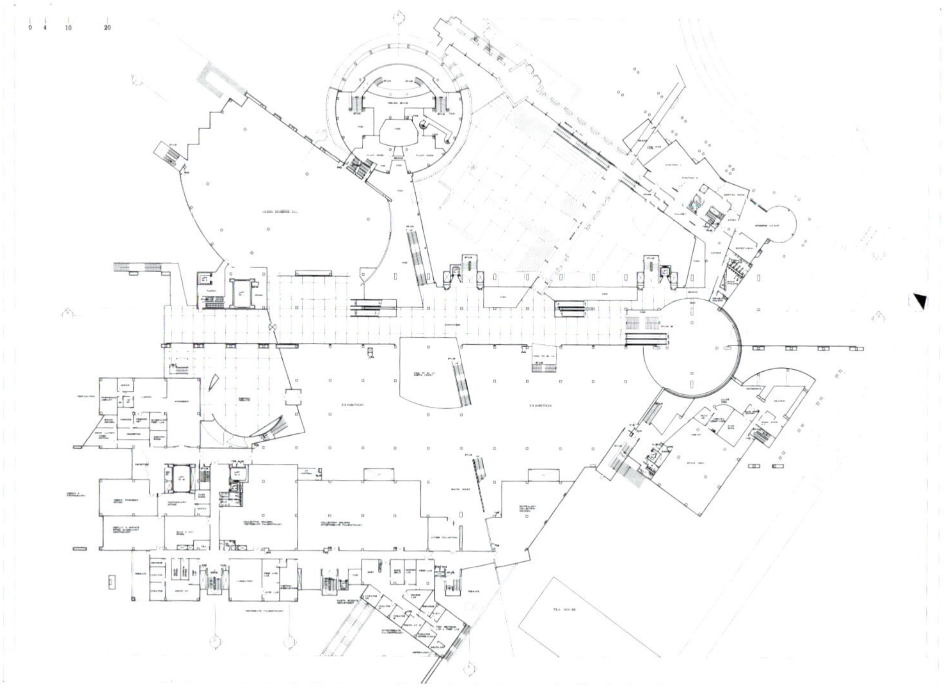

1

2

1 Floor plan
2 Aerial view of model
3 Courtyard and river edge
4 Courtyard and planetarium
5 River front

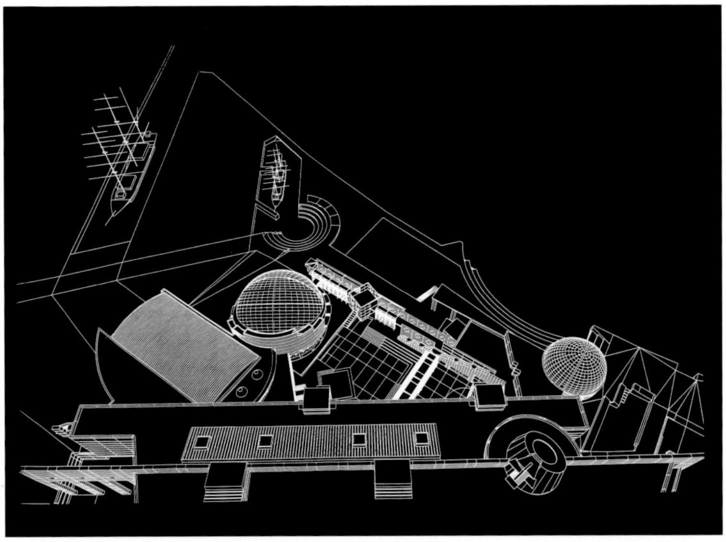
3

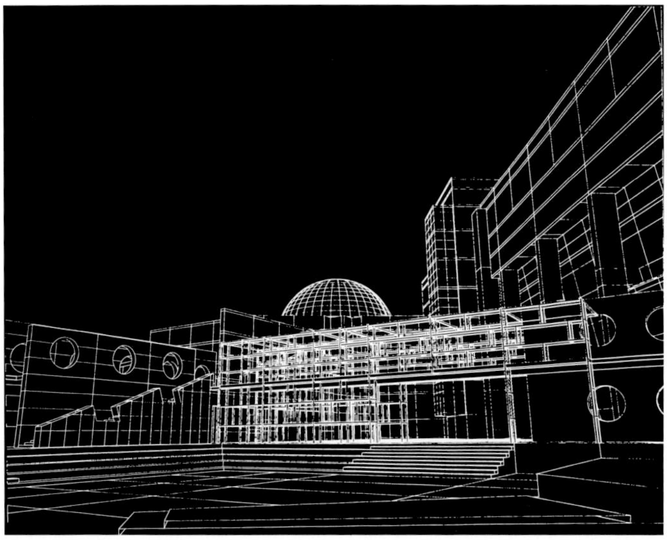
4

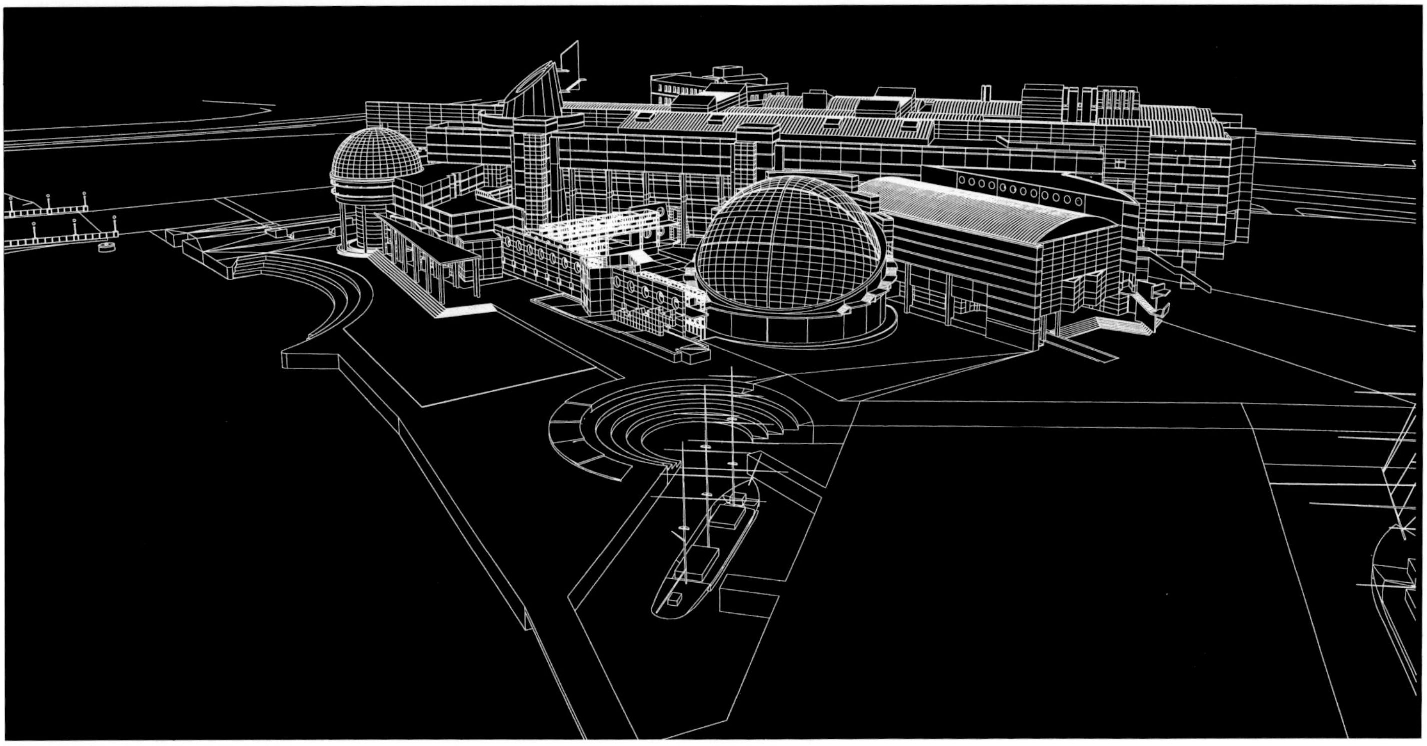
5

6 Cutaway photo of model
7 Model
8 Section
9 Model
10 Section

6

7

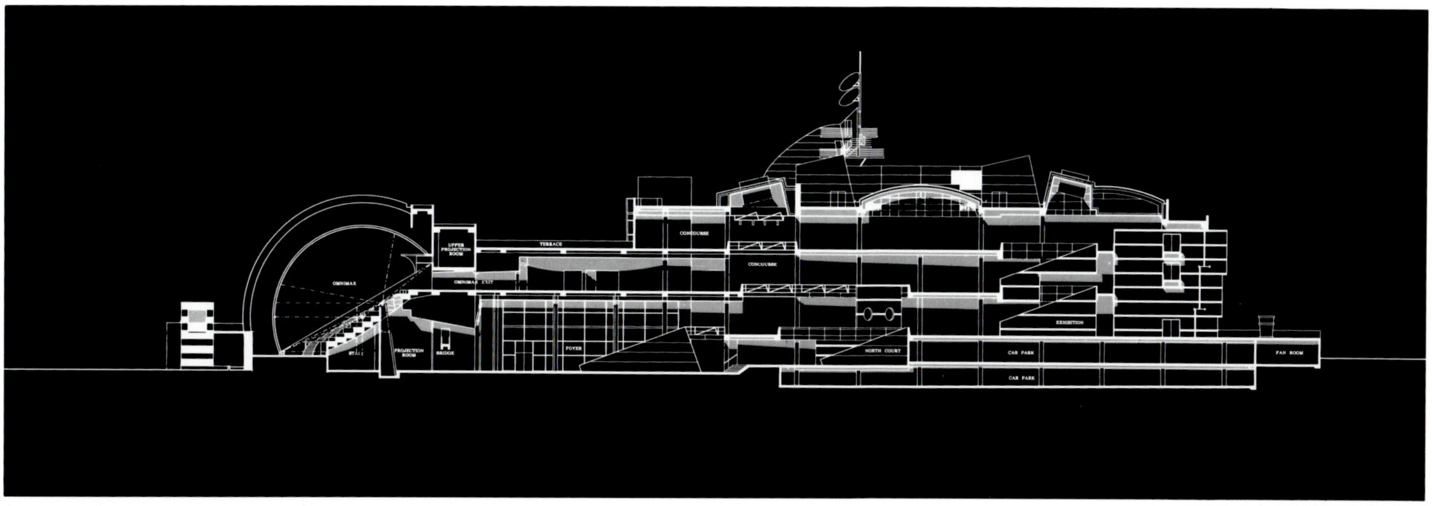
UPPER PROJECTION ROOM
TERRACE
CONCOURSE
CONCOURSE
OMNIMAX
OMNIMAX EXIT
PROJECTION ROOM
BRIDGE
FOYER
NORTH COURT
EXHIBITION
CAR PARK
FAN ROOM
CAR PARK

8

9

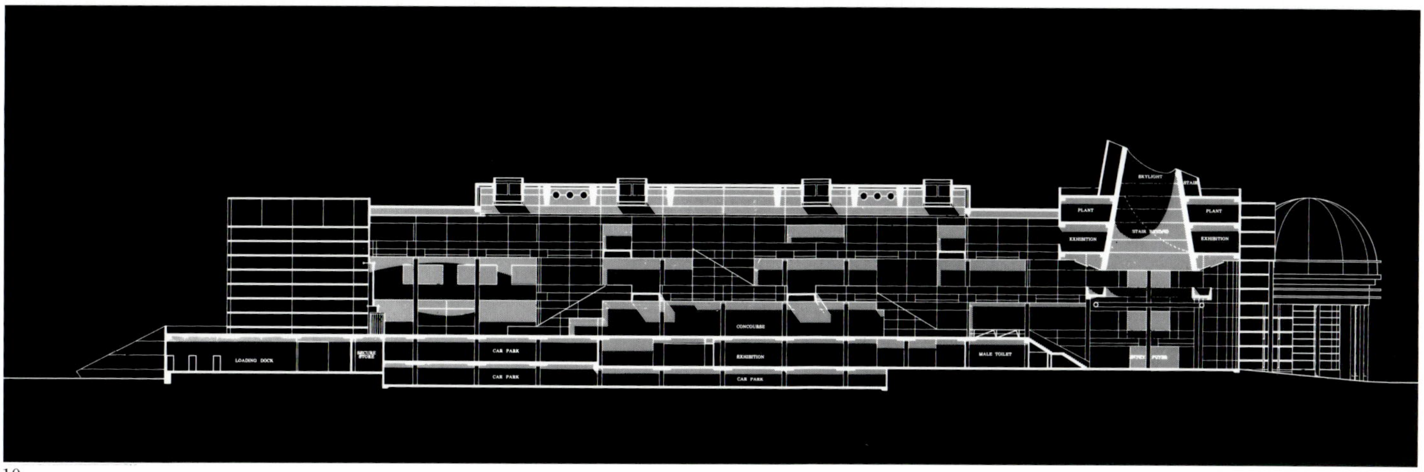
SKYLIGHT
STAIR
PLANT
PLANT
EXHIBITION
EXHIBITION
CONCOURSE
LOADING DOCK
SECURE STORE
CAR PARK
EXHIBITION
MALE TOILET
CAR PARK
CAR PARK

10

Station Pier

Design 1985
Port Melbourne, Victoria
State Government of Victoria
Associated architects: Mitchell/Giurgola & Thorp

Two large piers remain at Port Melbourne as useful reminders of Melbourne's original form of international connection. They are no longer used to accommodate outgoing Australian travellers or incoming immigrants.

Their planned re-use is for a mixture of leisure, recreation and housing. Connecting the piers back into their hinterland are a new commercial mixed-use village on one side and a carpet of low-rise housing planned around new waterways on the other. The stretch of water between the piers accommodates aquaria, a major marina, museums and a fun fair. The marina incorporates a series of townhouses built over the water.

The axes of the piers are reversed into the land form to construct one layer of plan organisation. Surrounding street alignments are brought into the scheme to draw existing and new morphology together.

1

2

1 Site and location plan
2 Aerial view from the land
3 Axial connections
4 Existing morphology integrated
5 Plan view

3

4

5

Crown Casino, Southbank

Design 1992

South Melbourne, Victoria

Hudson Conway

Associate architects: Bates Smart McCutcheon; Perrot Lyon Mathieson Pty Ltd

40,000 square metres

Concrete frame and post-tensioned floor slabs, bandstone granite and metal cladding

We called Melbourne's first casino design the "fifth garden". Facing the riverfront promenade, a large three-storey high edge of building houses the restaurant and hotel functions and entertainments that benefit from an outlook. The next layer within consists of casino gaming, cinemas and virtual reality areas.

Above the low-rise mass, a 400-room hotel is poised, facing the river and centre city beyond. The form is that of a ship, with rooms on each side of a central spine looking up and down the river, as well as over the pleasure gardens and games areas of the immediate roofscape. Pools, fountains, telescopic towers, belvederes and an interior flywheel are all objects of entertainment.

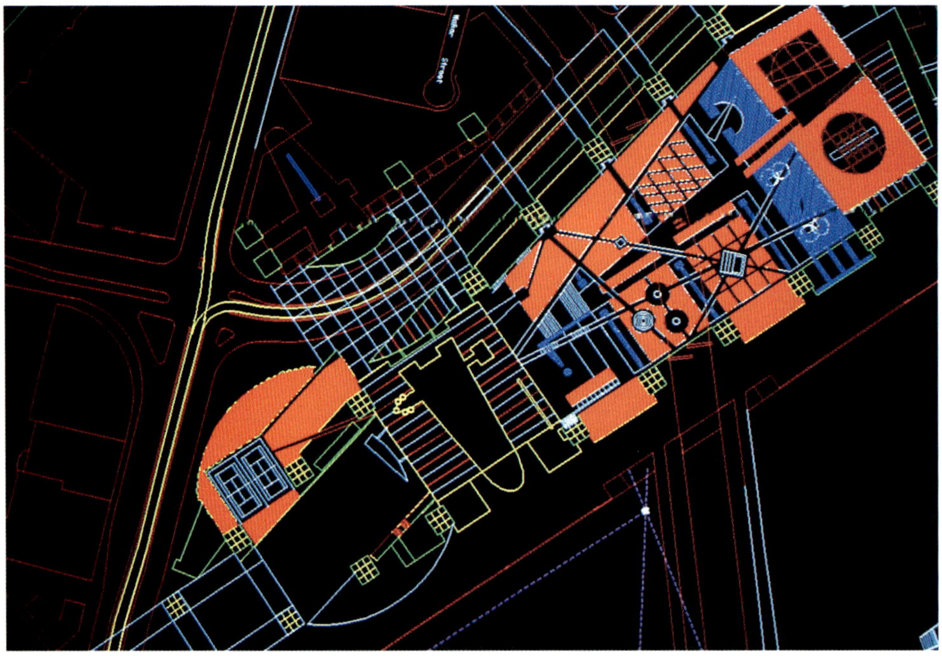

1

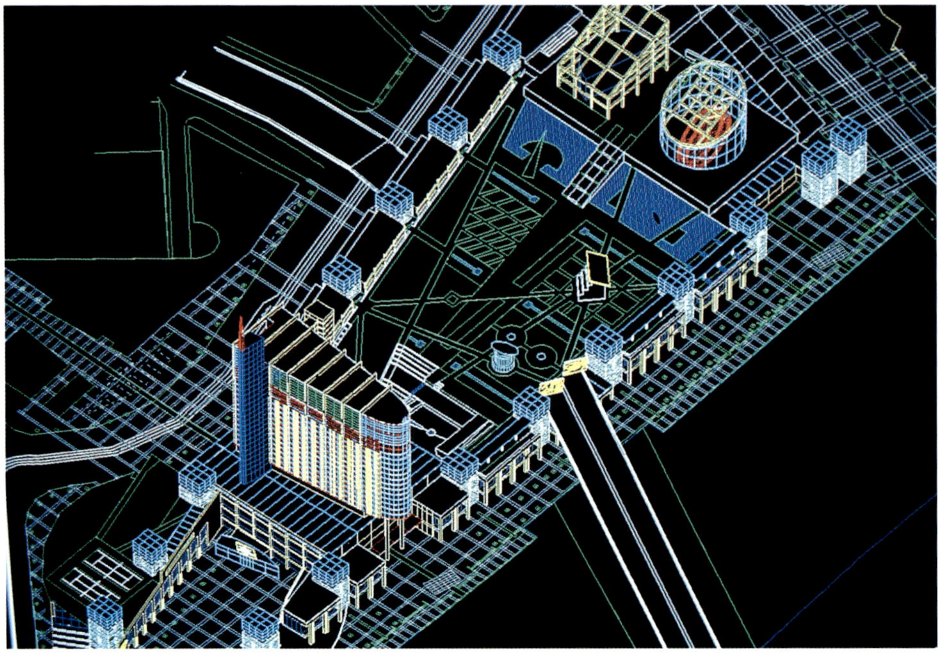

2

1 Plan

2 Axonometric

3 Photomontage

3

Garden Pavilion, Wales

Design 1993
Wales, United Kingdom
Welsh Garden Festival Institute of Architects
Architects: Daryl Jackson International Pty Ltd
1,500 square metres
Concrete and steel

The design consists of an exhibition pavilion constructed on a former valley slag heap in Wales. Views down the valley are significant, and the reinterpretation of an industrial landscape is a major challenge.

A structured platform projects the visitor into a space above the cliff face, with exhibits displayed in a small square above. A narrow defile cut into the waste connects these two elements. The assemblage heightens the tactile oppositions of base, cantilever and connection.

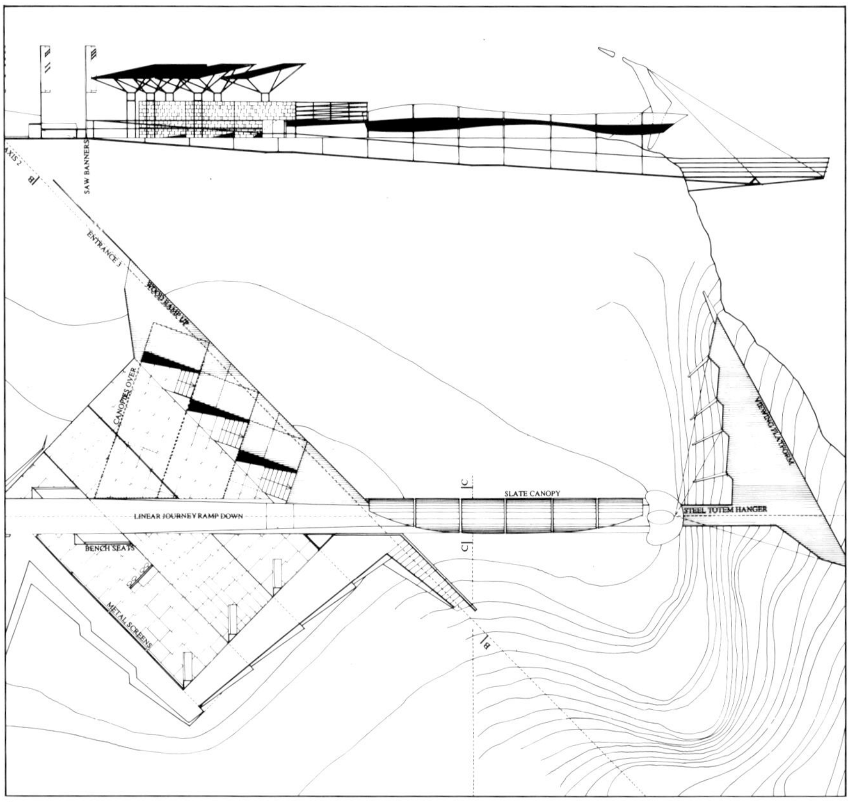

1

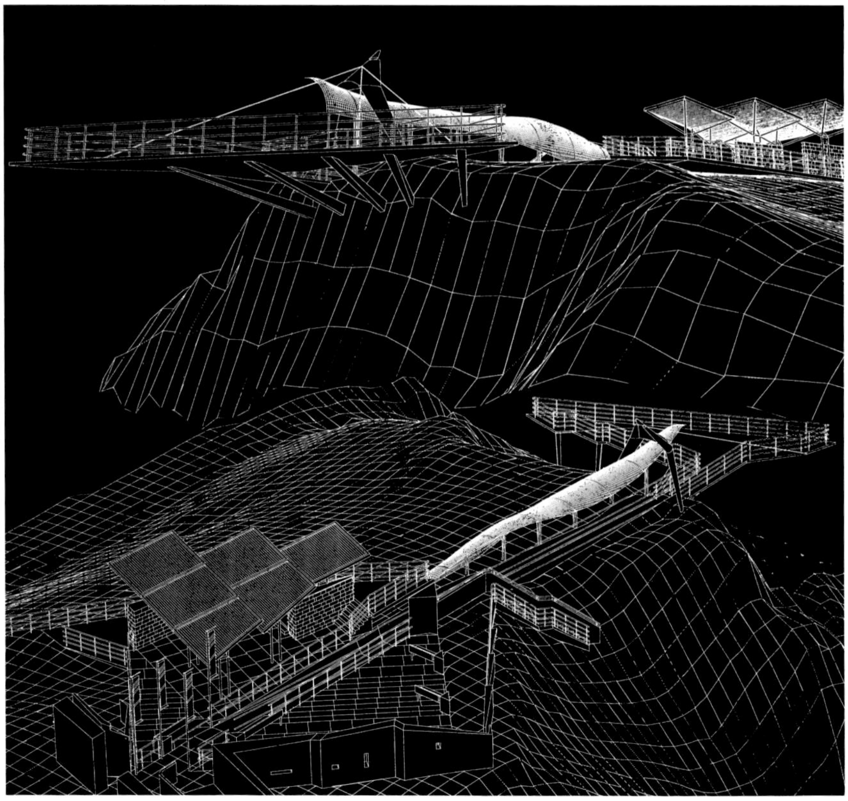
2

1 Plan and section
2 Computer modelling
3 From below
4 Looking in from the edge
5 Aerial view

3

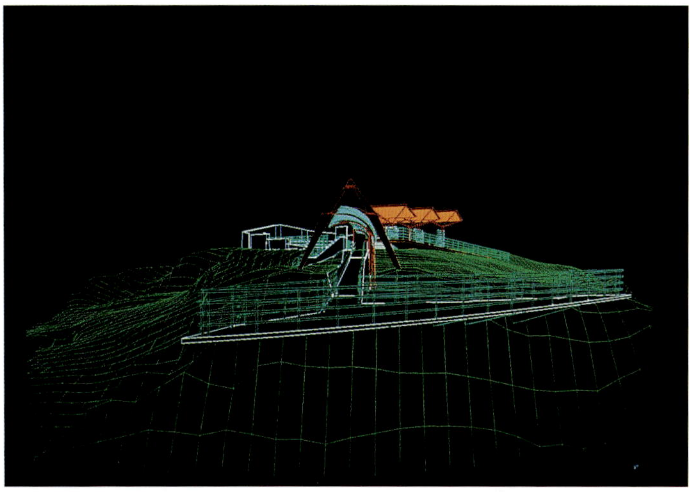

4

5

State Library/Museum of Victoria

Design 1985
Melbourne, Victoria
State Library and Museum Building Committee (Major Projects Unit)
40,000 square metres
In situ concrete; metal cladding; glass
Competition entry

This competition entry illustrates an expansion of the State Library and Museum to an adjacent site across Little Lonsdale Street. Three wings of a former Edwardian hospital were to be conserved and integrated. The design explores the "transfer" of the library's central octagon as a displacement which unites old and new and anchors the composition. There is no replication.

The library section of the scheme explores the idea of a top-lit series of floor plates, dividing the book stacks and offering identity to each section. The ground floor is an open gallery which serves the library's public information and exhibits areas as well as the key elements of the museum's temporary exhibits area. Each upper level element is served via centrally placed escalators and lifts offering the visitor an interior experience through the linear galleria.

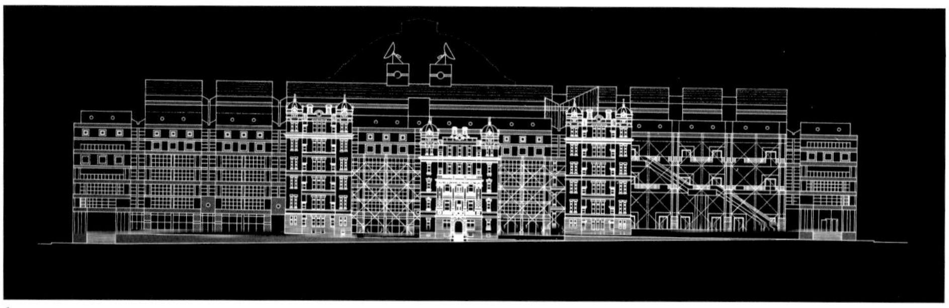

1

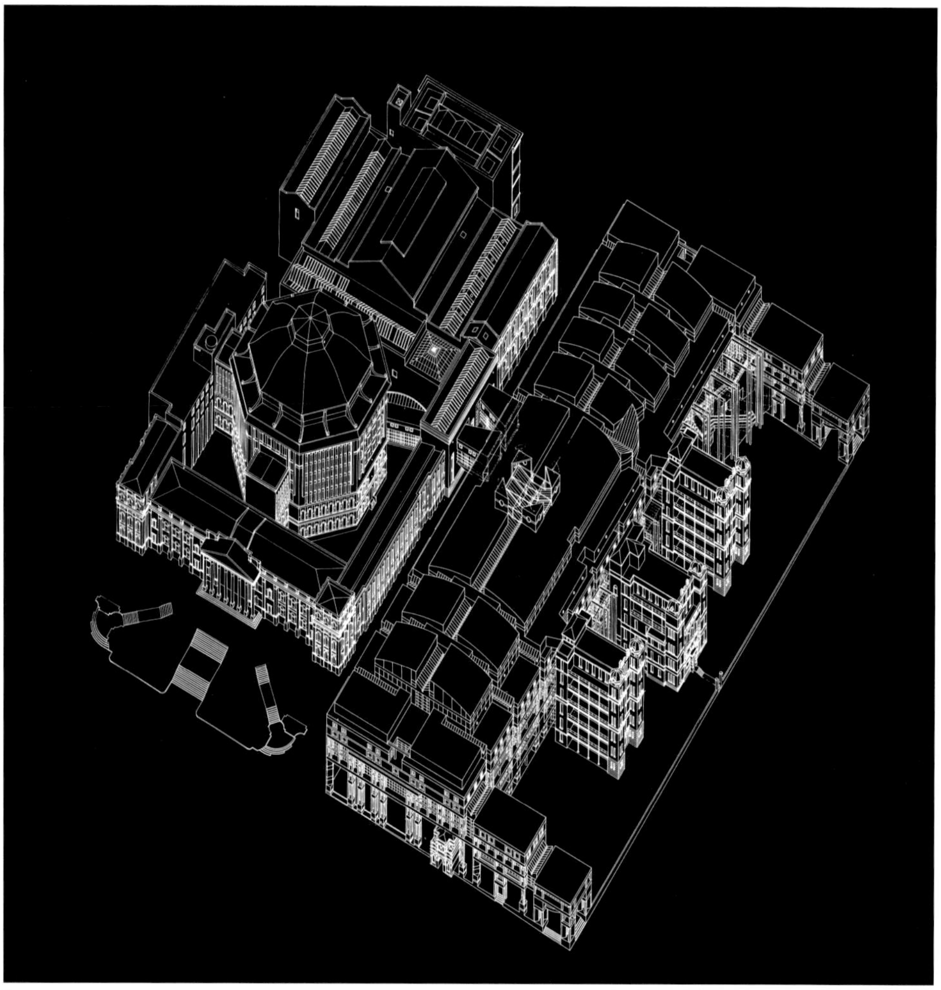

2

1 Elevation
2 Axonometric study
3 Floor plan
4 Roof plan
5 Wire frame perspective

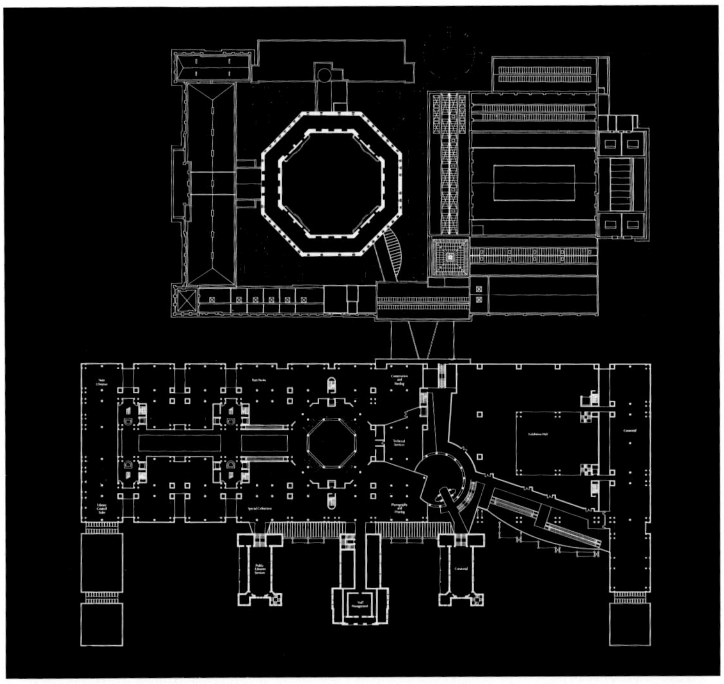

3

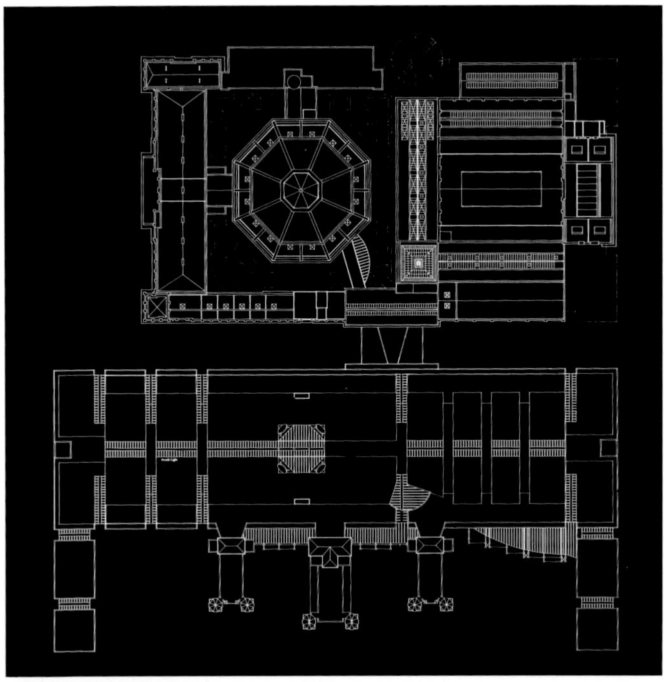

4

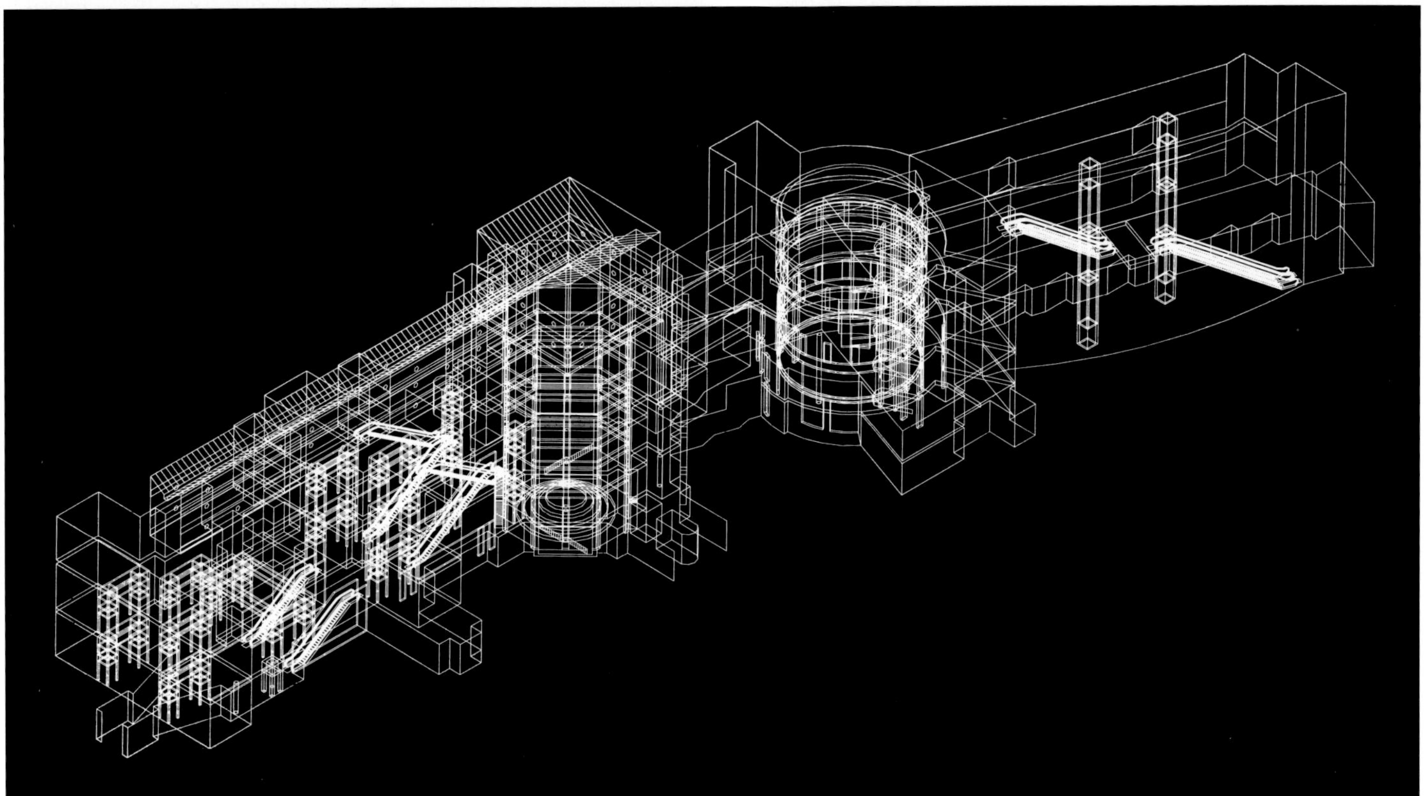

5

Aquarium, Darling Harbour

Design 1986
Sydney, New South Wales
Darling Harbour Authority
4,000 square metres
Architects: Daryl Jackson Robin Dyke Pty Ltd

At the base of Pyrmont Bridge to the north, a new aquarium was designed to reinforce the urban plinth and provide an outstanding visitor experience. A waterfront tower takes the visitors to an upper floor level where the journey starts with a rain shower. Gradually one descends to the fish tanks below and exits.

1

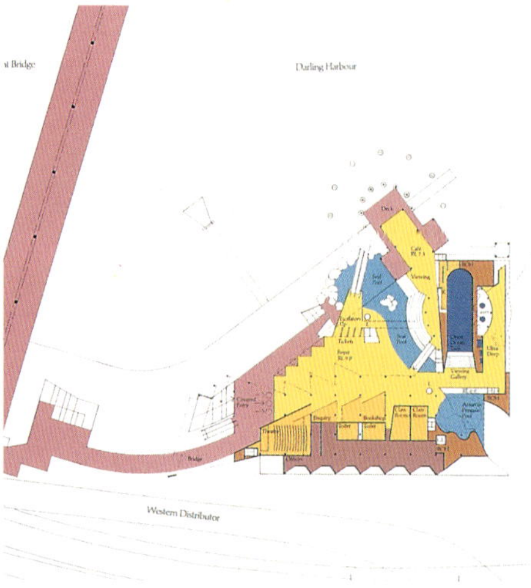

2

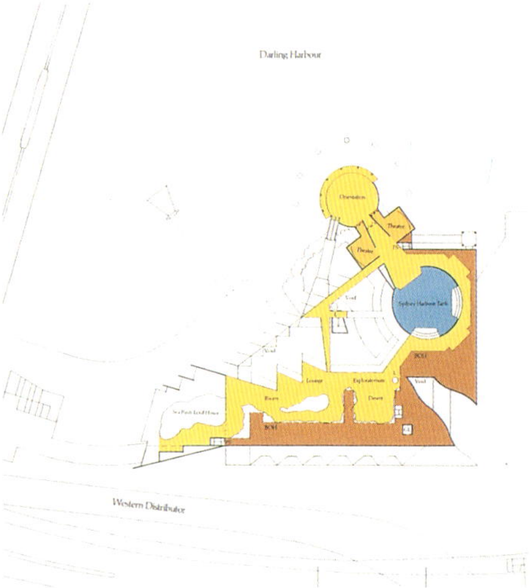

3

4

1 Roof plan
2-3 Floor plans
4 Site plan
5 Perspective
6 Interior section 1
7 Interior section 2

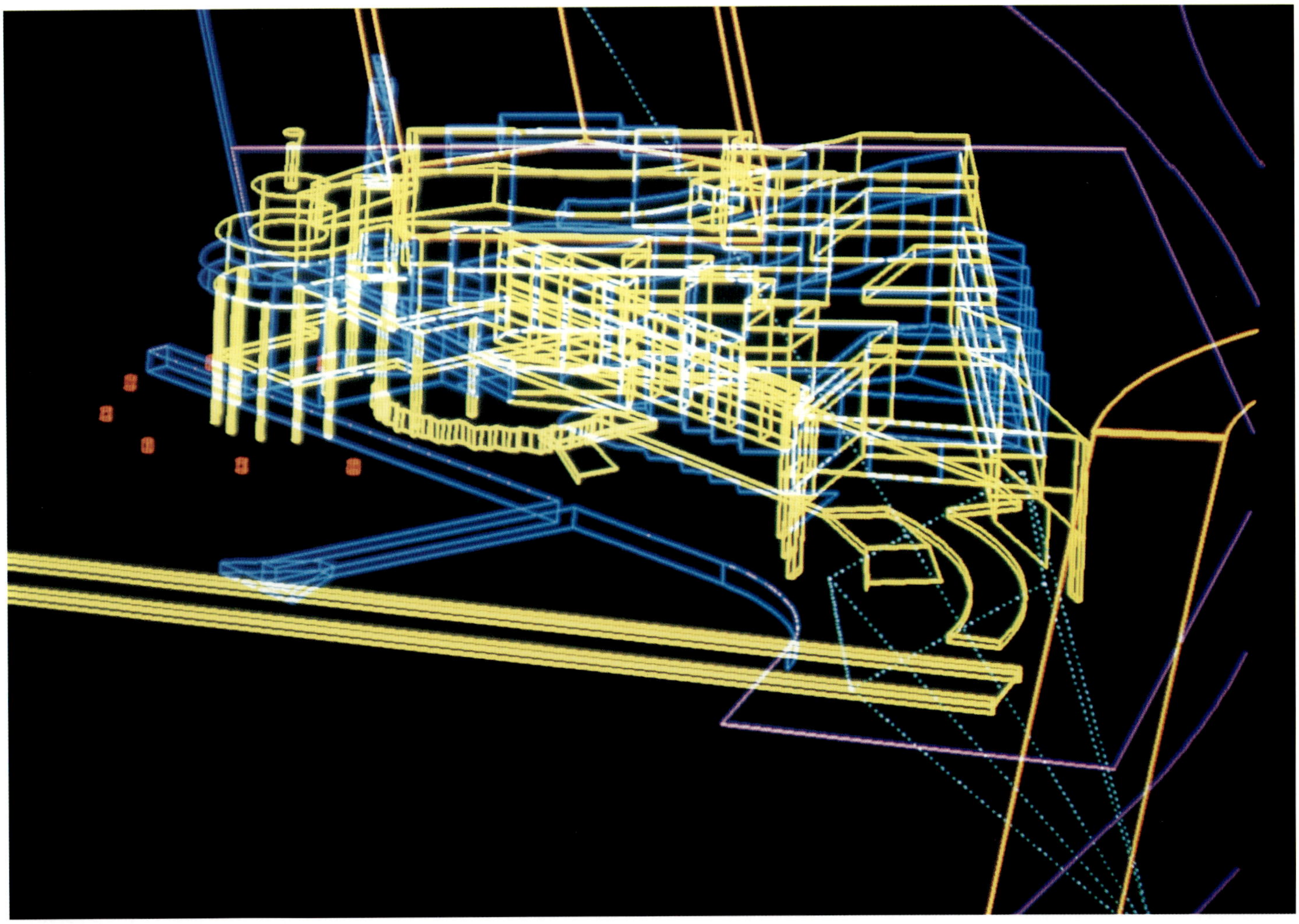

5

6

7

Darling Harbour Casino

Design 1986
Sydney, New South Wales
150,000 square metres
Architects: Daryl Jackson Robin Dyke Pty Ltd

The casino site offers the only opportunity to connect Darling Harbour with the western edge of the city. Stepped terraces rise from the water's edge to span the port freeway, connect into the city grid, and re-establish the solid base of the sandstone promontory on which Sydney is founded. The urban composition bounces an axis off the Pyrmont wall through the Conference Centre, reflecting its semi-circular form across the water in the design syntax of the hotel/casino elements. The axis draws the two buildings together to fend off the freeway and dramatise the built form relationships. The tower's stepped and curved form defines the edge of the city and mediates with the water through its maritime allusions.

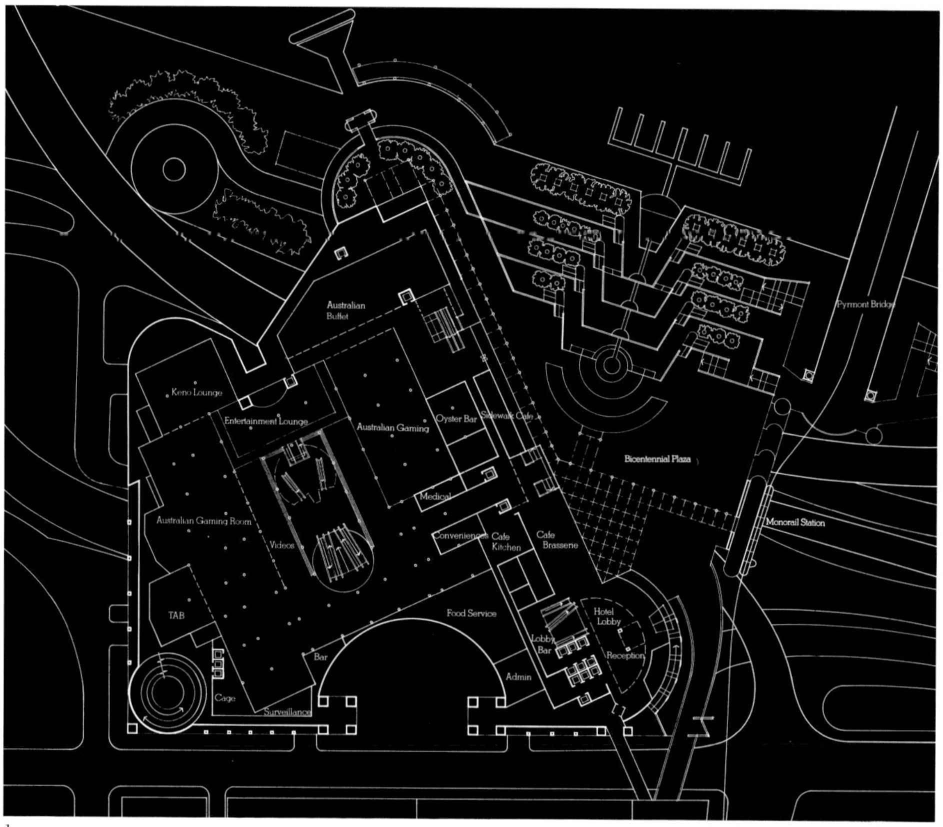

1

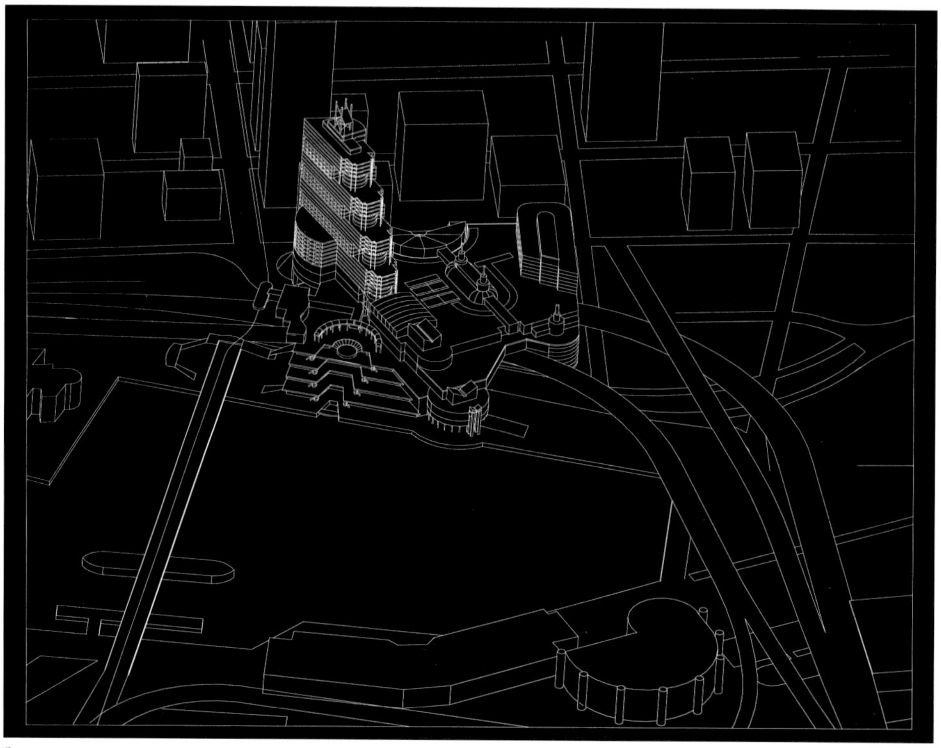

2

1 Floor plan
2 Axonometric study
3 Aerial view of model
4-5 Views of model

3

4

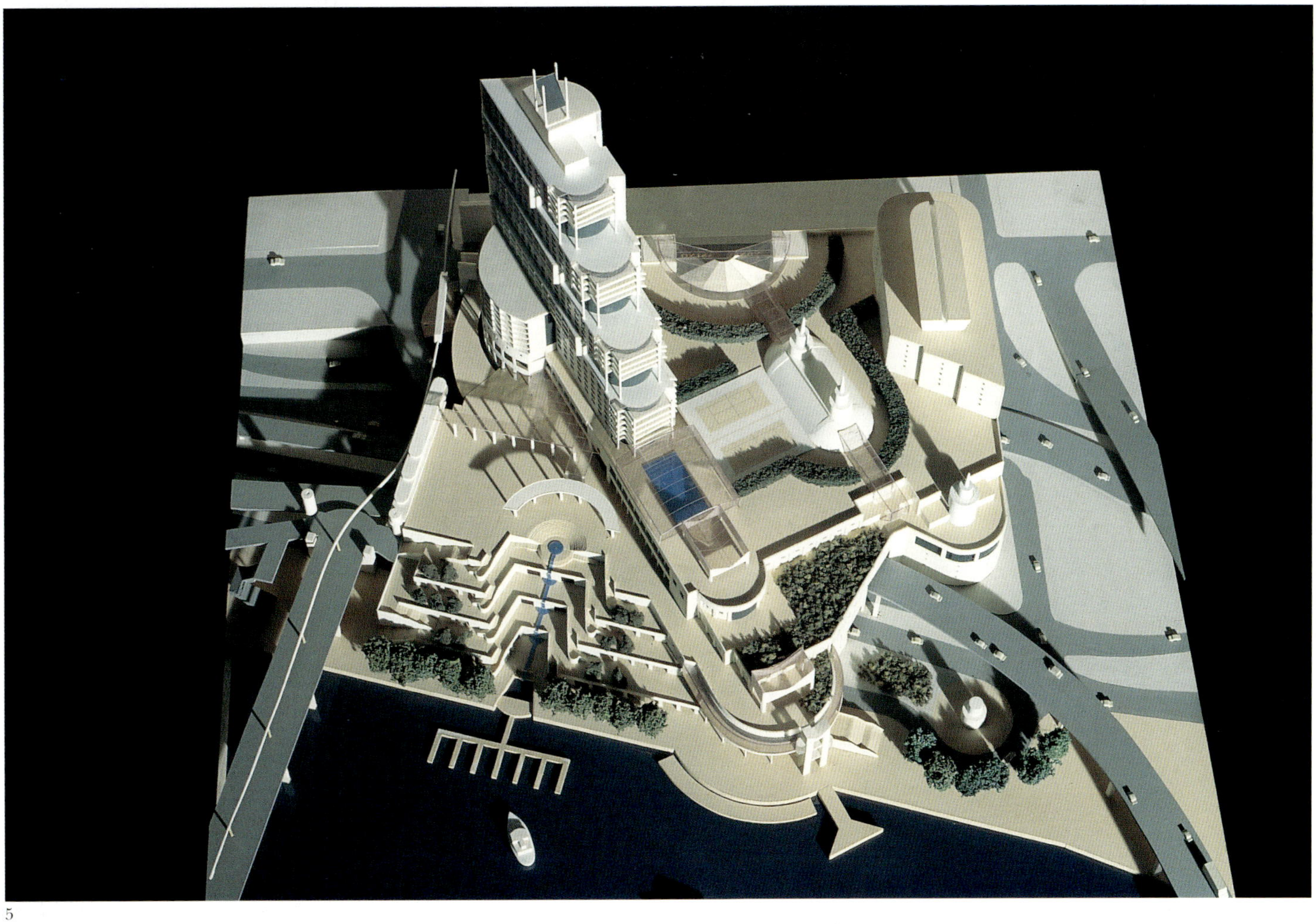

5

Merlin Street

Design 1986
Sydney, New South Wales
Uras Holdings
15,000 square metres
Architects: Daryl Jackson Robin Dyke Pty Ltd

Inner city precincts are now valued for entertainment. Merlin Street is a "walk through" of cinemas, live theatre, nightclubs, games, bars, restaurants and street events. A large Omnimax and an indoor roller ride are the major formal elements, acting in combination with the circular outdoor plaza and small lake.

Located in Darling Harbour, the project was intended to be complementary to other entertainment venues. Designed as a stage set, the architecture is urban theatre, incorporating sound and light, kinetics, signage, human movement, young and old, teenagers and families, as a microcosm of the metropolis.

1

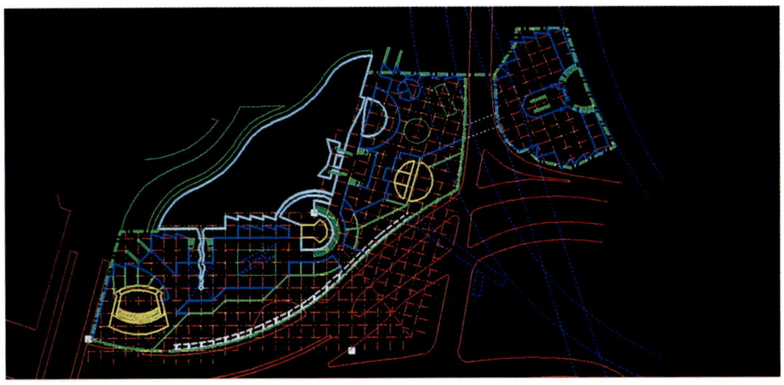

2

3

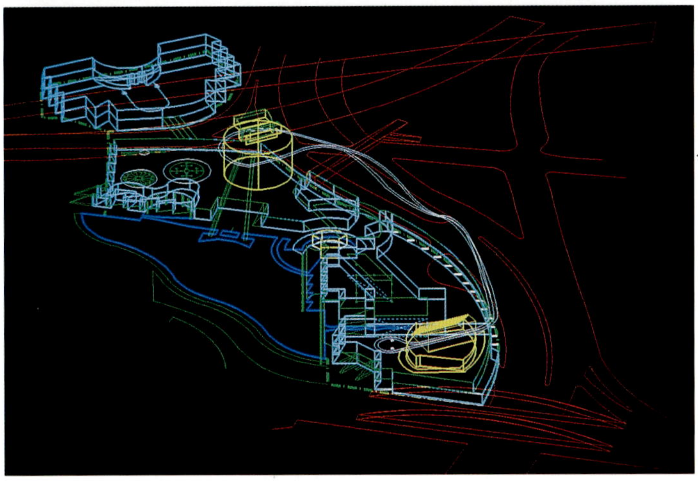

4

5

1 View of model
2 Site plan
3 Aerial view of model
4 Axonometric study
5 Model detail

Sega, Sydney

Design 1995
Darling Harbour, Sydney
Architects: Daryl Jackson Robin Dyke Pty Ltd
Competition entry

Interactive games, simulation experiences, approximations known as virtual realities are all in search of the definitive architectural envelope. This study places a large cone at a public point of entry. Restaurants, redemptions, realisations for the whole family dictate the interior micro-environment which consists of a two-level black box "experience theatre".

Externally, the signification is via graphics and illustration. No worthwhile virtual reality needs natural light, or even a present context, so it's light and sound, the set and the stage, the life of the rock musician as the analogy for everyone.

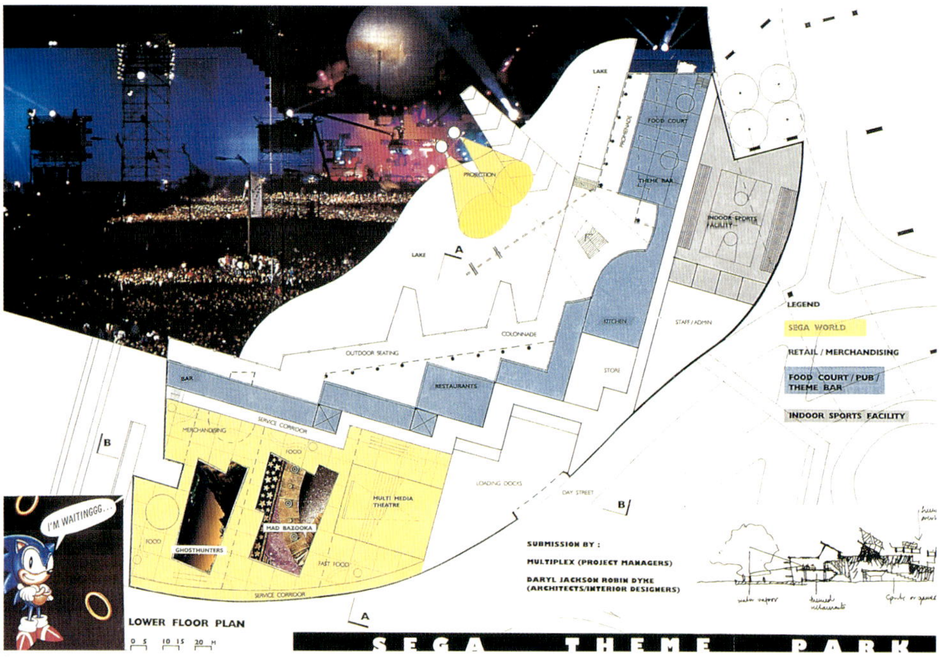

1

2

1 Site plan
2 Concept drawing
3-4 Design/concept sketches
5 Concept drawing

SEGA
freeway overhead
water vapour
themed restaurants
sports or games
SEGA VIRTUAL REALITY THEME PARK

3

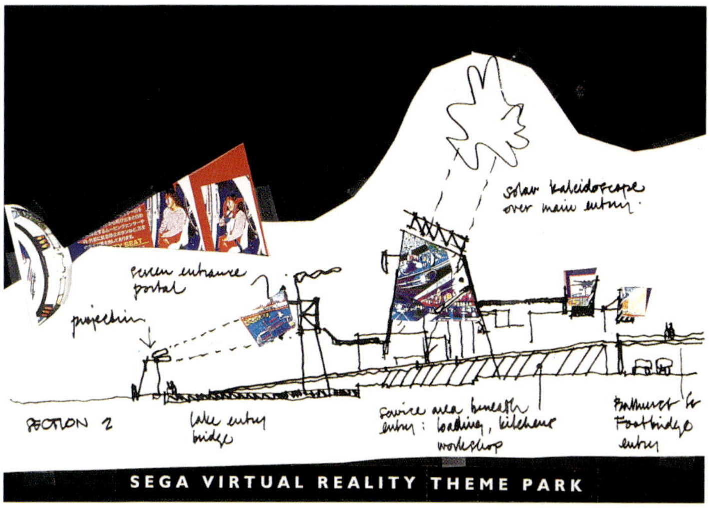
solar kaleidoscope over main entry
screen entrance portal
projection
SECTION 2
lake entry bridge
service area beneath entry: loading, kitchens workshop
Bathurst St Footbridge entry
SEGA VIRTUAL REALITY THEME PARK

4

ASTRONOMICON
SEGA WORLD
MAD BAZOOKA
GHOST HUNTER
RAILCHASE

5

Canberra Magistrates Court

Design 1992
Canberra, Australian Capital Territory
Architects: Daryl Jackson Alastair Swayn Pty Ltd

The courthouse plan is pre-ordained by the historic association of the bar, or barrier, separating the appellants from the judiciary. Judges' chambers attend to the rear of the arrangements; the public enter the court from the public foyer.

On this site in Canberra, the required number of courts are stacked vertically around a central light shaft in a six-level structure. Security is significant, but views across the city and landscape are brought into the composition to make the stress of waiting and negotiating somewhat more comfortable. The building is a block pertaining to site boundaries, its solid mass sculpted internally to reveal the plan arrangement.

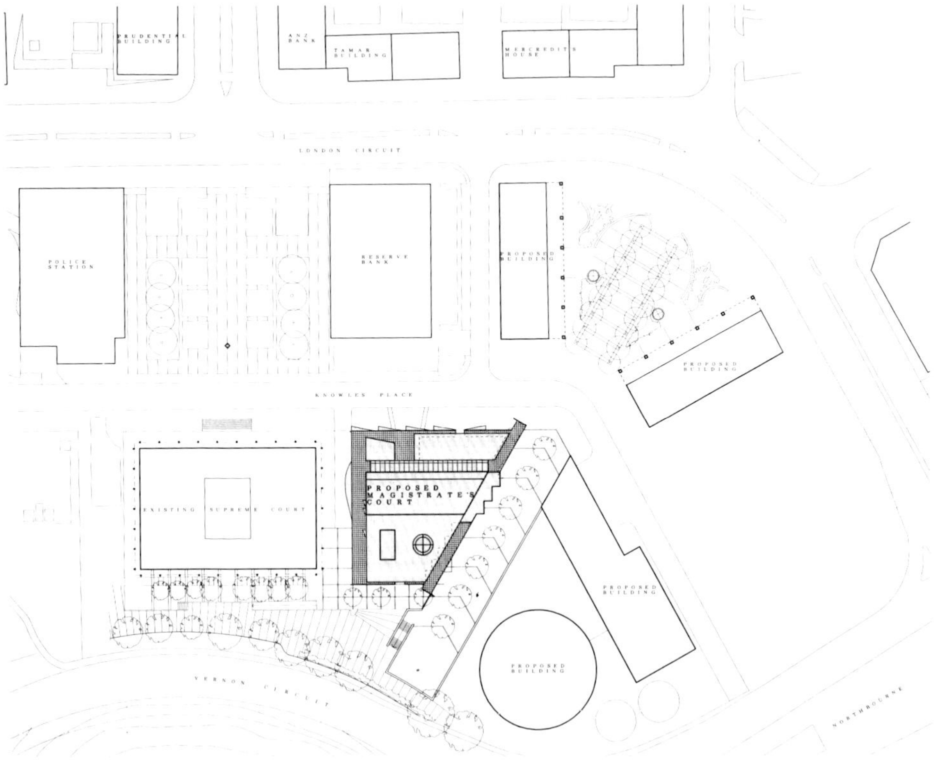

1

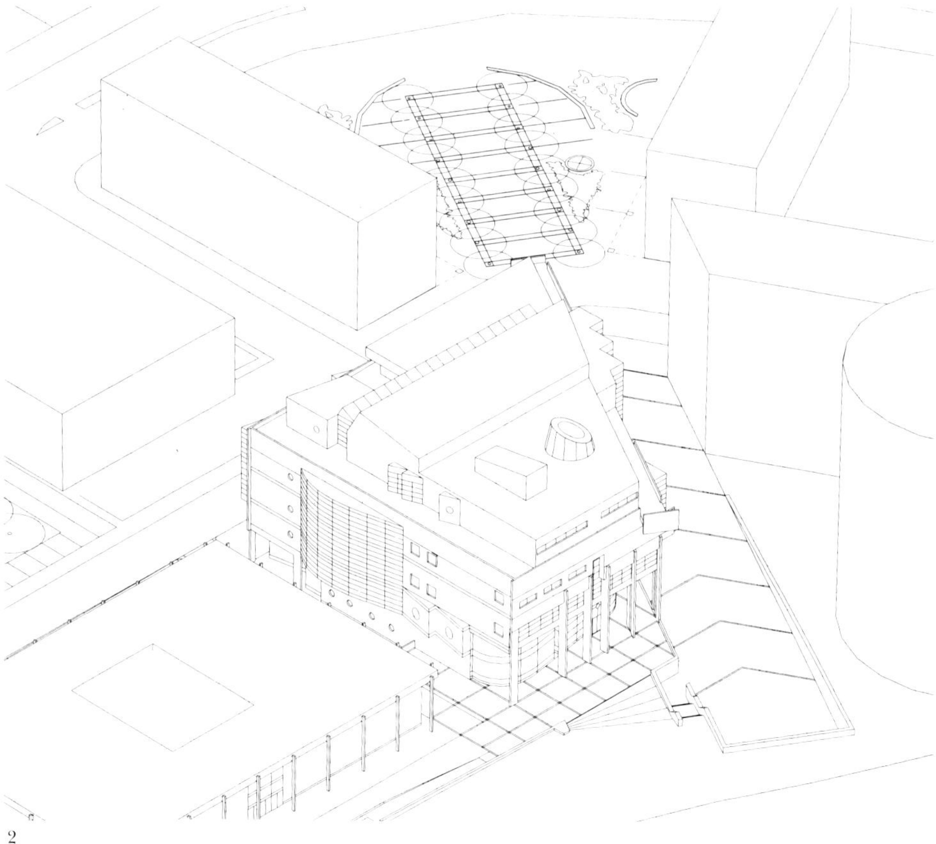
2

1 Site and location plan
2 Axonometric study
3 Floor plans
4-7 Axonometric facade details

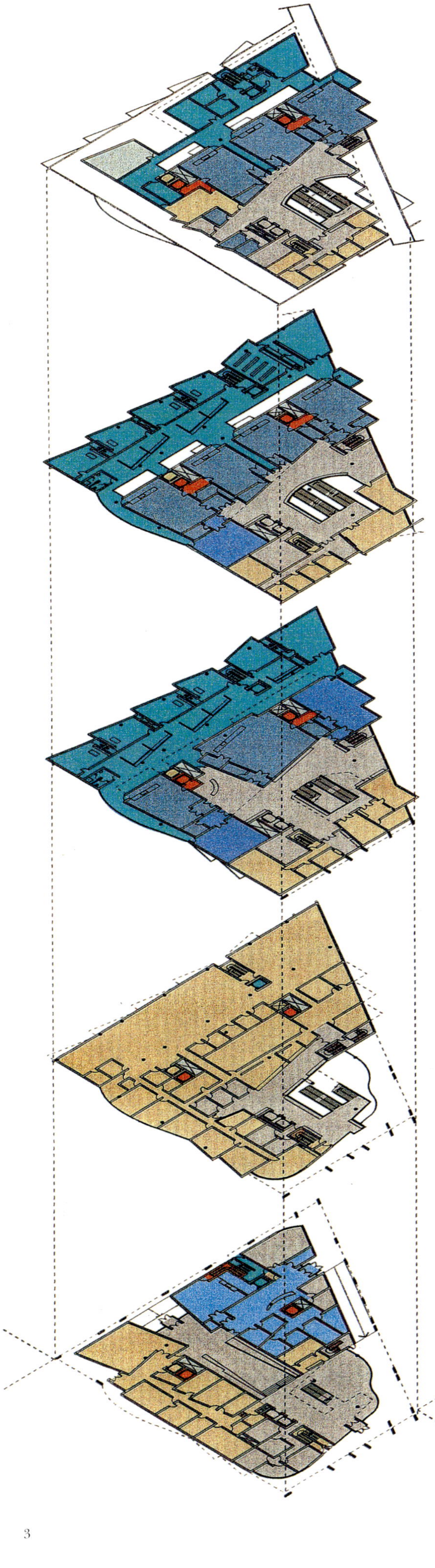

3

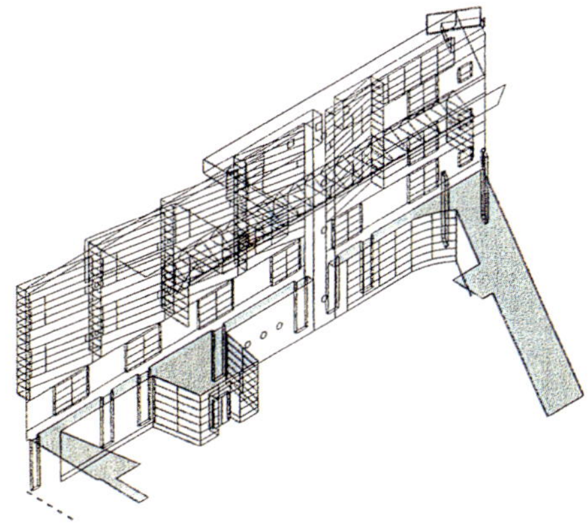

4

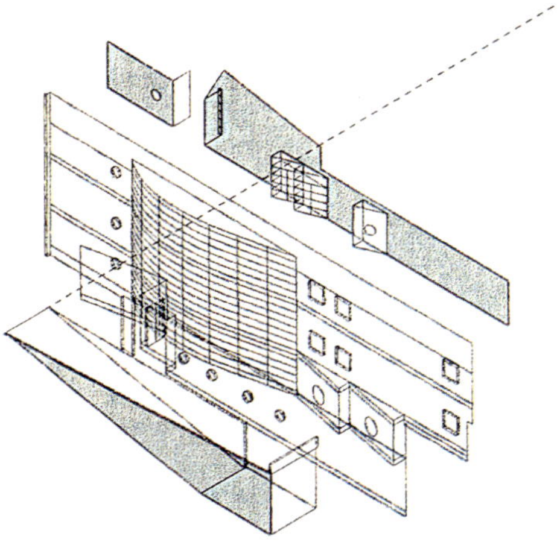

5

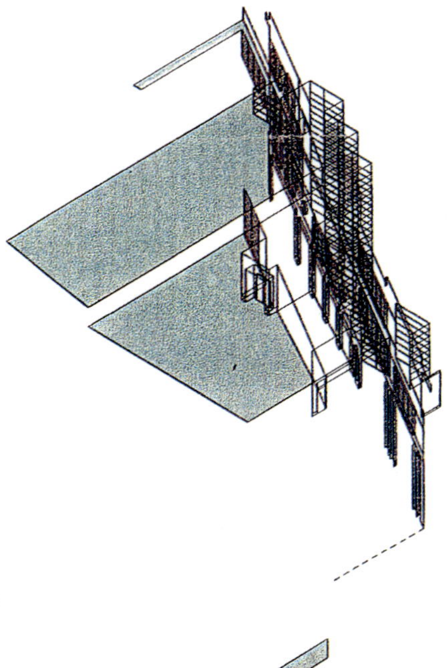

6

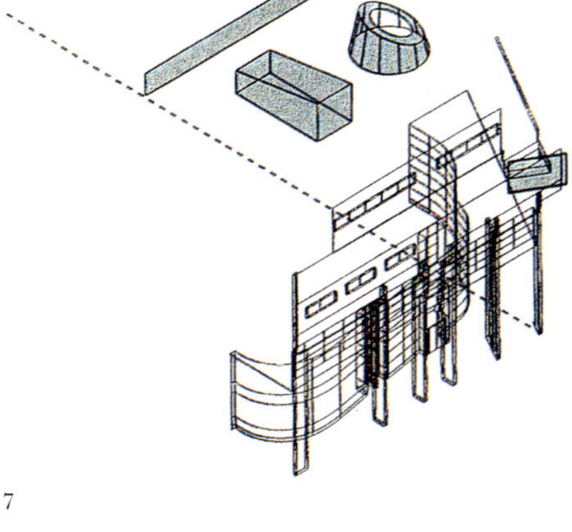

7

Brandenburg, Germany

Design 1994
Brandenburg, Germany
LEG Brandenburg
Architects: Daryl Jackson International Pty Ltd
Planning study

Replanning a section of the city of Brandenburg in East Germany involved inventing a range of uses for a number of large, 19th century water-powered grain mills. The 'Mill Islands' on the Havel River constitutes an extraordinary water/land environment, eminently suitable for tourist and recreational activities, hotels, sports and housing.

The "structure" plan uses the cross axial arrangement of view corridors, or "open space shafts", to heighten the opportunities to experience the mill structures as part of the reconstructed urban context. The waterways constitute a special asset upon which hotel, restaurant and new waterfront housing is placed. A village form of clustered precincts emerges, to be built over time as the economy permits.

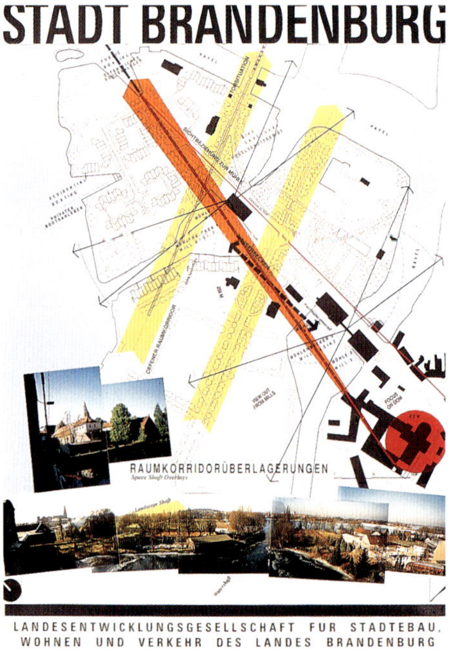

1

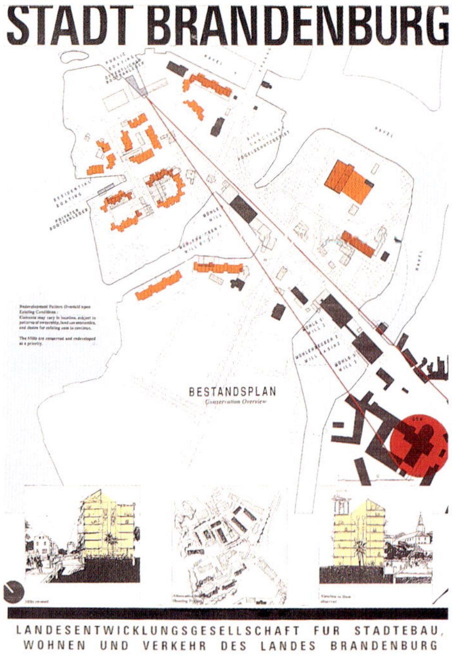

2

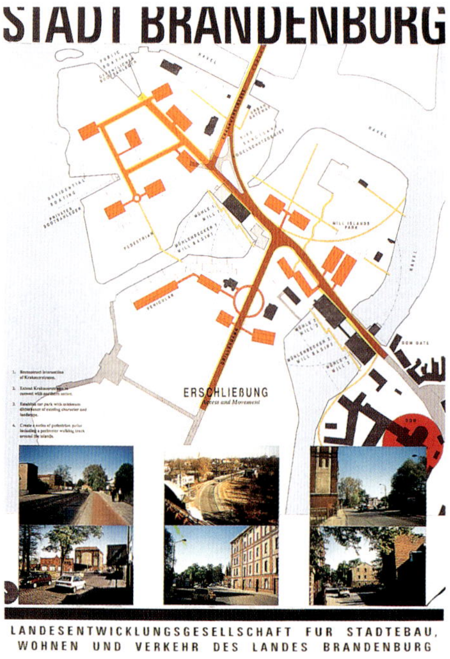

3

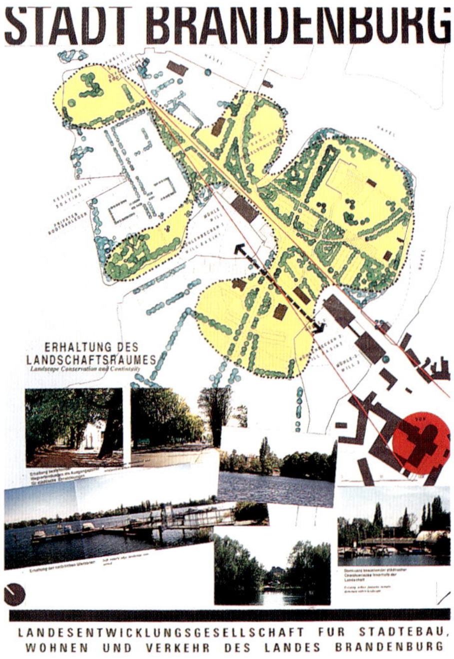

4

1-4 Stage 3 presentation
5 Urban criteria

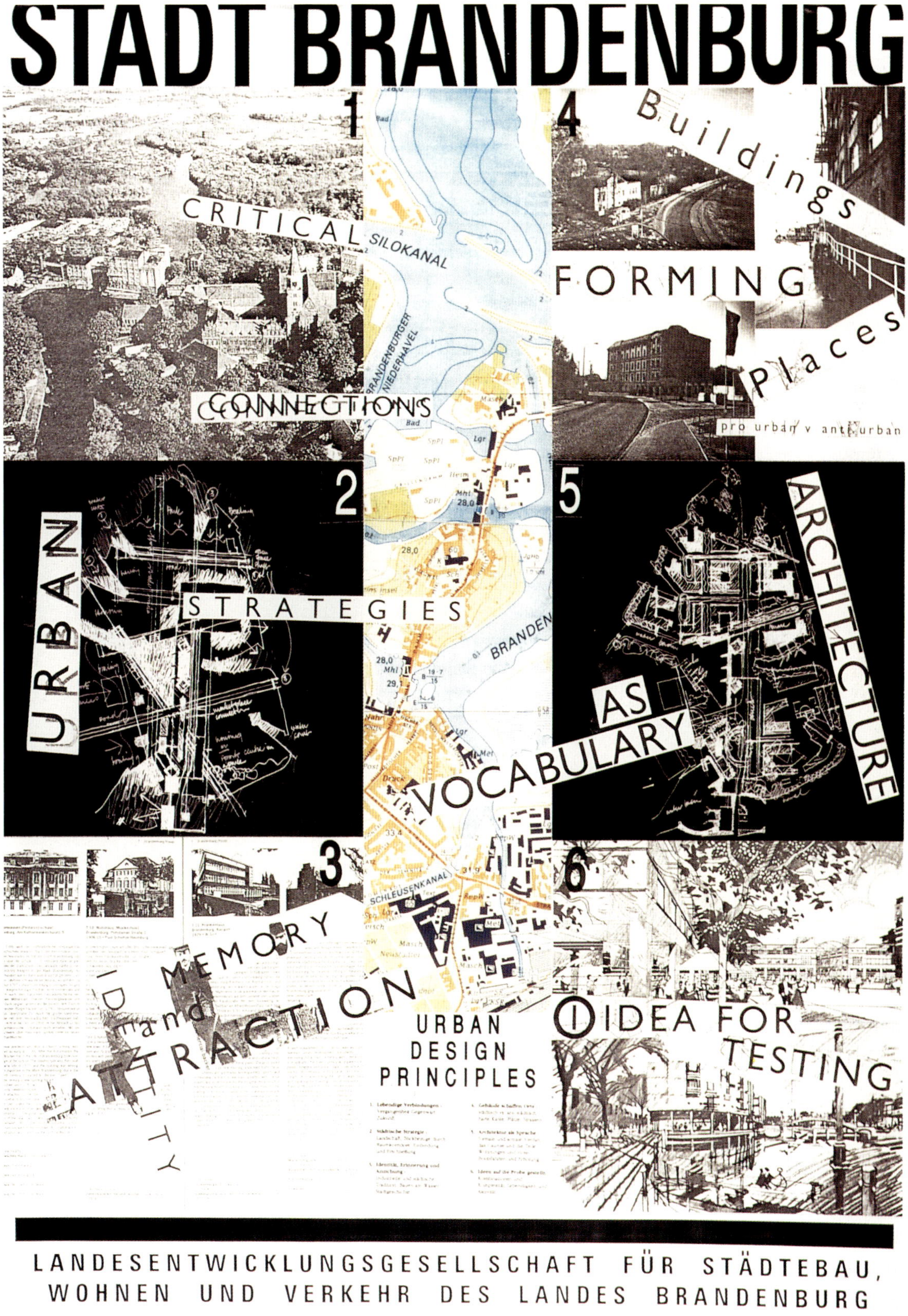

5

Anzac Parade

Design 1990
Canberra, Australian Capital Territory
Architects: Daryl Jackson Alastair Swayn Pty Ltd
Planning study

Canberra's principal urban avenue, and the one that Walter Burley Griffin intended to house the key symbols of his prize-winning design for Australia's capital city, is in need of renewal, or rather, completion. This project has to include a number of existing monuments to the fallen; in a rhythmic way, it uses them to provide greater urban/landscape density to the movement of visitors.

Within the parade, the seven Australian States are represented as a series of individually designed, yet matching partners. The plaza before the National War Memorial is flagged, with the seven-pointed "star". Where the parade crosses Griffin's Constitution Avenue, a large square is established to mark the coming together of "memory for the fallen" and 'recognition of the living'.

The parade ends in a large grass triangle which abuts Lake Burley Griffin. Out in the water, that distinctive constellation of stars, the Southern Cross, lights up at night to reflect back into the sky.

1

1 Overall master plan
2 Explanatory diagrams

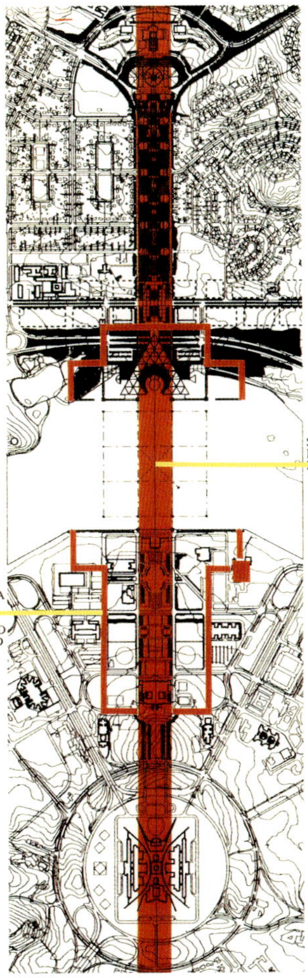

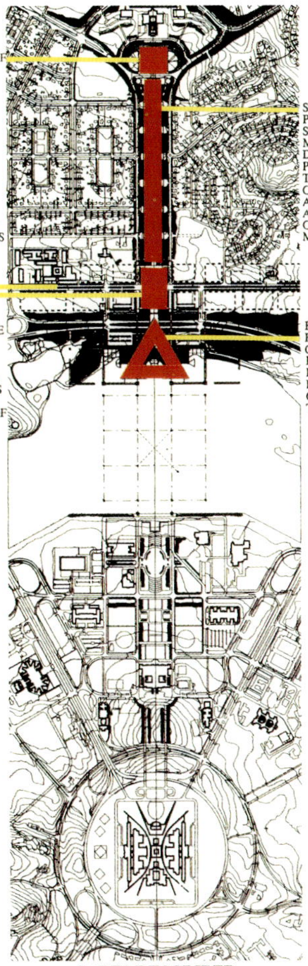

PARTS DESCRIBED

LAND/WATER AXIS INTERSECTION

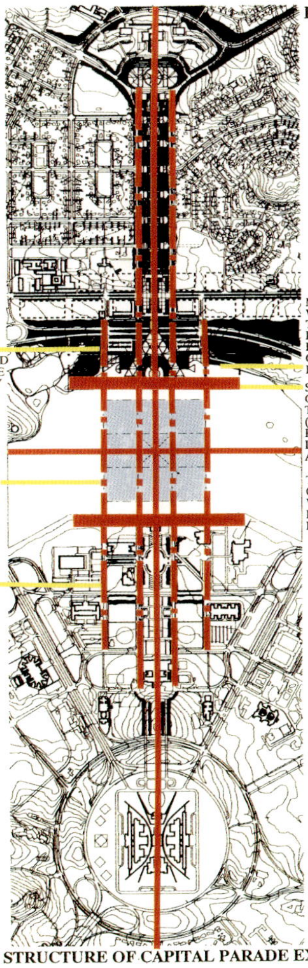

SPATIAL STRUCTURE OF CAPITAL PARADE EXTENDED

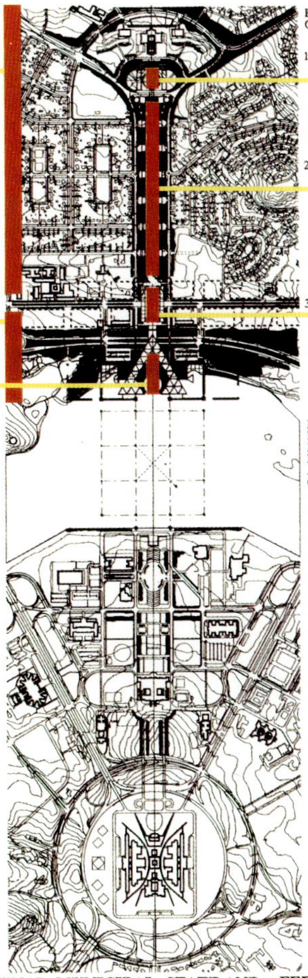

ANZAC PARADE: COMMUNAL; MUNICIPAL; STATE AND FEDERAL STRUCTURES

2

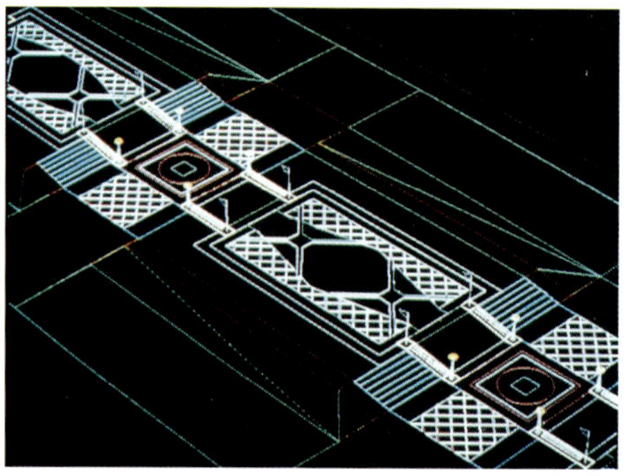

3

3 Concourse
4 Mall view
5 Plaza
6 Forecourt
7 Lakefront
8 Parade
9 Proposal

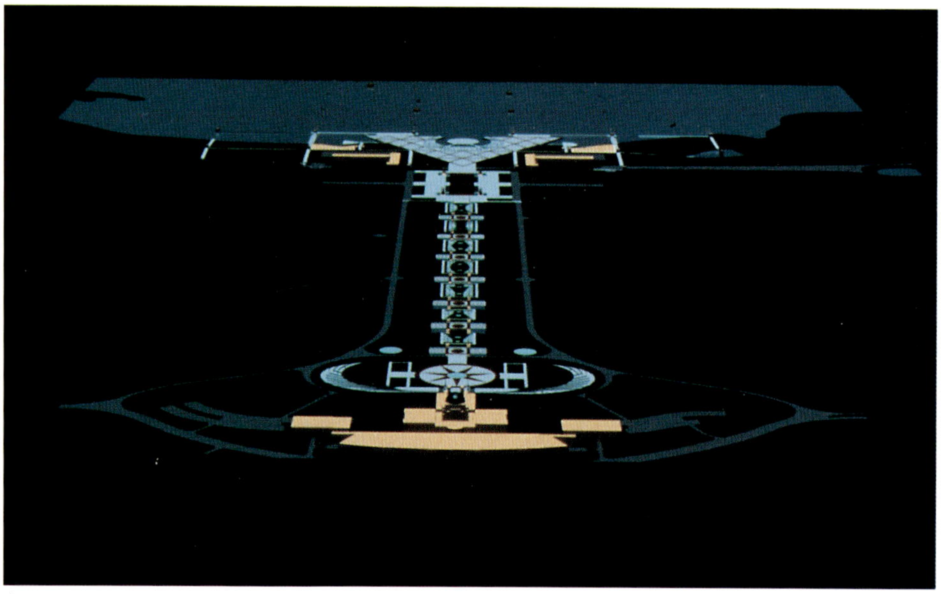

4

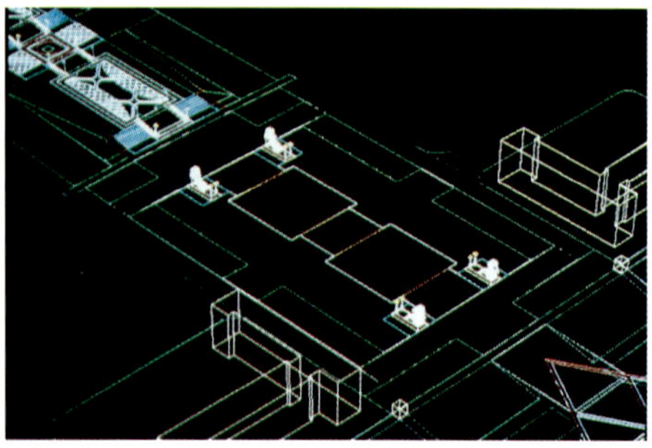

5

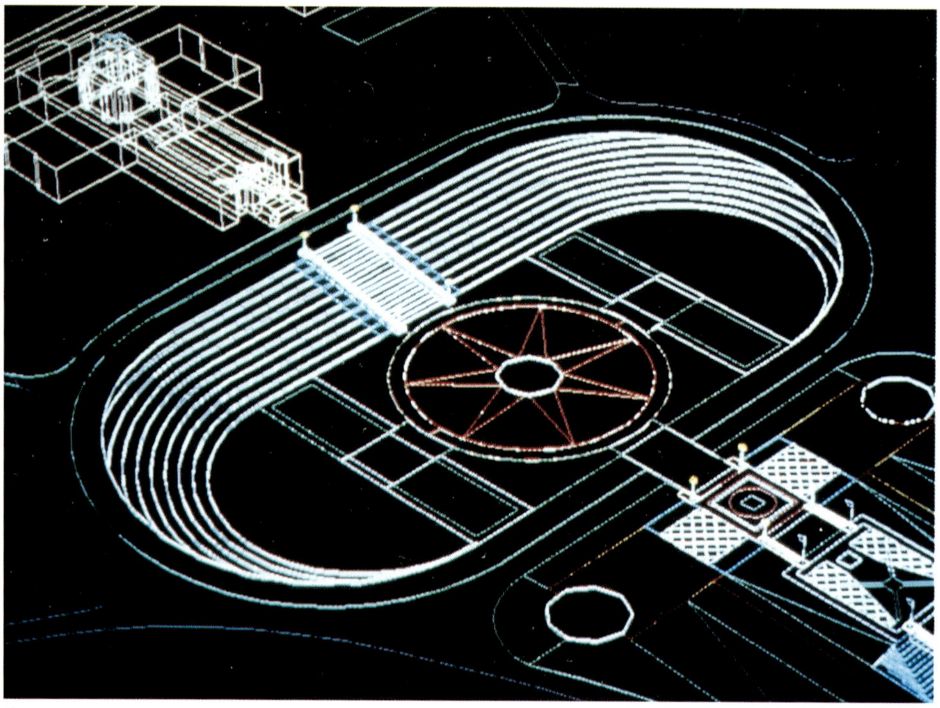

6

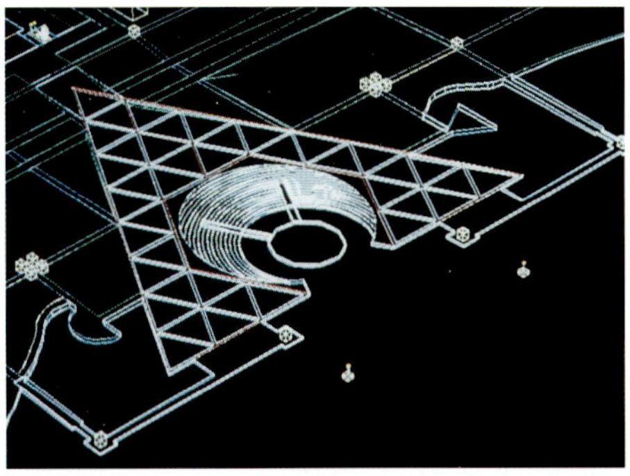

7

8

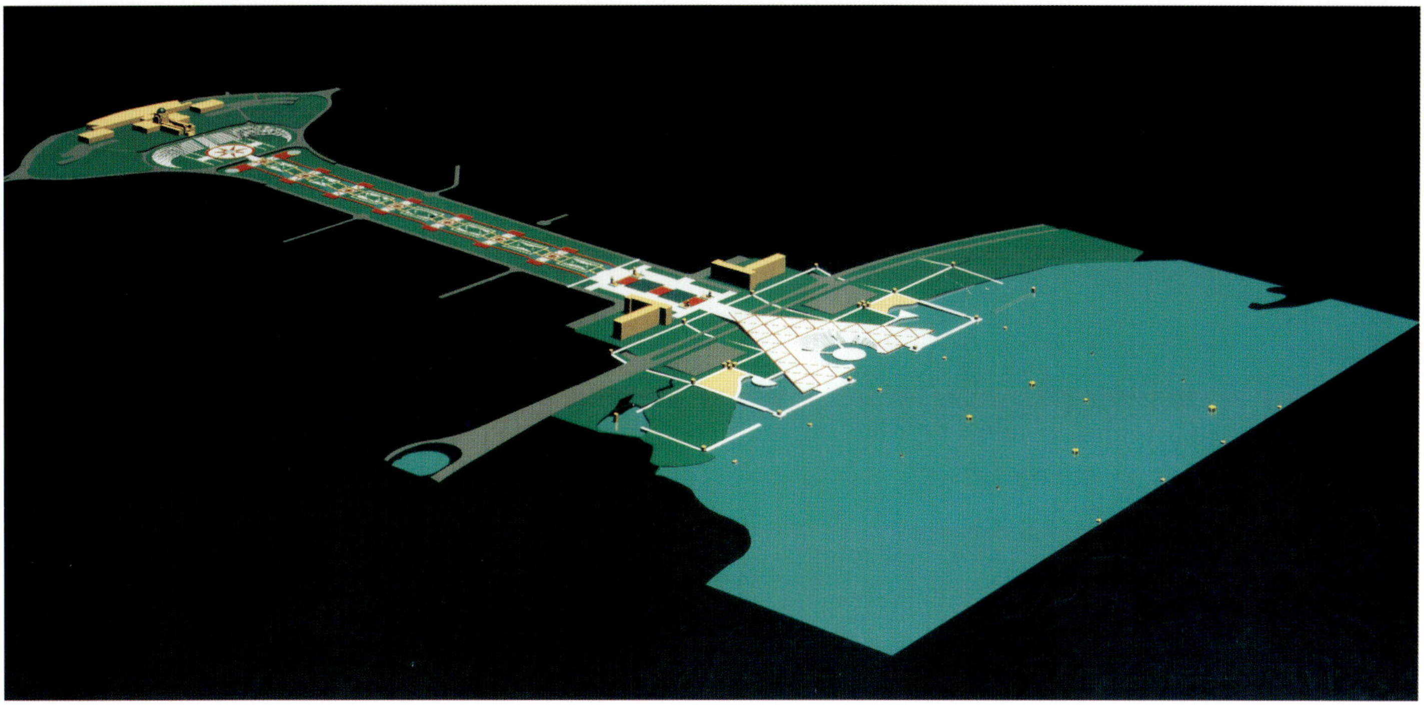

9

Perth Harbour-City Foreshore

Design 1991
Perth, Western Australia
Competition entry

Winning back the water's edge from the lakeside drive (now an arterial road) and getting the urbs to cross the park and make contact was the basis for this urban design competition.

A number of transformations are indicated. The ferry terminal becomes home for a massive "flywheel" (ferris wheel) on axis with the view point in Kings Park; the urban square around St George's Anglican Cathedral leapfrogs the park to become a model for an elaborate water image; other hard edge inserts are used to balance the waterfront feel with the park backdrop.

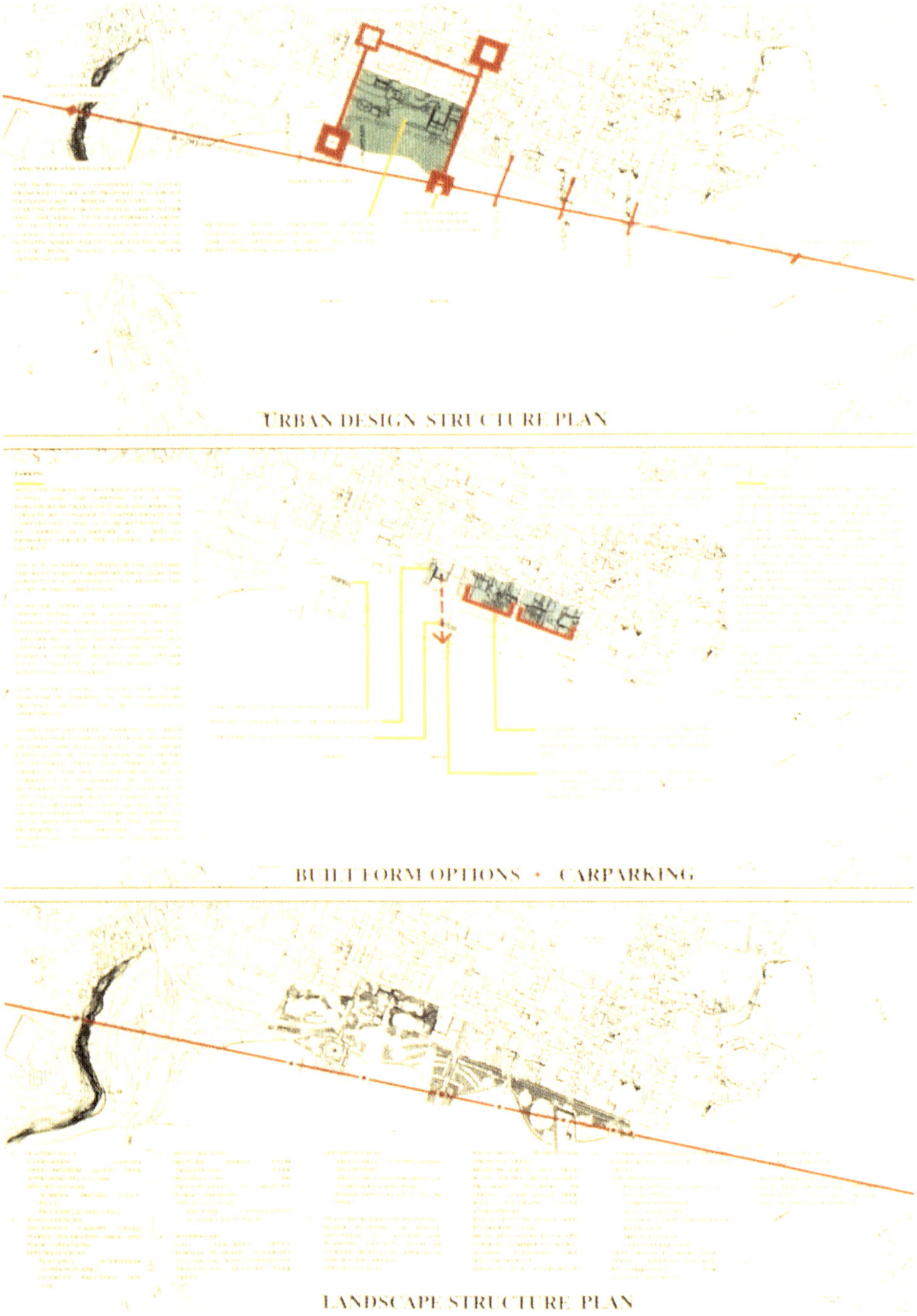

1

1 Explanatory diagrams
2 Site plan
3 Site and location plan

2

SWAN
RIVER
PT. LEWIS
THE NARROWS
OLD BREWERY
MILL PT
PT. BELCHES
PERTH
WATER
RIVER
PT. FRASER

3

Flinders Street Marketplace

Design 1988
Melbourne, Victoria
Merlin International Properties (Aust) Pty Ltd
20,000 square metres (GLA)
Associated architects: Architecture Oceania, Sydney
Reinforced concrete slabs, fire-protected steel beams, steel-encased concrete columns
Precast glazed walls, corrugated iron roofing

Constructing a new market floor above the existing platforms while maintaining the daily operation of commuter trains presents a difficult engineering exercise. The architecture unfolds as a series of roofed market halls, each with a large glass end facing the Yarra River which edges the station.

The main elevation steps down to the lower walk via a number of outdoor terraces, stair towers and escalators. The expression of colour banding to the masonry elements reflects the original fabric of the station, as built in 1910.

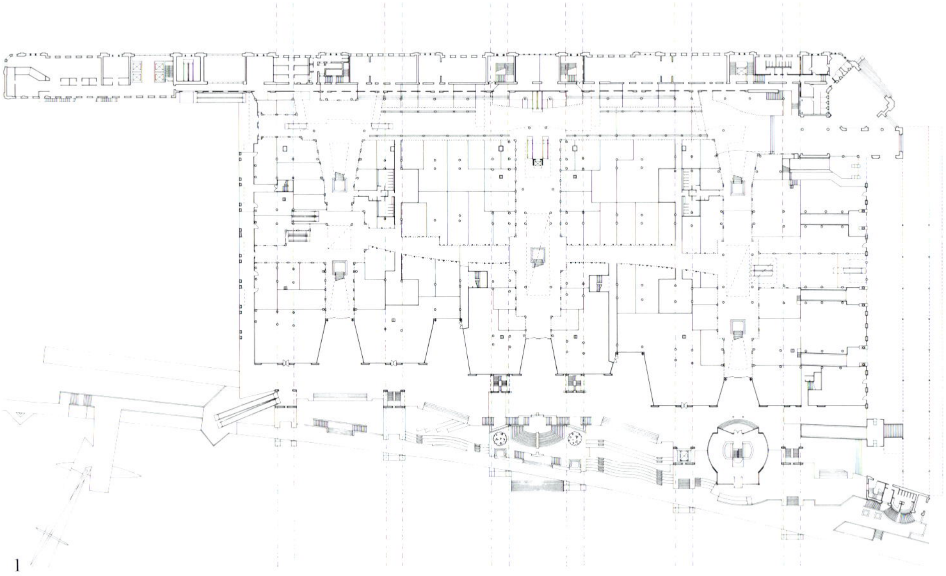

1

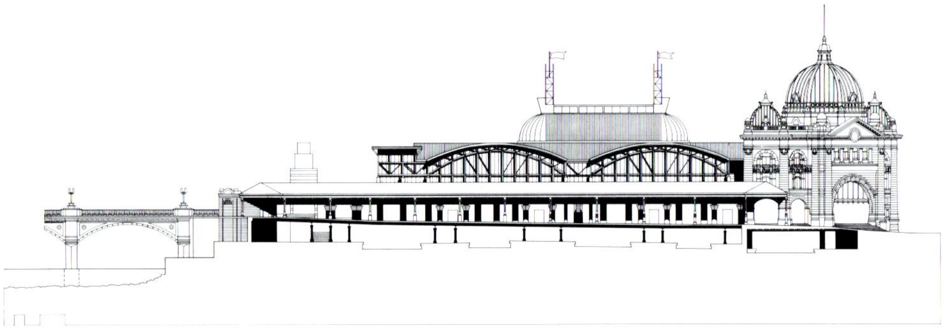

2

3

1 Entrance level plan
2 Swanston Street elevation
3 Yarra River view
4-5 Sections
6 Yarra River elevation

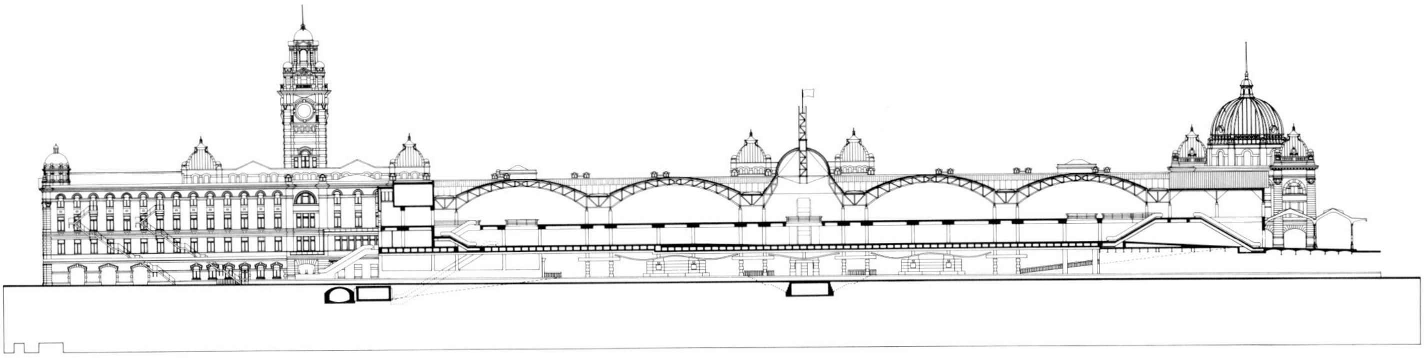

4

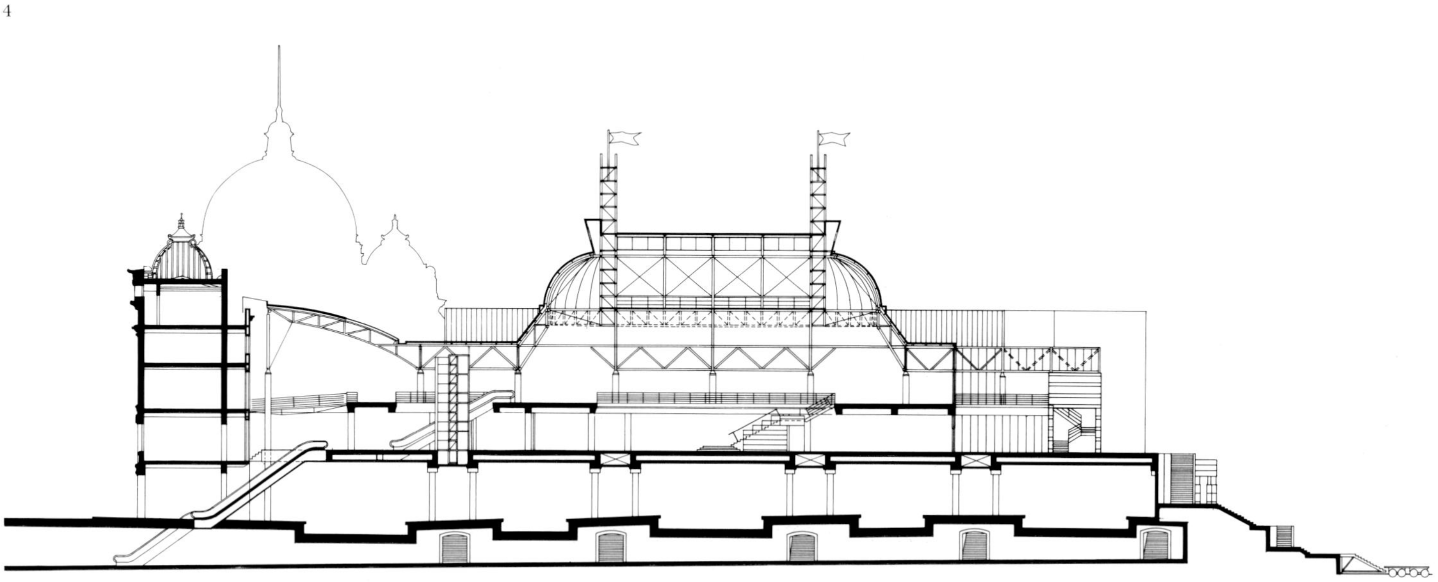

5

6

7 Model, south-west corner: view from Yarra River
8 Model: view of river facade
9 Aerial view of model

7

8

9

Brisbane Convention and Exhibition Centre

Design 1991
Brisbane, Queensland
Fletcher Construction
Competition entry

Continuing the rejuvenation of the South Bank area, this project extends the Expo 88 initiative. The long horizontal building sits above two layers of car parking, with a curving, metallic, shell-like form as the container for the grand exhibition halls. The Great Hall and convention facilities are concentrated at the southern end of the site to facilitate future joint operations with the South Bank entertainment area. The cubic forms of the Queensland Performing Arts Complex are incorporated into the design, and escalators connect the plaza to South Brisbane Station.

Two grand foyers at either end of the site introduce visitors to the festive, soaring interiors interspersed with arrival platforms, mezzanine lounges, kiosks and shops. With finely tuned glazing and walling, people are able to see and be seen along all street frontages, both day and night.

1

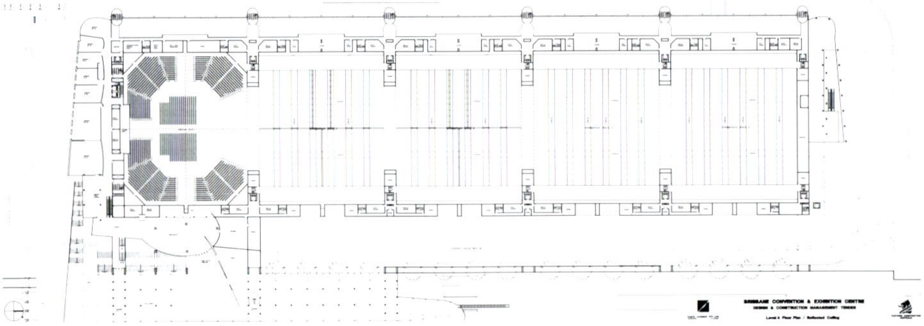

2

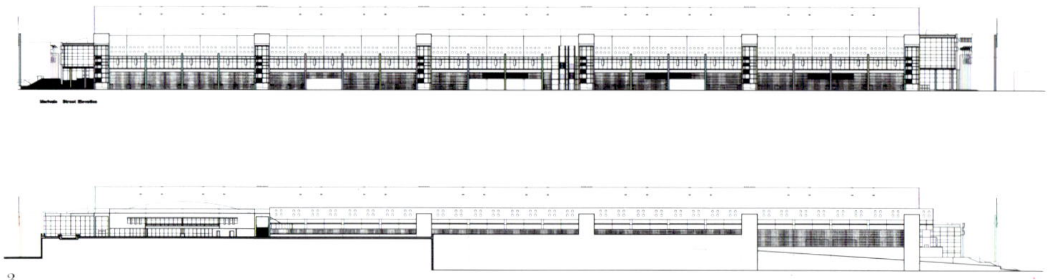

3

1 Internal perspective of foyer
2 Ground-floor plan
3 Elevations
4 Section
5 Perspective drawing, south-west corner

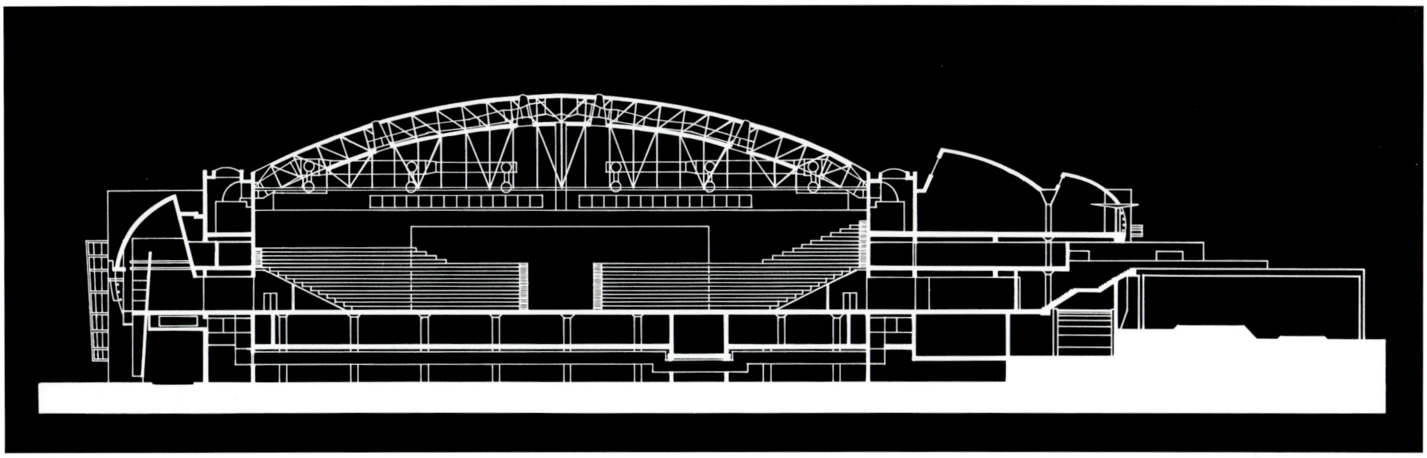

4

5

Daryl Jackson Office

Design 1985
Melbourne, Victoria
Daryl Jackson Architects Pty Ltd
1,000 square metres

The Melbourne office is situated on the top floor of a city warehouse. An open studio approach to the drawing office and meeting and social spaces allowed the structure to be cut back to the basics. Fan-shaped trusses span the interior and hold the corrugated iron ceiling sandwich in place. The work bays, computers and meeting tables stabilise the ideas on the floor below. A new staircase forms a vertical entry coil connecting the ground floor entrance to the studio level above.

1

2

1 Building entrance
2 Aerial view of office through roof trusses
3 Circulation staircase

3

FIRM PROFILE

Biographies

DARYL JACKSON

B.Arch (Melb Uni), Dip.Arch (RMIT), AO, LFRAIA, HonFAIA, ARIBA

Daryl Jackson is the Principal Director of Daryl Jackson Architects Pty Ltd and in this capacity provides the lead in establishing the design philosophy and management principles for the professional development of the practice.

Under his leadership, the Australian-based practice operates through offices in Brisbane, Canberra, Melbourne and Sydney. Daryl Jackson's offices have acquired a national reputation for architecture of excellence, as demonstrated by their consistent receipt of distinguished national and State architecture awards. Subjects of these awards have included such projects as the Great Southern Stand at the Melbourne Cricket Ground; 120 Collins Street, Melbourne; the Walter and Eliza Hall Institute; the Royal Melbourne Hospital redevelopment; and the Australian Film, Television and Radio School in Sydney.

The extensive range of educational design and briefing experience includes master planning for the University of the Northern Territory; Griffith and Bond universities in Queensland; and Swinburne and Melbourne universities in Victoria. In addition, a considerable array of sports architecture is now completed at the Australian Institute of Sport in the Australian Capital Territory; new stadia for Woolloongabba in Brisbane and Subiaco in Perth are further testimony to the diversity of the practice.

For the past 30 years, Daryl Jackson has been involved in a number of diverse, large-scale architectural planning and urban design projects in Australia, the United Kingdom and the Middle East. A separate practice, Daryl Jackson International, has offices in London and Berlin to undertake work in the United Kingdom and Eastern Europe.

Mr Jackson's built works, together with his considerable teaching, writing and lecturing have had a significant influence on the course of Australian architectural development. In 1990, public recognition of the quality of his services to architecture resulted in the conferring of an Order of Australia and an Honorary Fellowship of the American Institute of Architects.

With his extensive participation in various significant cultural organisations, including positions as Chairman of the Australian Film Institute, Trustee of the National Gallery of Victoria, and Member of the Victorian Council of the Arts, Mr Jackson continues to contribute to a heterogeneous notion of Australian culture.

BRIAN BRITT
B.Arch (NSW Inst. of Techn.), ARAIA

Brian is an Associate Director of the Sydney Office of the practice.

With 25 years in the profession, Brian has acquired a wide range of experience working for a number of architectural firms in Sydney and London. In 1984, he joined Daryl Jackson Robin Dyke as project architect for the Australian Film, Television and Radio School.

In 1987, Brian was responsible for the establishment of the Gold Coast office and was instrumental in the design development and documentation of the first academic building at Bond University.

In recent years, he has principally been concerned with leading teams for design development, documentation and contract administration of academic, public and government projects. Most recently, Brian has worked in New South Wales on Bathurst Police Station, Port Macquarie Court House, Albury Court House, Administration and Amenities Building for ICI at Botany, replanning and refurbishment of Newtown Telephone Exchange, Rooty Hill Community Complex, and an apartment complex adjacent to the Rocks area in Sydney. Works in progress include refurbishing the Sydney GPO for Australia Post and a research and design complex at the CSIRO site in North Ryde.

ROMAN BUGRYN
B.Arch (RMIT)

Roman is an experienced project architect who has travelled extensively and worked overseas, including twelve months in London and two years in Riyadh, Saudi Arabia.

Prior to joining the practice, he worked for Shepherd Robson in London on a large urban redevelopment project at Wood Green. More recently, he was an Associate Director with a small interior design/architectural practice in Melboume where he established office procedures and managed interior related projects.

At Daryl Jackson Pty Ltd, he has worked on the Australian Embassy in Riyadh, Saudi Arabia, dealing with all phases of the project, from concept design and documentation to construction on site. He also worked on a project to develop a Festival Marketplace over the existing Flinders Street Station platforms, including the upgrading of the existing historically significant station building and the refurbishment of the platforms.

He has tutored in design at Melbourne University.

GARY CARTER
Dip.Arch (Qld Inst. of Techn.)

Gary is an Associate Director of the Queensland office of the practice and works in all areas of project development. As Project Director, Gary is responsible for the day-to-day management of projects in the Brisbane office, with special emphasis on design implementation, construction detailing, and project delivery.

With over 20 years experience in the building industry, Gary has had the opportunity to be associated with highly acclaimed architectural projects. He has served as Project Architect on the Suncorp Building Society Head Office, Fortitude Valley; and the design and documentation of the concert hall for the Performing Arts Centre. In addition, Gary was a team member on documentation of the award-winning Belconnen Library, ACT.

Since coming to work at Daryl Jackson Pty Ltd, Gary Carter contributed to works at Bond University and the State Library - Queensland Cultural Centre. In 1990 he was appointed an Associate Director of the national practice.

During 1995, Gary was involved as Project Architect for the Food Technology Building at South Brisbane TAFE, and the Brisbane Cricket Ground Redevelopment.

PHILIP CHADWICK
B.Arch (RMIT), ARAIA

Philip Chadwick is an Associate of the practice responsible for the management, documentation and contract administration phases of major projects. Philip is an experienced facilitator, practiced in programming and management, liaison and negotiation.

Philip has been with the practice for over ten years and in that time has contributed to a number of buildings. He has been responsible for the Commercial Union Office Building; Stonier's Winery, Merricks; and the Information Technology and the Electrical Engineering Building, University of Melbourne. Philip has also documented the Swinburne College of TAFE, and the Royal Melbourne Hospital.

Philip is presently part of a team designing the $750 million Crown Casino to be established on Melbourne's Southbank.

PETER COEHLO
B.Arch (Madras Uni)

Peter is an Associate and CAD/Systems Manager of Computer Services with the practice.

Prior to his arrival in Australia, Peter lived in India where he was Gold Medalist in the final year of his degree. For eight years he worked for Misereor in Delhi as an architect and advisor on various aspects of architectural practice for projects in India, Bhutan, Nepal, and the Andaman and Nicobar Islands. In addition, he worked for two years for Schooley Caldwell and Associates (USA) in the Delhi office as Project Architect for USIS Building, Calcutta.

Peter came to Australia in 1985 and joined Daryl Jackson Pty Ltd in 1986. Since then he has been involved in a variety of architectural project types. Major commercial projects Peter has supervised on our CAD system include 120 Collins Street, Melbourne; Commercial Union Head Office, Melbourne; 90 Collins Street, Melbourne; Melbourne Cricket Ground Great Southern Stand; Museum of Victoria, Southbank; Information Technology and Electrical Engineering Building, University of Melbourne; and several residential projects in Melbourne.

Most recently, Peter has been involved with the Royal Melbourne Hospital Redevelopment; Methodist Ladies College Music School, Melbourne; and Frankston Cultural Centre.

In addition to his architectural skills, Peter has qualifications in computer management systems relating to mainframes, Unix, DOS and Novell networks.

PETER COLE
Dip.Arch (RMIT), ARAIA

Peter Cole is a Director of the practice, and is responsible for managing projects from design through documentation to final completion. Peter's architectural experience includes two years in London, and he has travelled extensively through Europe, Asia and North America.

With 18 years of experience in this practice, Peter has managed every phase of a range of projects that include the Frankston Cultural Centre; an inner urban housing scheme at Ascot Vale; libraries for the cities of Northcote, Footscray and Frankston; and a complex of clinical consulting suites in Richmond.

Peter's experience has also included managing medium to large sports and recreation projects, including the Box Hill Indoor Recreation Centre, Ringwood Pool, Harold Holt Pool Alterations and Extensions, and the Melbourne Cricket Ground Great Southern Stand, all in Victoria. Interstate work has included two major projects for the Australian Institute of Sport in Canberra (the Training Halls and the Indoor Training Pool); Bond University Pool and Sports Centre, Queensland; and the Western Australian Indoor Sports Centre. He has also worked on Queensland's Bond University Student Union and faculty buildings for law and arts.

Feasibility and master planning study experience includes Bond University Master Plan in Queensland; Camberwell Sports Centre and Warrnambool Aquatic Centre Feasibility Studies; Box Hill Indoor Recreation Centre Master Plan and Melbourne University Sports Union Master Plan, and the Frankston Cultural Centre.

ROBIN DYKE
B.Arch (Hons) (NSW Inst. of Techn), ARAIA

Robin Dyke is a Principal Director responsible for projects undertaken in Sydney. He graduated from the New South Wales Institute of Technology in 1973 with first class honours and, as the top architecture graduate in Australia, was awarded the RAIA Silver Medal.

His early experience with Harry Seidler and Associates included acting as Project Architect on the MLC Centre for three years, as well as assisting in the design of many major projects. From 1978, Robin operated his own practice, building such projects as the NSWIT Students Union, Twin Cinema Warringah Mall and Hampden Court Apartments in North Sydney for which he received an RAIA Merit Award in 1983.

Robin has been Design Director on such recent projects as Prairiewood Aquatic Centre; Flight Bays, Sydney International Airport; Rooty Hill Sports Centre; and the Prince of Wales Hospital redevelopment.

RICHARD HYWEL EVANS
B.Arch & Dip.Arch (Architectural Assoc. London), ARIBA

Richard Hywel Evans is the key UK Director of Daryl Jackson International in London and is responsible for the design, development and continuity of projects together with the Principal.

Following his honours degree in architecture at the AA, Richard worked with Richard Horden Associates on the Eland House redevelopment; in Sydney with Philip Cox Richardson and

Partners on scheme design for Darling Harbour; and subsequently in Melbourne with Daryl Jackson on the design of Bond University, Queensland.

Since the London office of Daryl Jackson International was established in 1989, Richard has worked with Daryl on the prize-winning design for the Wales Garden Festival Pavilion (RIBA competition), won first prize in the Brandenburg Mill Island Competition, and third prize in a cultural centre competition in Pirmasens, Germany. At present the office is completing a range of sports/recreation projects in London.

IAN HARTLEY
B.Arch (Melb Uni)

Ian Hartley is an Associate of the practice, managing projects from conceptual design to completion. He has travelled extensively in Europe and Asia and his architectural experience prior to joining this practice includes two years in London and a range of projects involving design and documentation in the fields of commerce, research, housing, education and health.

Since joining the practice in 1981, Ian has contributed to the Eastern Suburbs Geriatric Centre; Presbyterian Ladies College New Science Wing; Melbourne Graduate School of Management; New Residential Wing for University College, University of Melbourne; training halls for the Australian Institute of Sport, Canberra; and medical research laboratories at the Royal Melbourne Hospital.

More recently, Ian has been Project Architect for Bond University Recreation and Hotel Centre (production phases), and the Royal Melbourne Hospital Redevelopment, which provided the hospital with a new Clinical Services Centre. He has managed developments in health and housing; the master planning for the Austin and Repatriation Medical Centre and the master planning for Ridley College, University of Melbourne.

In addition to his work with the practice, Ian has tutored in design at the University of Melbourne and has been an advisor to a number of institutions associated with the Anglican Diocese of Melbourne.

LYNDON HAYWARD
B.Arch (RMIT), ARAIA

Lyndon Hayward is an Associate Director of the practice and has an impressive record in the team leadership of large projects.

Lyndon is responsible for the project documentation of major projects within the office, including management of briefing, design, documentation and delivery. He has been responsible for 90 Collins Street, Melbourne and 120 Collins Street, Melbourne.

Lyndon has worked with the practice for 10 years; opening the London office of Daryl Jackson International in 1989 to overseeing work in Britain, Hungary and Italy.

Lyndon has undertaken post graduate studies in Landscape Architecture; travelled extensively to gardens of Europe and Japan and has lectured on Renaissance and Japanese gardens.

Currently, Lyndon is Project Architect of the Melbourne Casino project, responsible for over 120 architects and interior designers and the delivery of all architectural services on the $1.3 billion project.

Lyndon brings to the practice expertise in project management of major architectural projects; as team leader, he works closely with client principals to facilitate achievement.

TIMOTHY JACKSON
B.Arch (Hons) (Melb Uni), ARAIA

Timothy Jackson is a Director of the practice whose skills in conceptual design and design stages have been developed over a wide range of projects.

Prior to joining Daryl Jackson Pty Ltd in 1988, he worked for Denton Corker Marshall, Melbourne, and the Public Works Department of the Victorian State Government.

The projects Tim has been actively involved in at Daryl Jackson Pty Ltd include the Information Technology and Electrical Engineering Building, University of Melbourne; Wesley College, Glen Waverley Campus; Stonier's Winery, Merricks; and the Jackson House, Bermagui, NSW.

Tim has travelled extensively in Europe and the USA. He is a respected, capable and creative designer who is a valuable asset on any project team. In addition to his role at Daryl Jackson Pty Ltd, Tim also manages his own architectural practice, specialising in residential projects.

MANFRED LOBERT
Dip.Aeronautical Eng. (RMIT), B.Arch (Melb Uni), ARAIA

Manfred Lobert is an Associate Director of Daryl Jackson Pty Ltd, responsible for the development and review of project design, detailing and technology.

Manfred spent several years in Europe and has now been with the practice for over 20 years. He has developed broad practical experience in the detail design process relating to architectural and technical design issues across the spectrum of design professions. His particular expertise is in membrane and cable stayed structures, including suspended glazing systems.

Manfred has gained extensive experience on such projects as the Australian Bicentennial Travelling Exhibition; Penguin Visitor Centre, Phillip Island; Bond University, Queensland; the Great Southern Stand, Melbourne Cricket Ground; and the Museum of Victoria, Southbank. Most recently, he has been involved with Crown Casino, Southbank, Melbourne.

In addition to his work with the practice, Manfred has also tutored in building construction at the School of Architecture, Melbourne University and is a committee member of the Australian Institute of Steel Construction.

PETER QUIGLEY
B.Arch (Melb Uni), ARAIA

Peter Quigley is a Director of Daryl Jackson Pty Ltd, and is responsible for the project management, design development, documentation and contract administration of major projects. Peter is an experienced facilitator, practiced in programming, management, liaison and negotiation.

As a Project Director, Peter assumes control of a project at the briefing stage and is responsible for its development through to the completion of construction and occupation by the client. His role ensures that staff, clients, consultants and builders have a singular
and constant point of contact and responsibility.

In addition to his involvement with specific projects, Peter is responsible for the continuing professional development of the office in the areas of technology, contract administration and architectural practice.

Prior to joining the practice, Peter gained extensive experience in the design and construction of hospital projects, including seven years as Project Architect for the construction of the Harold Stokes Block at the Austin Hospital, Melbourne, a major development which involved an extensive range of hospital facilities. He was also involved with several smaller hospital projects at Swan Hill, Bendigo and Shepparton in Victoria.

Recent experience includes the management of a number of commercial and institutional projects, including the Hyatt Hotel, Canberra, the development of the corporate headquarters for Commercial Union Insurance, the Swinburne University Hawthorn Campus, the Royal Melbourne Hospital redevelopment, the Little Chapel Street Car Park for the City of Stonnington, the MLC Music School, and buildings at the Glen Waverley and Prahran campuses
of Wesley College.

Peter's commitment to architecture is further demonstrated by his involvement with the Victorian Chapter of the Royal Australian Institute of Architects where he is a member of the Professional Development Board, the Practice Committee and the Standing Committee (Complaints). He is an examiner with the Victorian Architects Registration Board and has lectured in professional practice at the Royal Melbourne Institute of Technology.

MARK ROEHRS
B.Arch (Hons) (Uni. of Qld), ARAIA

Mark is an Associate Director of the Queensland office of Daryl Jackson Pty Ltd, and has considerable experience in the briefing, planning and design of educational and institutional projects.

Prior to joining Daryl Jackson Pty Ltd in 1987, Mark gained experience on many architectural project types, including restaurants, retail, hospital extensions and houses. In his current capacity, he has been the Briefing and Design Architect on such projects as Swinburne College of TAFE, Melbourne; School of Information Technology and Electrical Engineering, University of Melbourne. He also led the planning process for the Northern Territory University Master Plan, and the Royal Brisbane Hospital and Royal Women's Hospital Herston Campus Master Plan.

Most recently, Mark has been the Briefing and Design Architect for the Arts/Law Building and Science Building, Northern Territory University; the Music School, Methodist Ladies College, Melbourne; Redland Shire Council Capalaba Centre Library and Meeting Rooms, Queensland; and the Redland Shire Council Cleveland Centre Library and Municipal Offices.

In addition to his work with the practice, Mark has been a design tutor at Melbourne University, and has delivered occasional guest lectures at Royal Melbourne Institute of Technology, Melbourne University and Queensland University.

BILL RYAN

Dip.Arch (RMIT), ARAIA

Bill Ryan is a Director of the practice responsible for planning and design. He has travelled extensively on a number of occasions, and prior to joining the practice in 1969, was responsible for the design of a diverse range of major projects in Australia, Canada and the United Kingdom.

Bill's significant experience extends over a range of areas, including commercial, educational, government, sports and community facilities. Projects include 90 Collins Street, Melbourne; the Walter and Eliza Hall Institute of Medical Research; City Edge Housing, South Melbourne; the Canberra School of Art; and the Australian Institute of Sport Training Halls and Indoor Training Pool, in the Australian Capital Territory.

More recently, Bill has worked on the Information Technology and Electrical Engineering Building at the University of Melbourne; the Swinburne University, Hawthorn; the Royal Melbourne Hospital redevelopment; and the Subiaco Football Stadium, Western Australia.

In addition to his work with the practice, Bill tutors in design at both the Royal Melbourne Institute of Technology and the University of Melbourne; acts as a juror for the RAIA (Victorian Chapter) Awards; and is a Fellow of the Royal Melbourne Institute of Technology.

BOB SINCLAIR

Dip.Arch (RMIT), ARAIA

Bob Sinclair is a Director of the practice responsible for project design and design development. In 20 years participation with Daryl Jackson, Bob Sinclair has been responsible for the design character of significant buildings such as the Canberra School of Art (awarded First Zelman Cowan Architecture Prize, 1981); the Australian Defence Force Academy Indoors Sports Building (Canberra Medallion, 1987); the Australian Chancery, Riyadh, Saudi Arabia; the Belconnen College (Certificate of Merit, 1988); the Hyatt Hotel, Canberra (winner of numerous State and national awards); and Bond University, Queensland.

Recently, Bob has been Design Director involved in the competition submission for the Museum of Victoria and the submission for the Brisbane Convention Centre. For the last two years Bob has been responsible for the design of Melbourne's new Crown Casino, working with a team of 120 architects and interior designers. The casino is expected to open in 1996.

Together with Bob's extensive involvement in the practice, he has participated in a diverse range of activities committed to architecture and design education. He has been a tutor in design at the Royal Melbourne Institute of Technology and Deakin University, and continues in this capacity at the University of Melbourne. In addition, he has held the positions of Chairman of the Editorial Panel, Australian Architect Monographs, 1985; Member of the Royal Australian Institute of Architects Board of Architectural Education (Victorian Chapter), 1988; Convenor, University of Melbourne Education Working Party, 1990; Chairman, Royal Australian Institute of Architects Housing Awards (Victorian Chapter), 1993; and is an examiner for the Architects Registration Board.

OLIVER STIRLING

B.Arch (Hons) (Oxford Uni), ARIBA

Oliver Stirling is an Associate of Daryl Jackson International, London. Oliver brings to the practice a sensible design appreciation and plays a fundamental technical role in the design development, contract documentation and administration of work going through the London and European offices.

Prior to joining the practice, Oliver worked for Richard Horden Associates, London. In 1989, he joined Daryl Jackson International and in 1990 was appointed an Associate of the practice.

He has recently carried out the design and management of the European Serviced Offices, Budapest, and completed the renovation and extensions to Cannons Gymnasium, London.

ALASTAIR SWAYN

Dip.Arch (Liverpool Polytechnic), DIPCabd, ARAIA, ARIBA

Alastair Swayn is the Director responsible for the initial planning, building audits and adaptive re-use of projects, and is the Manager of the Canberra office of the practice.

Alastair was born in Scotland. Before migrating to Australia, he travelled widely in Europe, Canada and South Africa. In 1973 he moved to Australia to work in Sydney with Collard Clark and Jackson. He was involved in the documentation and design development of a number of schools and health centres which eventually led him to move to Canberra to carry out the supervision of some of the larger projects.

He joined Daryl Jackson Pty Ltd in 1979 to become the site architect for the McLachlan Offices project, and in 1981 he was appointed Manager of the Canberra office, enabling him to take full responsibility for the organisation of all projects in the Canberra area.

Alastair has extensive experience in successfully transforming drawing board designs into finely finished buildings. Among the notable buildings with which Alastair has been involved are McLachlan Offices, Barton; Australian Institute of Sport Indoor Training Pool; Singapore Embassy; Lake Ginninderra College; Centenary House, Barton; Tuggeranong Pool; Boiler House Lecture Theatre, University of Canberra; Australian National University Sports Union additions; and the redesign of the Administrative Building, Parkes.

BILL SZYDLIK

B.Arch (RMIT), ARAIA

Bill Szydlik is a Director of the Canberra practice, responsible for detailed design, design development, documentation and overall management of projects.

Bill joined the Melbourne office in 1982 after having been tutored by Daryl Jackson in his final year of design at the Royal Melbourne Institute of Technology. He has a strong background in architectural design, having worked alongside our principal designers, Daryl Jackson and Bob Sinclair. In 1984 he spent 11 months travelling in the USA, Europe, Japan, China and India studying architectural design.

Bill was appointed a Director of the practice in 1993. He has been Design/Project Architect on a range of projects, including Belconnen Housing, Canberra; Refurbishment of the Department of Foreign Affairs; the Australian Institute of Sport Grandstand; and Bonython Primary School. More recently, Bill has worked on Tuggeranong Pool; Centenary House; the Australian Institute of Sport Visitor Centre; and the University of Canberra School of Law.

DAVID TROTT

Dip.Arch (RMIT), ARAIA

David Trott is a Director of the practice and Manager of the Queensland office of Daryl Jackson Pty Ltd, with over 20 years experience in the building industry. David is responsible for the management, design, implementation, documentation and administration of all projects in Queensland.

David joined the Melbourne office of Daryl Jackson Pty Ltd in 1978, after travelling throughout Europe and the United Kingdom, furthering his architectural studies.

Early in 1988, David relocated to Queensland to establish and manage the Brisbane office, and principally to undertake the development of Bond University. This role involved the management of the office, implementation of design and documentation of all buildings and administration of all contracts. This undertaking included the master planning of the university, the establishment of most of the Stage 1 buildings and the Research Park, and all urban works.

Recently, David has been responsible for the management and co-ordination of the Master Planning Review for Griffith University, the Redevelopment Master Planning Study for Cairns Base Hospital, the Redevelopment Master Planning Study for the Herston Complex (incorporating Royal Brisbane Hospital, Royal Women's Hospital and Royal Children's Hospital), the redevelopment of the Brisbane Cricket Ground (the Gabba), and the Food and Technology Building at South Brisbane TAFE.

Associates & Collaborators

Appreciation is extended to these associated architectural practices who have participated in joint venture submissions and works illustrated in this book.

Architecture Oceania, Melbourne
(Flinders Street Marketplace, Melbourne)

Basil Carter
(Australian Film, TV and Radio School)

Bates Smart McCutcheon and Perrot Lyon Mathieson Pty Ltd, Melbourne
(Crown Casino)

Di Carlo Potts, Sydney
(Royal Melbourne Hospital)

Godfrey Spowers, Melbourne
(Walter and Eliza Hall Institute)

Hassells Pty Ltd, Melbourne
(120 Collins Street, Melbourne)

McGlashan Everist, Melbourne
(Wesley College Senior School, Glen Waverley)

Mel Yepterv, Budapest
(European Serviced Offices, Budapest)

Meldrum Burrows, Melbourne
(Australian Chancery, Riyadh, Saudi Arabia)

Mitchell/Giurgola & Thorp, Canberra
(Station Pier Redevelopment, Port Melbourne)

Peter Hunt Architects, Perth
(Western Australian Indoor Sports Centre; Department of Land Administration Offices; Commercial Union)

Tompkin Shaw & Evans, Melbourne
(Melbourne Cricket Ground Great Southern Stand)

Woodhead (Aust) NT Pty Ltd
(Northern Territory University Master Plan; Northern Territory University Arts/Law Building)

Chronological List of Buildings & Projects

*Indicates work featured in this book
(see Selected and Current Works).

1994

Queen Victoria Market Hall Refurbishment
Melbourne, Vic.

Hellas Soccer Stadium
South Melbourne, Vic.

Box Hill Indoor Recreation Centre
Box Hill, Vic.

Swinburne University of Technical And Further Education
Melbourne, Vic.

Sydney General Post Office Redevelopment Study
Sydney, NSW
(Daryl Jackson Robin Dyke Pty Ltd)

Moonee Valley Racecourse Planning Study
Moonee Ponds, Vic.

Wesley College, Early Childhood Development
Waverley, Vic.

Swinburne University
Mooroolbark, Vic.

***Museum of Victoria, Carlton Gardens**
Melbourne, Vic.
Competition

King Street (Little Chapel Street) Prahran Car Park
Prahran, Vic.

Swinburne University Urban Design Report
Lilydale, Vic.

Dandenong Civic Precinct Redevelopment Plan
Dandenong, Vic.

Ridley College Master Plan
Parkville, Vic.

***Sega, Sydney**
Sydney, NSW
Submission
(Daryl Jackson Robin Dyke Pty Ltd)

1993

***Wales Garden Pavilion**
Wales, United Kingdom
Competition Entry
(Daryl Jackson International)

***Brandenburg**
East Germany
Competition Entry
(Daryl Jackson International)

Sunshine City Centre Development Plan
Sunshine, Vic.

Methodist Ladies College Woodwing Alterations
Kew, Vic.

Sunshine Social Security Building
Sunshine, Vic.

***The Gabba Master Planning Study**
Woolloongabba, Qld
(Daryl Jackson Queensland)

1992

Wesley College Special Interest Music Centre
Elsternwick, Vic.
(In association with McGlashan Everist Architects)

Wesley College Preparatory School
Prahran, Vic.

Wesley College Master Planning
All campuses, Vic.

Methodist Ladies College Master Plan
Kew, Vic.

Wesley College Prahran Quadrangles
Prahran, Vic.

***Frankston Civic Centre**
Frankston, Vic.

***Swinburne University Master Plan, Lilydale**
Lilydale, Vic.

Melbourne University Recreation Facilities Study
Parkville, Vic.

***Arts/Law Building, Northern Territory University**
Brinkin, NT
(In association with Woodhead (Aust) NT)

***Methodist Ladies College Music School**
Kew, Vic.

***Royal Melbourne Hospital Master Plan Strategy Review**
Parkville, Vic.
(In association with Di Carlo Potts)

***Crown Casino, Southbank**
South Melbourne, Vic.
(In association with Bates Smart McCutcheon Perrot Lyon Mathieson)

***Information Technology & Electrical Engineering Building, University of Melbourne**
Parkville, Vic.

***Griffith University Plan Reviews**
Brisbane, Qld

***Flight Bays, Sydney International Airport**
Mascot, NSW
(Daryl Jackson Robin Dyke Pty Ltd)

***Canberra Magistrates Court**
Canberra, ACT
Competition entry

Prairiewood Aquatic Centre
Prairiewood, NSW
(Daryl Jackson Robin Dyke Pty Ltd)

1991

Eastside Planning Study
Jolimont, Vic.

Swinburne University Student Union Facility Redesign
Hawthorn, Vic.

Royal Melbourne Hospital Bone Marrow Donor Research Unit
Parkville, Vic.

Eastern Precinct Car Park Planning Study, Melbourne University
Parkville, Vic.

Jakarta Office Building
Jakarta, Indonesia
Project

Subiaco Oval Master Plan and Stage 1 Development
Subiaco, WA
(In association with Peter Hunt Architects, Perth)

Sports Club
Jeddah, Saudi Arabia
Project

Grattan Street Housing Study
Carlton, Vic.

***Footscray Library**
Footscray, Vic.

***Boiler House Lecture Theatre, University of Canberra**
Bruce, ACT
(Daryl Jackson Alastair Swayn Pty Ltd)

***Department of Land Administration Offices**
Midlands, WA
(In association with Peter Hunt Architects, Perth)

***European Serviced Offices**
Budapest, Hungary
(Daryl Jackson International and Mel Yepterv, Budapest)

***Brisbane Convention and Exhibition Centre**
Brisbane, Qld
Competition

***Perth Harbour-City Foreshore**
Perth, WA
Competition entry

***Museum of Scotland**
Edinburgh, Scotland
Competition entry

Bunkers Hill Offices
Sydney, NSW
(Daryl Jackson Robin Dyke Pty Ltd)

New South Wales University Student Housing
Sydney, NSW
(Daryl Jackson Robin Dyke Pty Ltd)

1990

***Northern Territory University Master Plan**
Brinkin, NT
(In association with Woodhead (Aust) NT)

***TAFE Complex, Swinburne University, Hawthorn**
Hawthorn, Vic.

Aqua Del Ray Resort
Whitsundays, Qld
Submission

***Anzac Parade**
Canberra, ACT
(Daryl Jackson Alastair Swayn Pty Ltd)
Competition entry

***South Brisbane TAFE, Food Technology Building**
South Brisbane, Qld
(Daryl Jackson Alastair Swayn Pty Ltd)

***Centenary House**
Canberra, ACT
(Daryl Jackson Alastair Swayn Pty Ltd)

***IBM Southgate**
South Melbourne, Vic.

Thredbo Village
Thredbo, NSW
(Daryl Jackson Robin Dyke Pty Ltd)

1989

Olympic Village Study
Melbourne, Vic.

***Jackson House, Bermagui**
Bermagui, NSW

***Australian Institute of Sport Grandstand**
Bruce, ACT
(Daryl Jackson Alastair Swayn Pty Ltd)

***Cannons Gymnasium**
London, UK
(Daryl Jackson International)

***Seymour Powell Studio**
London, UK
(Daryl Jackson International)

***Stonier's Winery**
Merricks, Vic.

1988

Carter House
Mission Beach, Qld

***Wesley College Senior School**
Glen Waverley, Vic.
(In association with McGlashan Everist)

W.G. Wright Recreation Centre
Dandenong, Vic.

Bond University Student Centre Building
Burleigh Forest, Qld
(Daryl Jackson Queensland)

Bond University Recreation Centre Building
Burleigh Forest, Qld
(Daryl Jackson Queensland)

***Melbourne Cricket Ground Great Southern Stand**
Melbourne, Vic.
(In association with Tompkins Shaw & Evans)

***Museum of Victoria, Southbank**
South Melbourne, Vic.
Competition entry

***Tuggeranong Pool**
Tuggeranong, ACT
(Daryl Jackson Alastair Swayn Pty Ltd)

***Olympic Dockland**
Melbourne, Vic.

***Flinders Street Marketplace Design Study**
Melbourne, Vic.
(In association with Architecture Oceania)

Student Housing, King Street and Princes Street
Randwick, NSW
(Daryl Jackson Robin Dyke Pty Ltd)

1987

Ambulance Officers Training Centre
Doncaster, Vic.

***Commercial Union Offices Stage 2**
Melbourne, Vic.
(In association with Peter Hunt Architects, Perth)

***Porta Di Roma Redevelopment**
Rome, Italy

Gollings Studio
Richmond, Vic.

***National Water Sports Centre**
Carrum, Vic.

1986

***120 Collins Street Offices**
Melbourne, Vic.
(In association with Hassell Group Associated Architects)

Cape Schanck Condominiums (Stages 1 & 2)
Cape Schanck, Vic.

***Cox House, Portsea**
Portsea, Vic.

***Bond University Master Plan**
Burleigh Forest, Qld
(Daryl Jackson Robin Dyke Pty Ltd)

***Penguin Visitor Centre**
Phillip Island, Vic.

Deakin University New Master Plan Study
Geelong, Vic.
(In association with McGlashan Everist)

State Bank, Mornington Branch
Mornington, Vic.

***Darling Harbour Casino**
Sydney, NSW
(Daryl Jackson Robin Dyke Pty Ltd)
Project design

***Aquarium, Darling Harbour**
Sydney, NSW
(Daryl Jackson Robin Dyke Pty Ltd)
Project design

***Merlin Street**
Sydney, NSW
(Daryl Jackson Robin Dyke Pty Ltd)
Project design

University College Library
Parkville, Vic.

Melbourne University Architecture School Atrium
Parkville, Vic.

Barbarino's Restaurant
Doncaster, Vic.

Trellini's (Elizabeth Street) Retail Interior
Sydney, NSW
(Daryl Jackson Robin Dyke Pty Ltd)

***Lake Ginninderra College**
Belconnen, ACT

***Australian Bicentennial Exhibition**

***Hyatt Hotel, Canberra**
Yarralumla, ACT
(Daryl Jackson Alastair Swayn Pty Ltd)

Taronga Park Zoo Reptile House
Taronga Park, NSW
(Daryl Jackson Robin Dyke Pty Ltd)

1985

Davies House
Vinifera, Vic.

Footscray Mall Stage 1, Maddern Square
Footscray, Vic.

***Australian Film, Television and Radio School**
North Ryde, NSW
(Daryl Jackson Robin Dyke Pty Ltd in association with Basil Carter)

***Cape Schanck National Golf Club**
Cape Schanck, Vic.

***Cape Schanck Golf Club**
Cape Schanck, Vic.

***Western Australian State Indoor Sports Centre**
Mt Claremont, WA
(In association with Peter Hunt Architects, Perth)

Thompson House
Red Hill, Vic.

St Monica's Parish Centre
Canberra, ACT
(Daryl Jackson Alastair Swayn Pty Ltd)

Melbourne University Art Gallery Interior
Parkville, Vic.

Philip Institute Library/Computer Facility
Bundoora, Vic.
(In association with Godfrey Spowers)

Swinburne University (Stage 1)
Hawthorn, Vic.

University College Principal's Residence
Parkville, Vic.

***State Library/Museum of Victoria**
Melbourne, Vic.
Competition

***Station Pier**
Port Melbourne, Vic.
(In association with Mitchell/Giurgola Thorp, Canberra)
Project

Kew Recreation Centre
Kew, Vic.

Snowy Mountains Hydro Electricity Authority Offices
Cooma, NSW
(Daryl Jackson Alastair Swayn Pty Ltd)

***Commercial Union (Stage 1)**
Melbourne, Vic.
(In association with Peter Hunt Architects, Perth)

Carlyon Stables
Mornington Peninsula, Vic.

Daiwa Security Recreational Hostel
Molesworth, Vic.

***Australian Chancery, Riyadh**
Riyadh, Saudi Arabia
(In association with Meldrum Burrows)

1984

Ministry of Housing
Flemington, Vic.

Melbourne Clinic, Psychiatric Consulting Section
Richmond, Vic.

Carey Grammar School Multi-Purpose Sports Hall
Doncaster, Vic.

***Daryl Jackson Office**
Melbourne, Vic.

Rosebud Police Station
Rosebud, Vic.

Conservatorium of Music, Melba Hall, University of Melbourne
Parkville, Vic.

***Monash University Multi-Disciplinary Centre**
Clayton, Vic.

***Belconnen Housing, Canberra**
Belconnen, ACT
(Daryl Jackson Alastair Swayn Pty Ltd)

1983

Victoria State College Library
Burwood, Vic.

Remand Centre
Melbourne, Vic.

Northcote Public Library
Northcote, Vic.

Royal Melbourne Hospital Entry Building
Parkville, Vic.
(In association with Godfrey Spowers)

1982

Nelson Road Public Housing
South Melbourne, Vic.

***Australian Institute of Sport Training Halls**
Canberra, ACT
(Daryl Jackson Alastair Swayn Pty Ltd)

Commonwealth Bank
Mornington, Vic.

Ringwood Swimming Pool and Recreation Centre
Ringwood, Vic.

***Graduate School of Management, University of Melbourne**
Parkville, Vic.

***Walter and Eliza Hall Institute**
Parkville, Vic.
(In association with Godfrey Spowers)

1981

Eastern Suburbs Geriatric Centre
East Burwood, Vic.

Commonwealth Bank
Rosanna, Vic.

***Singapore Embassy/Chancery**
Yarralumla, ACT
(Daryl Jackson Alastair Swayn Pty Ltd)

Esprit de Corps
Abbotsford, Vic.

Riddell Exhibition Promotions
Melbourne, Vic.

***Australian Institute of Sport Indoor Training Pool**
Canberra, ACT
(Daryl Jackson Alastair Swayn Pty Ltd)

Fuller House
Kew, Vic.

Waverley Aged Persons Housing
Waverley, Vic.

1980

Austcom Office Development
Jolimont, Vic.

Diocesan Church Centre
Ballarat, Vic.

***Cox House, Hawthorn**
Hawthorn, Vic.

***Australian Defence Force Complex**
Campbell, ACT
(In association with Department of Administrative Services Construction Group, ACT Region)

***Engehurst Competition**
Sydney, NSW

1979

South Port Nursing Home
South Melbourne, Vic.

Latchford Barracks
Bonegilla, Vic.

State Bank UPS Generator Building
Melbourne, Vic.

Woodleigh School Library
Baxter, Vic.

1978

Deakin University General Purpose Academic Building
Geelong, Vic.

University of Melbourne Old Physics Building Redevelopment
Parkville, Vic.

Deakin University Lecture Theatre
Geelong, Vic.

***Canberra School of Art**
Acton, ACT
(Daryl Jackson Alastair Swayn Pty Ltd)

***McLachlan Offices, Canberra**
Barton, ACT
(Daryl Jackson Alastair Swayn Pty Ltd)

1977

***Abrahams House**
Brighton, Vic.

Griffiths House
Main Ridge, Vic.

Deakin University Union/Administration Building (Stage 1)
Geelong, Vic.
(In association with McGlashan Everist)

Wesley College Primary School
(In association with McGlashan Everist)

Swinburne University Sports Building (Stage 1)
Hawthorn, Vic.

Taylors Lakes Sales and Reception Centre
Taylors Lakes, Vic.

Woodleigh School Multi-Purpose Building
Baxter, Vic.

Ashburton Public Library
Ashburton, Vic.

Riley House
Sorrento, Vic.

1976

Collingwood Bandstand Reconstruction
Collingwood, Vic.

Carringbush Public Library
Collingwood, Vic.

Balwyn Public Library
Balwyn, Vic.

Porter House
Shoreham, Vic.

***Royal Melbourne Tennis Club**
Richmond, Vic.

***Jackson House**
Shoreham, Vic.

1975

Boyle House
Mornington, Vic.

St Alipius Balwyn New Teaching and Library Facilities
Balwyn, Vic.

***Belconnen Housing**
Belconnen, ACT

Royal Melbourne Hospital Housing
Parkville, Vic.

St Paul's Woodleigh (Stage 2) Science Lab Senior School
Baxter, Vic.

Presbyterian Church Disabled Housing Units
North Essendon, Vic.

St Alipius Primary School
Ballarat, Vic.

***Emu Ridge Housing**
Belconnen, ACT

1974

Lauriston Girls Junior School
Armadale, Vic.

St Patrick's College Library
Ballarat, Vic.

St Paul's Woodleigh Secondary School Stage 1 Classrooms
Baxter, Vic

Spring Street Sports Pavilion Reserve
Keilor, Vic.

Box Hill Indoor Recreation Centre
Box Hill, Vic.

Tenaden Tutorial Building
Upwey, Vic.

Endeavour Hills Kindergarten
Endeavour Hills, Vic.

Association of Modern Education School
Western Creek, ACT

Green Gully Sport Pavilion
Keilor, Vic.

SSB College
Baxter, Vic.

Ian Parsons House
Mornington Peninsula, Vic.

St Paul's Woodleigh Administration Building
Baxter, Vic.

Yooralla Pre-School
Glenroy, Vic.

1973

Benalla School Ballandella Day Training Centre
Benalla, Vic.

Kingswood Senior College
Box Hill, Vic.

Presbyterian Ladies College Music School
Burwood, Vic.

Mac Parsons House
Mornington, Vic.

Collingwood Swimming Pool
Collingwood, Vic.

1972

Belconnen East Link Town Centre: Urban Design Study
Belconnen, ACT

Methodist Ladies College Laboratory Extension
Kew, Vic.

Narre Warren Pre-School
Narre Warren, Vic.

Kingswood Middle School
Box Hill, Vic.

Mt Scopus College Library
Burwood, Vic.

Mt Scopus College Hall and Synagogue
Burwood, Vic.

Mt Derrimut Homestead Alterations
Mt Derrimut,, Vic.

1971

Yooralla School
Glenroy, Vic.

Hedstrom Tully Estate Planning
Donvale, Vic.

ANZ Bank
Glen Waverley, Vic.

***Canberra School of Music**
Acton, ACT

1970

University of Melbourne Student Housing
Carlton, Vic.

Princes Hill High School
North Carlton, Vic.

Methodist Ladies College Resource Centre
Kew, Vic.

Ballarat College of Advanced Education Student Union
Ballarat, Vic.

Ballarat College of Advanced Education Student Housing
Ballarat, Vic.

Wesley College Redevelopment Study
Prahran, Vic.
(In association with McGlashan Everist)

Eltham Pre-School/Health Centre
Eltham, Vic.

1969

Lower Eltham Park Sports Pavilion
Eltham, Vic.

Collingwood Council Depot
Collingwood, Vic.

Chanel Home of Compassion
Suva, Fiji

Mt Derrimut Animal Husbandry Unit
Sunshine, Vic.

YMCA
Suva, Fiji

St Hilda's New Residential Wing, Melbourne University
Parkville, Vic.

1968

Murray House
Templestowe, Vic.

Lauriston Girls School Gym/Music School
Armadale, Vic.

Collingwood Council Elderly Citizens Club
Collingwood, Vic.

Collingwood Council Swimming Centre
Collingwood, Vic.

Muntz House
Shepparton, Vic.

ES&A Bank
Hawthorn, Vic.

Merchant Builders Display Housing
Elliston, Vic.

1967

Habitat Housing
Malvern, Vic.

Pacemaker Display Homes
Waverley, Vic.

Harold Holt Memorial Swimming Pool
Malvern, Vic.
(In association with Kevin Borland)

1966

Auret House
Wandin Yallock, Vic.

Boyle House
South Yarra, Vic.

Bragge House
Bulleen, Vic.

Buchanan House
Thomastown, Vic.

Siemon House
Mt Waverley, Vic.

Lauriston Girls School Special Studies Building
Malvern, Vic.

Fett House
East Malvern, Vic.

LA Peyre House
Tatura, Vic.

1965

Davies House
Goschen, Vic.

Nicol House
Lilydale, Vic.

1964

Hampton Methodist Church Hall
Hampton, Vic.

Awards

Merit Award
Royal Australian Institute of Architects (Qld Chapter)
Department of Land Administration Offices, Redlands, WA
1994

Australian Tourism Award
Penguin Parade, Phillip Island, Vic.
1994

BOMA Award
National Building Owners and Managers Association
120 Collins Street, Melbourne, Vic.
1993

BOMA Award
Victorian Building Owners and Managers Association
120 Collins Street, Melbourne, Vic.
1993

Sir Zelman Cowan Award
Royal Australian Institute of Architects
National award for the most outstanding architectural work
MCG Great Southern Stand, Melbourne, Vic.
1992

Victorian Architecture Medal
Royal Australian Institute of Architects (Vic. Chapter)
MCG Great Southern Stand, Melbourne, Vic.
1992

Award Winner
Royal Australian Institute of Architects (Vic. Chapter)
MCG Great Southern Stand, Melbourne, Vic.
1992

Award Winner
Royal Australian Institute of Architects (Vic. Chapter)
120 Collins Street, Melbourne, Vic.
1992

Canberra Medallion
Royal Australian Institute of Architects (ACT Chapter)
Boiler House Lecture Theatre, University of Canberra, ACT
1992

Australian Tourism Award
The Hyatt Hotel, Canberra, ACT
1992

Finalist, The F.D.G. Stanley Award
Royal Australian Institute of Architects (Qld. Chapter)
Food Technology Building, South Brisbane College of TAFE, Qld
1992

International Award
Royal Australian Institute of Architects
Australian Chancery Complex, Riyadh, Saudi Arabia
1991

Canberra Medallion
Royal Australian Institute of Architects (ACT Chapter)
Australian Institute of Sport Grandstand, Canberra, ACT
1991

Honorary Fellowship, AIA
Conferred upon Daryl Jackson in recognition of his esteemed character and distinguished world class achievements in the field of architecture.
1990

BOMA Award
National Building Owners and Managers Association
The Hyatt Hotel, Canberra, ACT
1990

Australian Heritage Award
Australian Council of National Trusts
The Hyatt Hotel, Canberra, ACT
1990

Merit Award
Membrane Structures Association of Australia
Penguin Parade, Phillip Island, Vic.
1990

National President's Award
Royal Australian Institute of Architects
The Hyatt Hotel, Canberra, ACT
1989

National Interior Design Award
Royal Australian Institute of Architects (with Hirsch Bedner Inc.)
The Hyatt Hotel, Canberra, ACT
1989

Conservation Award
Royal Australian Institute of Architects (ACT Chapter)
The Hyatt Hotel, Canberra, ACT
1989

Heritage Award
Australian Capital Territory Tourism Award
The Hyatt Hotel, Canberra, ACT
1989

International Accommodation Award
Australian Capital Territory Tourism Award
The Hyatt Hotel, Canberra, ACT
1989

Victorian Tourism Award
Penguin Parade, Phillip Island, Vic.
1989

Merit Award
Royal Australian Institute of Architects (NSW Chapter)
Australian Film, Television and Radio School, North Ryde, NSW
1989

National Australian Council for the Rehabilitation of the Disabled Award
Sarina's Restaurant, Taronga Park Zoo, NSW
1989

Merit Award
Royal Australian Institute of Architects (ACT Chapter)
Lake Ginninderra College, Belconnen, ACT
1988

Citation, Library Design Awards
Royal Australian Institute of Architects and Australian Library Promotion Council
Northcote Library, Northcote, Vic.
1988

Commendation
Australian Consulting Engineers Association National Award
Australian Bicentennial Exhibition
1988

Commendation
Membrane Structures Association of Australia National Award
Australian Bicentennial Exhibition
1988

Commendation
Institution of Engineers (Vic. Division) Award
Australian Bicentennial Exhibition
1988

RAIA Gold Medal
Royal Australian Institute of Architects' highest award to an architect who has made a significant contribution to the development of architecture in Australia.
1987

Canberra Medallion
Royal Australian Institute of Architects (ACT Chapter)
Australian Defence Force Academy Indoor Sports Complex, Campbell, ACT
1987

Honorary Diploma and Bronze Medal
Third World Biennale of Architecture Interarch 85, Sofia, Bulgaria
Australian Institute of Sport Training Halls, Canberra, ACT
1985

President's Award Citation
Royal Australian Institute of Architects
Esprit de Corp Offices and Warehouse
1985

Canberra Medallion
Royal Australian Institute of Architects (ACT Chapter)
Singapore High Commission & Chancery, Yarralumla, ACT
1985

Canberra Medallion
Royal Australian Institute of Architects (ACT Chapter)
Australian Institute of Sport Indoor Training Pool, Canberra, ACT
1984

Sir Zelman Cowan Award
Royal Australian Institute of Architects National Award for the most outstanding architectural work
Australian Institute of Sport Indoor Training Pool, Canberra, ACT
1984

Robert Haddon Award
Royal Australian Institute of Architects (Vic. Chapter)
Abrahams House, Brighton, Vic.
1982

Merit Award
Royal Australian Institute of Architects
(ACT Chapter)
McLachlan Offices, Barton, ACT
1982

Citation, Library Design Awards
Royal Australian Institute of Architects
and Australian Library Promotion Council
Ashburton Branch Library, Ashburton,
Vic.
1982

Timber in Architecture Award
Timber Promotion Council of Australia
Jackson House, Shoreham, Vic.
1982

Sir Zelman Cowan Award
Royal Australian Institute of Architects
National Award for the most outstanding
architectural work
Canberra School of Art, Acton, ACT
1981

Canberra Medallion
Royal Australian Institute of Architects
(ACT Chapter)
Canberra School of Art, Acton, ACT
1981

Citation
Royal Australian Institute of Architects
(Vic. Chapter)
Royal Melbourne Hospital Staff Housing,
North Melbourne, Vic.
1979

Citation, Library Design Awards
Royal Australian Institute of Architects
and Australian Library Promotion Council
Balwyn Branch Library, Balwyn, Vic.
1979

Prize Winner
Parliament House Design Competition
Selected as one of ten prize winners for
Stage One Competition
1979

Bronze Medal
Royal Australian Institute of Architects
(Vic. Chapter)
State Bank College, Baxter, Vic.
1978

Citation
Royal Australian Institute of Architects
(Vic. Chapter)
Collingwood Swimming Pool,
Collingwood, Vic.
1978

Merit Award
Royal Australian Institute of Architects
(ACT Chapter)
Canberra School of Music, Acton, ACT
1977

Bronze Medal
Royal Australian Institute of Architects
(Vic. Chapter)
City Edge Housing, South Melbourne, Vic.
1976

Citations
Royal Australian Institute of Architects
(Vic. Chapter)
Boyle House, Mornington, Vic.
St Paul's School, Woodleigh, Vic.
Yooralla Special Day School, Glenroy, Vic.
South Drummond Street Conservation
Study, Carlton, Vic.
1976

Citation
Royal Australian Institute of Architects
(Vic. Chapter)
Library Resource Centre, Methodist
Ladies College, Kew, Vic.
1974

Bronze Medal
Royal Australian Institute of Architects
(Vic. Chapter)
Princes Hill High School, North Carlton,
Vic.
1973

Bronze Medal
Royal Australian Institute of Architects
(Vic. Chapter)
Lauriston Girls School, Melbourne, Vic.
1970

Citation
Royal Australian Institute of Architects
(Vic. Chapter)
(In association with Kevin Borland)
Harold Holt Memorial Swimming Pool,
Malvern, Vic.
1969

Bibliography

Articles

"120 Collins Street." *Constructional Review* (vol. 65, no. 1, February 1992): pp. 20–27. (Photographs by John Gollings)

Andrews, John. "Building Australia." *Design World* (no. 19, 1990): pp. 56–62. (Bond University; Australian Chancery, Riyadh Saudi Arabia; Hyatt Hotel, Canberra)

"Anzac Parade Urban Design Competition." *Landscape Australia* (February 1992): pp. 48–49.

"Australia's Bicentennial Exhibition." *Lightweight Structures*. Connell Group, 1988.

"Australian Chancery Complex, Riyadh." *Architecture Australia* (November 1991): pp. 54–56. (Winner of RAIA International Award. Photographs by John Gollings)

"Australian Chancery Complex, Riyadh." *Tasarim* (Turkey, no. 26, August, 1992): pp. 58–67. (Photographs by John Gollings)

"Australian Film, Television and Radio School." *Constructional Review* (vol. 62, no. 4, November 1989): pp. 46–53. (Photographs by Tom Balfour of Max Dupain and Associates)

"Australian Institute of Sport, ACT, Athletics Field Grandstand, Canberra." *Innovative Building* (vol. 7, no. 3, March 1992): pp. 1, 16.

Bagnall, Diana "Diplomatic Unity." *Vogue Living* (vol. 14, no. 7, September 1990): pp. 96–105, 158. (Australian Chancery, Riyadh, Saudi Arabia. Photographs by John Gollings)

Bagnall, Diana. "Architecture in Living." *Vogue Living* (vol. XXXIII, no. 1, February 1990): p. 18. (Cox House, Portsea)

"Bank College." *Constructional Review* (vol. 5, no. 3, August 1978): pp. 40–45. (Photographs by John Gollings)

"Baths." *Architecture in Australia* (vol. 58, no. 5, October 1969): pp. 813–818. (Harold Holt Memorial Swimming Pool. Photographs by Ian McKenzie)

Beck, Haig & Jackie Cooper. "Daryl Jackson: 1987 Gold Medallist." *Architect* (Victoria, April 1987): pp. 8–9.

Biagi, Marco. "Ville Moderne: Tradizione Liberata." *Ville Giardini* (no. 287, December 1993): pp. 14–21. (Jackson House Bermagui)

"Bond University Library, Humanities and Administration Buildings." *The Japan Architect* (Japan, no. 402, October 1990): pp. 45–51.

"Bond University." *Constructional Review*, (vol. 63, no. 3, August 1990): pp. 10–23. (Photographs by John Gollings)

"Bond University." *Nikkei Architecture* (Japan, 1:20, 1992): pp. 224–231.

Brennan, Betsy. "Capital Conversion." *Vogue Living* (October 1988): pp. 134–139. (Hyatt Hotel, Canberra. Photographs by John Hay)

Brennan, Betsy. "Romancing the Dune." *Vogue Living* (no. 10, December/January 1990/91): pp. 96–103. (Carter House, Mission Beach, Queensland. Photographs by Scott Frances)

Britt, Brian. "The Australian Film, Television and Radio School." *Profiles in Building*. James Hardie & Coy Pty. Ltd, 1989: pp. 10–14.

Buchanan, Peter. "Big Top Down Under." *Architectural Review* (London, vol. 177, no. 1059, May 1985): pp. 64–67. (Australian Bicentennial Touring Exhibition).

"Canberra School of Art." *Architecture Australia* (vol. 70, no. 6, December 1981): pp. 4, 6–8. (Winner of the Sir Zelman Cowen Award 1981. Photographs by Max Dupain)

"Canberra School of Art." *Architecture Australia* (vol. 70, no. 6, December 1981): pp. 46–47.

"Canberra School of Music." *Architecture Australia*, vol. 65, no. 6, January 1977): pp. 15–20. (Photographs by Max Dupain)

"Canberra's Architecture." *Architecture Australia* (vol. 72, no. 5, September 1983): pp. 47–48. (Canberra School of Art; National Swimming Training Centre)

"Centenary House." *Constructional Review* (vol. 67, no. 1, February, 1994: pp. 26–31. (Photographs by Eric Sierins)

"Commercial Union Assurance." *Corporate and Office Design* (Autumn/Winter 1989): pp. 40–43. (Commercial Union, Melbourne)

Cooper, Jackie. "Architecture Ergonomics." *Vogue Living* (no. 8, October 1991): pp. 138–139. (Gollings Studio, Richmond. Photographs by John Gollings)

"Daryl Jackson International Limited: Penguin Parade." *Architectural Review* (London, vol. CLXXXIX, no. 1130, April 1991): p. 73.

"Daryl Jackson International Limited: Welsh Walk." *Architectural Review* (London, vol. CLXXXIX, no. 1130, April 1991): p. 71–72.

"Daryl Jackson Pty Ltd." *Design Ink* (no. 8, March 1992): pp. 22–25.

"Daryl Jackson Pty Ltd: Two Projects." *Architecture Australia* (vol 78, no. 2, March 1989): pp. 48–55. (Hyatt, Hotel Canberra; Australian Bicentennial Exhibition. Photographs by John Gollings)

"Daryl Jackson." ("Australian Interior Design 1991: A Survey.") *Design World* (no. 20, 1991): pp. 64–68.

"Daryl Jackson." *Space Design* (Japan, no. 293, February 1989): pp. 26–27.

"Daryl Jackson: RAIA Gold Medal 1987." *Architecture Australia* (special commemorative issue, vol. 76, no. 7, November 1987): pp. 51–82. (Articles by Haig Beck and Daryl Jackson: 12 early buildings; Lake Ginninderra College, Belconnen; Monash Gallery Building, Monash University, Clayton; the Walter and Eliza Hall Institute of Medical Research, Parkville; Australian Defence Force Academy Indoor Sports Centre, Canberra; Bond University, Gold Coast; Cape Schanck Golf Club; Ringwood Pool, Melbourne; Carey Grammar Sports Hall, Melbourne; 120 Collins Street Office Tower, Melbourne; Commercial Union Office Building, Melbourne)

Deas, Greg. "Public Sector Architecture." *Architecture Australia* (July 1990): pp. 42–44. (Belconnen College, Canberra)

Dickinson, Michael. "Downtown Looks Up: the Missing Ingredient." *Bulletin* (June 30, 1987). (Daryl Jackson's personal view for the City Perfect)

Drew, Philip. "Complementing the Best of Sport." *Business Review Weekly* (January 15, 1993): pp. 68–69. (MCG Southern Stand. Photographs by John Gollings)

Duncan, Jenepher & Conrad Hamann. "Seven in the Seventies." *Architecture Australia* (vol. 71, no. 1, January 1982): pp. 51–59. (Review of an exhibition)

"Emu Ridge Government Housing." *Constructional Review* (vol. 53, no. 1, February 1980): pp. 40–45.

"Financial Management Consulting Group." *Corporate and Office Design* (Autumn/Winter 1989): pp. 146–149. (Financial Management Consulting Group, Melbourne. Photographs by Mark Chow)

"Food Technology Building." *Constructional Review* (vol. 66, no. 2, May 1993): pp. 48–51. (Photographs by Richard Stringer)

Friss-Clark, Anny. "Stonier's Merricks Vineyard." *Corporate and Office Design* (Spring/Summer 1991): pp. 94–97. (Stonier's Winery, Merricks. Photographs by Tim Griffith)

Gardner, Carl. "Australian Converts." *RIBA Journal* (London, vol. 98, no. 6, June 1991): pp. 64–66. (Cannons Sports Club and Seymour Powell Studio, London. Photographs by Rory Carnegie)

Georgiev, Peter. "Great Southern Stand Wins Victorian Architecture Medal." *Architect* (Victoria, June 1992): p. 4.

"Grandstand in a Bush Setting." *Architecture Australia* (December 1990): p. 10. (Athletics Field Grandstand, Australian Institute of Sport, ACT)

Green, Louise. "The National Golf Club." *Corporate and Office Design* (Spring/Summer 1990): pp. 216–218. (National Golf Club, Cape Schanck. Photographs by John Gollings)

Greenwood, Helen. "Hide-Art." *Plenty* (vol. 5, November/January 1990): pp. 42–44. (Abrahams House, Brighton. Photographs by Ashley Evans)

Griffiths, Anna. "Stonier's Winery." *Design Ink* (no. 7, December 1991): pp. 24–31. (Photographs by Tim Griffith)

Grose, James. "National Sports Centre Swimming Halls, Bruce." *Architecture Australia* (December 1984).

"High School." *Constructional Review* (vol. 47, no. 2, June 1974): pp. 24–26. (Princes Hill High School, Carlton)

"Hit or Miss." *Architect* (Victoria, vol. 3, no. 36, January/February 1975): pp. 4–8. (Royal Melbourne Tennis Club, Richmond)

"Housing City Edge." *Constructional Review* (vol. 50, no. 3, May 1977): pp. 26–33.

"Hyatt Hotel, Canberra: Daryl Jackson Pty Ltd." *Architecture Australia* (vol. 78, no. 11, December 1989): pp. 28–30. (Winner, President's Award for Recycled Buildings; Winner, Belle Interiors Award in Association with Hirsch Bedner Incorporated. Photographs by John Gollings)

Hyatt, Peter. "Pool Hall Operators." *Steel Profile* (no. 38, December 1991): pp. 26–31. (Dandenong Pool. Photographs by Peter Hyatt)

Hyatt, Peter. "Shrines of Remembrance." *Steel Profile* (no. 41, September, 1992): pp. 16–23. (MCG Southern Stand. Photographs by Peter Hyatt)

"I.T.E.E. Building." *Constructional Review* (vol. 67, no. 2, May 1994): pp. 50–55. (Information Technology & Electrical Engineering Building, University of Melbourne. Photographs by John Gollings)

Jackson, Daryl & Geoff Nairn. "Adelaide 2000 Competition." *Architecture Australia* (vol. 75, no. 6, September 1986): pp. 45–49.

Jackson, Daryl & Patrick McCaughey. "Daryl Jackson: Architecture, Drawings and Photographs." *Architect* (Victoria, vol. 8, no. 2, June/July 1984): pp. 18–23.

Jackson, Daryl. "Daryl Jackson: Four Projects." *Architecture Australia* (vol. 79, no. 2, March 1990): pp. 27–42. (Australian Film, Television and Radio School, Sydney; Bond University, Queensland; Penguin Parade, Phillip Island; Australian Chancery, Riyadh, Saudi Arabia. Photographs by John Gollings)

Jackson, Daryl. "Desert Diplomat." *World Architecture* (London, issue no. 13, 1991): pp. 58–61. (Australian Chancery, Riyadh, Saudi Arabia)

Jackson, Daryl. "Design in the Eighties: The Search for an Urban Australia." *Architect* (Victoria, September 1988): pp. 4–5.

Jackson, Daryl. "Extract." *Edge Magazine* (no. 2, 1991). (Review of firm)

Jackson, Daryl. "From Edge to Centre: Sense and Stylism in Current Australian Architecture." *UIA International Architect* (Japan, no. 4, 1984): pp. 4–5.

Jackson, Daryl. "Response to Philip Drew's Paper by Daryl Jackson." *Architecture Australia* (vol. 73, no. 4, June 1984): pp. 80–84. (Following the article "Terra Australis Nondum Cognita" by Philip Drew)

Jackson, Daryl. "Two New Buildings." *Architecture Australia* (vol. 69, no. 5, November 1980): pp. 48–57. (AME School, Canberra and Collingwood Pool, Melbourne. Photographs by John Gollings)

Jackson, Daryl. "Urban Frontiers." *Melbourne Lygon Arts Festival* (vol. 1, no. 2, 1989): pp. 62–65.

Jackson, Davina. "Dynamic Recycling." *Vogue Living* (vol. XXVII, no. 2, April/May 1994): pp. 138–141. (Boiler House Lecture Theatre, University of Canberra. Photographs by John Gollings)

Jahn, Graham. "Far East, Down Under." *Architectural Record* (USA, May 1991): pp. 58–65. (Library Administration Building, Bond University, Queensland)

Keens, Leta. "St Monica's Church." *Corporate and Office Design* (Autumn/Winter 1991): pp. 215–217. (Photographs by John Gollings)

Kerr Forster, Pannell. "Building a Name — Client Profile: Daryl Jackson Pty Ltd." *Current Affairs* (vol. 12, October 1990): p. 8.

"Lake Ginninderra College, ACT." *Constructional Review* (vol. 61, no. 2, May 1988). (Photographs by John Gollings)

"Latchford Barracks." *Constructional Review* (vol. 57, no. 2, May 1984): pp. 10–19. (Photographs by Max Dupain)

"Lauriston Girls School." *Architecture in Australia* (vol. 59, no. 4, August 1970): pp. 657–658.

Luker, Paul. "Business Builds its Future Leaders." *Business Review Weekly* (vol. 9, no. 26, July 3, 1987): pp. 88–90. (Melbourne University Graduate School of Management. Photographs by John Hay)

MacMahon, William. "The Bare Minimum." *Interior Architecture* (issue 32, 1991): pp. 88–99. (Gollings Studio, Richmond. Photographs by John Gollings)

"MCG Southern Stand: Sir Zelman Cowen Award Winner." *Architecture Australia* (December, 1992): pp. 38–40.

"McLachlan Offices." *Constructional Review* (vol. 54, no. 2, May 1981): pp. 12–19. (Photographs by Max Dupain)

"Medical Research Building: The Walter and Eliza Hall Institute of Medical Research, Parkville." *Trends.* James Hardie & Co. Pty Ltd (vol. 2, no. 3, November 1987): pp. 14–15.

Missingham Greg & Norman Day. "Daryl Jackson Architecture: Two Reviews Prompted by the Exhibition." *Transition* (vol. 3, no. 3/4, April/June 1984): pp. 77–82.

"Modern Australian Architecture." *Process Architecture* (Tokyo, no. 22, March 1981). (St Paul's Woodleigh; Jackson Walker Offices, Fitzroy; Collingwood Pool)

"Mt Scopus College." *Constructional Review* (vol. 50, no. 3, August 1977): pp. 38–41. (Photographs by Ian McKenzie)

"Murray House, Templestowe." *Architecture in Australia* (vol. 62, no. 5, October 1973): pp. 78–79.

Murray, P. "Architecture in the Antipodes." *RIBA Journal* (London, no. 91, February 1984): pp. 23–24.

"Music School, Canberra." *Architectural Review* (London, vol. 164, no. 979, September 1978): p. 152.

"New Educational Buildings: Menindee Central School." *Architecture Australia* (July 1990): p. 48.

"New Medical Research Building." *Constructional Review* (vol. 59, no. 2, May 1986): pp. 12–19. (Photographs by John Gollings)

"Oasis Recreational Centre." *Constructional Review* (vol. 64, no. 4, November 1991): pp. 36–41. (Dandenong Pool. Photographs by John Gollings)

"Old Physics Courtyard and Art Gallery." *Architecture in Australia* (vol. 64, no. 4, August 1975): p. 93. (Old Physics Building, University of Melbourne)

Osborne, Catherine. "Bond University." *Corporate and Office Design* (Spring/Summer 1990): pp. 52–55. (Photographs by John Gollings)

"Penguins on Parade." *Steel Profile* (no. 27, March 1989): pp. 10–17. (Penguin Parade, Phillip Island. Photographs by Peter Hyatt)

"Pleasures in Architecture: Engehurst." *Architecture Australia* (vol. 69, no. 2, May 1980): pp. 46–47. (Design competition entries for the "Pleasures of Architecture" RAIA Conference)

"Pluralism Down Under: The Work of Daryl Jackson." *Building* (London, vol. 245, no. 7314 (42), October 21, 1983): p. 22.

"Premiated Parliament House Entry." *Transition* (no. 3, March 1980): pp. 23–25.

Raftopoulos, Andrew & Michael Bialek. "Princes Hill High School." *Architect* (Victoria, vol. 3, no. 31, March/April 1974): pp. 13–16.

Rasch, Horst. "A Large House for Long Holidays." *Hauser* (no. 2, 1994): pp. 26–33. (Jackson House, Bermagui. Photographs by Reiner Blunck)

"Redevelopment of Royal Melbourne Hospital." *Constructional Review* (vol. 65, no. 4, November 1992): p. 8.

Remington, Kay. "Design for Designers." *Interior Design* (issue 7, 1987): pp. 104–112. (Daryl Jackson Offices, Melbourne. Photographs by William Rethmeier)

"Residential Wing, St Hilda's College." *Architect* (Victoria, vol. 3, no. 25, March/April 1973): pp. 14–17.

"Resource Centre." *Constructional Review* (vol. 47, no. 2, June 1974): pp. 30–33. (Methodist Ladies College Resource Centre, Kew).

"Ringwood Swimming Centre, Ringwood, Victoria." *Trends.* James Hardie & Co. Pty Ltd (vol. 2, no. 3, November 1987): pp. 6–7.

"Riyadh Chancery Complex." *Constructional Review* (vol. 63. no. 1, February 1990): pp. 22–29. (Photographs by John Gollings)

"Royal Tennis Club." *Constructional Review* (vol. 50, no. 3, August 1977): pp. 32–37. (Photographs by Ian McKenzie)

"School of Art." *Constructional Review* (vol. 54, no. 3, August 1981): pp. 20–27. (Canberra School of Art)

"Scuola in Australia." *Domus* (Italy, no. 564, November 1976): pp. 36–40. (Yooralla Hospital School for Crippled Children, Glenroy)

"Shelter for Bandsmen." *Architecture Australia* (vol. 65, no. 4, August/September 1971): pp. 70–71. (Collingwood Bandstand, Melbourne)

Sinclair, Bob. "Budapest Business Centre." *Architect* (Victoria, March 1993): p. 8.

Sinclair, Bob. "Commercial Union." *Architect* (Victoria, April 1992): p. 13.

"Singapore High Commission." *Constructional Review* (vol. 59, no. 1, February 1986): pp. 28–33. (Photographs by John Gollings)

Smith, Brian. "New Southern Stand for MCG." *Innovative Building* (vol. 6, no. 11, November 1991): p.10.

"Southern Stand, Melbourne Cricket Ground." *Constructional Review* (vol. 65, no. 2, May 1992): pp. 16–23. (Photographs by John Gollings)

Spence, Rory & Peter Davey. "Australia: Sydney/Melbourne." *Architectural Review* (London, special issue, vol. 178, no. 1066, December 1985): pp. 22–95. (Esprit de Corps Offices and Warehouse, Abbotsford)

Spence, Rory. "Three Australian Houses." *Architectural Review* (London, vol. 176, no. 1052, October 1984): pp. 26–31. (Jackson Houses, East Melbourne and Shoreham)

"St Paul's Woodleigh, Baxter." *Architectural Review* (London, vol. 164, no. 979, September 1978): p. 167.

"State Bank Staff College." *Architecture Australia* (vol. 67, no. 5, October/ November 1978): pp. 69–70. (Photographs by John Gollings)

Styant-Brown, Anthony. "Dynamic Order." *Architecture Australia* (March/April 1995): pp. 56–61. (IBM tenancy, Southgate, Melbourne. Photographs by John Gollings)

Sudjic, D. "Australia: The Great Indoors." *Blueprint* (London, September 1988).

"The Bond University, Queensland — A Study of Style with Steel." *Metal Building News* (vol. 5, no. 8, August 1990): pp. 1, 16–17.

"The Graduate School of Management." *Constructional Review* (vol 60, no. 2, May 1987): pp. 30–37. (Photographs by John Gollings)

"The Head Office for the Digital Equipment Corporation, Rhodes, Sydney." *Innovative Building* (vol. 7, no. 1, January 1992): p. 11–12.

"The Search for Identity." *Steel Profile* (no. 19, March 1987): pp. 10–15. (Profile/ interview with Daryl Jackson. Photographs by Peter Hyatt and John Gollings)

"The Singapore High Commission in Canberra by Daryl Jackson, Alastair Swayn and Peter Rees." *Architecture Australia* (vol. 74, no. 8, December 1985): p. 24. (The Sir Zelman Cowen Award Finalists)

Tombesi, Paolo. "Australian Architecture." *Casabella 550* (Italy, anno LII, October 1988): pp. 54–62. (Monash Gallery Building, Melbourne)

Towndrow, Jennifer. "Making Waves in the New World." *RIBA Journal* (London, vol. 97, no. 7, July 1990): pp. 10–23. (Review of current work)

"Training Centre and Special School." *Constructional Review* (vol. 50, no. 2, May 1977): pp. 18–25. (Yooralla Hospital for Crippled Children, Glenroy. Photographs by Ian McKenzie)

"Tribune in Canberra." *Baumeister* (Germany, October 1991): pp. 30–31. (Athletics Field Grandstand, Australian Institute of Sport, ACT)

Trimble, Judith. "Image and Function." *Architecture Australia* (July 1991): pp. 20–25. (Dandenong Pool. Photographs by John Gollings)

Turnball, Jeff. "Style and Repose: Unity in Plurality." *Architecture Australia* (vol 75, no. 5, July 1986): pp. 55–62. (Swimming Training Halls, Canberra; Catholic Diocesan Offices, Ballarat; Esprit de Corp, Abbotsford. Photographs by Jeff Turnball and John Gollings)

"Two Recent Projects by Jackson/Walker." *Architect* (Victoria, vol. 3, no. 42, July 1976): pp. 22–23. (Raiwaga Youth Centre; Ballarat Student Union and Student Housing)

"University Complex." *Constructional Review* (vol. 5, no. 3, August 1980): pp. 28–33. (Deakin University Administration and Lecture Theatre Building. Photographs by John Gollings)

"Up and Under." *Designers' Journal* (London, May 1991): p. 4. (Cannons Sports Club and Seymour Powell Studio, London)

Van Schaik, Leon. "Daryl Jackson Pty Ltd: Reflections on the Role of the Designer in the Corporate Firm." *Transition* (no. 22/23, Summer 1987): pp. 56–58.

"Warehouse Architectural Office." *Architecture in Australia* (vol. 62, no. 4, August 1973): pp. 76–78. (Jackson Walker Offices, Fitzroy)

Welsh, John. "Coastal Orders." *Building Design* (London, no. 1112, February 19, 1993): pp. 16–17. (Jackson House, Bermagui)

"Wesley Senior College." *Constructional Review* (vol. 65, no. 4, November 1992): pp. 36–41. (Photographs by Tim Griffiths)

Wheeler, Tony, "Pool." *Architecture Australia* (September/October, 1993): pp. 47–51. (Tuggeranong Pool. Photographs by John Gollings)

"YWCA Community Resource Centre, Suva, Fiji." *Architecture in Australia* (vol. 63, no. 6, December 1974): pp. 50–51.

"YWCA, Suva." *Constructional Review* (vol. 47, no. 3, September 1974): pp. 28–33.

Monographs

Day, Norman. *Modern Houses Melbourne.* Melbourne: Brian Zouch Publications, 1976. (Murray House; Boyle House; Parson House)

Griggs, Michael & Leon Paroissien (eds). *Old Continent New Buildings: Contemporary Australian Architecture.* Sydney: David Ell Press, 1983. (Jackson House, East Melbourne; Canberra School of Art; Southport Nursing Home)

Jackson, Daryl. *Architecture: Drawings and Photographs.* Melbourne: Macmillan Company of Australia, 1984.

Judd, Bruce & John Dean (eds). *Medium Density Housing in Australia.* Canberra: RAIA Education Division, April 1985. (City Edge Housing, South Melbourne; Royal Melbourne Hospital Staff Housing, Melbourne; Emu Ridge Housing, Canberra)

Pegrum, Roger. *Details in Australian Architecture* Volume 1. Canberra: RAIA Education Division, 1984, pp. 108–109, (Abrahams House, Brighton)

Pegrum, Roger. *Details in Australian Architecture* Volume 2. Canberra: RAIA Education Division, 1987, pp. 72–76. (Swimming Training Halls, Canberra)

Acknowledgments

The practice that began as Daryl Jackson Evan Walker in 1965 now exists as five offices throughout Australia and in the UK. During the period 1965–69, Evan Walker conducted a separate practice in Toronto, Canada. He returned to Melbourne to work with Daryl Jackson until he entered the Victorian State Parliament in 1979. The partnership was disbanded and Daryl Jackson Pty Ltd was established. Under the leadership of Daryl Jackson, projects are undertaken in Asia and the Pacific, as well as in Europe and the Middle East.

For their continued commitment to the standard of excellence achieved in this practice, special acknowledgment is given to the skills of the current Directors, Associates and all staff members.

London
(Daryl Jackson International)
Director: Richard Evans
Associate: Oliver Stirling

Melbourne
(Daryl Jackson Pty Ltd)
Directors: Bob Sinclair, Bill Ryan, Peter Quigley, Peter Cole and Timothy Jackson
Associate Directors: Roman Bugryn, Lyndon Hayward and Manfred Lobert
Associates: Philip Chadwick, Peter Coehlo and Ian Hartley

Sydney
(Daryl Jackson Robin Dyke Pty Ltd)
Director: Robin Dyke
Associate Director: Brian Britt

Canberra
(Daryl Jackson Alastair Swayn Pty Ltd)
Directors: Alastair Swayn and Bill Szydlik

Brisbane
(Daryl Jackson Pty Ltd)
Director: David Trott
Associate Directors: Mark Roehrs and Gary Carter

Thanks also to former Directors, Ron Billard and Jaro Safer, both of whom have left the practice.

Our gratitude is extended to clients with the vision and the trust to commission or select the work. In addition, we thank all consultants and contractors who have applied their talents to get the projects built.

Many photographers have contributed to the work in this book. Special thanks go to John Hay (Cox House, Portsea), A.J. Nutt & Associates with David Davies Photography (DOLA, Perth), John Gollings and Tim Griffith.

My appreciation to Elisabeth Kumm, who began working with The Images Publishing Group during the initial stages of this project; to Chris Viola, for his efforts in sourcing the images represented in this monograph; and to Karen Davis for her research, extensive text preparation, and management. The practice also thanks The Images Publishing Group for their invitation to participate in The Master Architect Series.

It is the work of these people and all the other architects, interior designers and secretarial staff in the firm that has given the practice a national and international reputation for high quality consultation and performance.

Index

Every effort has been made to trace the original source of copyright material contained in this book. The publishers would be pleased to hear from copyright holders to rectify any errors or omissions.

The information and illustrations in this publication have been prepared and supplied by Daryl Jackson Pty Ltd. While all reasonable efforts have been made to ensure accuracy, the publishers do not, under any circumstances, accept responsibility for errors, omissions and representations express or implied.